This, the frontispiece from Moses Harris' 1766 book *The Aurelian: or Natural History of English Insects; namely, Moths and Butterflies: together with the Plants on which they feed* is very well known to entomologists. It depicts a gentleman in the woods with a 'clap net' and a box containing his captures of the day; a friend is seen behind him collecting. The name 'Aurelian' is an early name for a Lepidopterist (one who is interested in butterflies) (© Royal Entomological Society).

John Tennent is the author of over two hundred scientific papers and three books on butterflies. He served in the British Army between 1967 and 1991, mostly overseas. He was awarded the British Empire Medal in the New Year's Honours List in 1981 for work in Belize, and made a Member of the Order of Logohu in the Papua New Guinea New Year's Honours List in 2015, for research into Pacific butterfly taxonomy.

He resigned from the Army in 1991 to pursue research into insects and the history of natural history in many parts of the world, usually on the path least travelled. He has recently carried out research into Pacific butterfly biogeography and systematics on islands of the southwest Pacific. He was elected a Fellow of the Royal Entomological Society in 1982, Fellow of the Linnean Society in 1995, a Member of the Institute of Biology in 1998, and a Fellow of the Royal Society of Biology in 2015. He gained a Master of Science degree in Biodiversity Management in 1998 and was invited to become a Scientific Associate of the Natural History Museum Entomology Department, London the same year.

He has described more than 130 butterfly species and subspecies new to science – many discovered by himself, and copies of his book on Vanuatu butterflies, published in 2009, were supplied *gratis* to every school in Vanuatu. He was awarded the Linnean Society HH Bloomer Medal for contributions to science in 2007.

With a wide variety of interests outside the service environment, poetry has been important to him since he was a small boy growing up in north Yorkshire.

The
Poetry Bug

Edited by
John Tennent

Parthian, Cardigan SA43 1ED
www.parthianbooks.com
Anthology © John Tennent 2015
Poems with kind permission © the writers
ISBN 978-1-910901-00-7
Edited by Carly Holmes
Cover by Robert Harries
Typeset by Elaine Sharples
Printed and bound by Printed in EU by Pulsio SARL
Published with the financial support of the Welsh Books Council.
British Library Cataloguing in Publication Data
A cataloguing record for this book is available from the British
Library.

CONTENTS

THE POETRY BUG

Preface

The silken thread that binds these poems is made by the only things that can make the stuff – insects and spiders (the latter given honorary insect status for the purposes of the anthology). On long field trips to various obscure parts of the world, I have seldom been without a poetry book of one kind or another. There are things that can be said in poetry which cannot be said so well in prose; poetry can be read and reread without it seeming boring or jaded, and – like good music – the familiarity of knowing what comes next is a delight.

I would dearly love to be able to commit vast tracts of poetry to memory, removing the need for carting a heavy book around the world, but sadly I am cursed with a depressingly poor memory. A few random verses from some favourite poems may stick in the memory for a while, but efforts to memorise anything substantial seem doomed to failure. My favourite poem has nothing to do with insects or entomology: Coleridge's 'The Rime of the Ancient Mariner'. I once made a concerted effort, whilst carrying out research for several months in the Solomon Islands, to commit the whole 130+ stanzas to memory, but by the time I reached stanza 30 something, I had largely forgotten the first few. The few stanzas now embedded in my inadequate brain include:

> *About, about, in reel and rout*
> *The death fires danced at night.*
> *The water, like a witch's oils,*
> *Burnt green, and blue, and white*

not because these lines are particularly memorable (though they are), but because they remind me of a midnight dash in an open boat across Roviana Lagoon in the New Georgia Island group to catch the weekly ferry back to the Solomon Islands capital Honiara, with a local "driver" whose faith in an Almighty was absolute. The bow wave thrust aside symmetrical streams of white and blue phosphorescence as we streaked across waters renowned for barely submerged coral heads, any one of which would have ripped out the bottom of our fibre-glass canoe. The sight was magnificent – the experience terrifying.

One of my favourite anthologies is Lord Wavell's *Other Men's Flowers*: more than 400 cluttered pages of poetry all of which Wavell, amazingly, had at one time or another committed to memory. How anyone can do so is incomprehensible to me, and I am deeply envious. Many poems are annotated with Wavell's own thoughts and experiences, which explain and enhance some of the poetry. Wavell believed that poetry should rhyme, a view that might be regarded as rather old-fashioned in these modern days, but there is nothing wrong with demanding that poetry should rhyme, that music should be tuneful, and that paintings should look like something identifiable. No doubt the intricacies of technical cleverness are very gratifying to the modern writer, composer and artist, but struggling with poetry that makes little sense, or listening to discordant music, or being unsure as to whether a modern painting should be this way up or that is not – to me at least – remotely satisfying.

My interest in insects – in particular butterflies – stems from a childhood spent roaming the fields and moors near my home in Robin Hood's Bay armed with a jam jar in which to imprison luckless individuals of almost anything that moved. Subsequently, interest in butterflies became paramount; not

2

just because of the things themselves (I maintain no private collection), but because it gave me access to the world's wild places: a reason to travel. The travel is as important as the research; there is something about rounding a corner on a forest trail in Indonesia and seeing what first looks like a startled farmyard cockerel take off vertically (the red junglefowl is a wild ancestor of our domesticated chicken); or cooking freshly caught tuna over an open fire on the beach of an island uninhabited by people, that can't be bought. Walking alone through a tropical forest, with nothing but the sounds of the myriad life forms that belong there, including irate cockatoos scolding noisily from the canopy before handing you over to their equally noisy colleagues in an adjacent territory, is an experience that far outweighs the discomfort, and sometimes danger, of getting there.

As to my interest in insect-inspired poetry: since I like both, it was a natural progression. Like insect research, poetry provides another – albeit rather different – means of travelling far away from the mundanity of the frankly sometimes rather tedious world we have constructed for ourselves.

The poems in this anthology come from a wide range of sources. Some will be familiar, whilst others, previously unpublished or drawn from some specialist or obscure sources (or both), will not be. Although the primary theme is insects, humour comes a close second. This is a very personal selection – but I hope it also has a general appeal. No attempt has been made to prepare sections of even approximately equal length – to a degree choice has been restricted by the number of poems available, but is fundamentally based on merit.

JT

An August Midnight

A shaded lamp and a waving blind,
And the beat of a clock from a distant floor;
On this scene enter – winged, horned, and spined –
A longlegs, a moth, and a dumbledore;
While 'mid my page there idly stands
A sleepy fly, that rubs its hands ...

Thus meet we five, in this still place,
At this point of time, at this point in space.
My guests besmear my new-penned line,
Or bang at the lamp, and fall supine.
'God's humblest, they!' I muse. Yet why?
They know Earth-secrets that know not I.

Thomas Hardy

Just as the butterfly, child of an hour,
      Flutters about in the light of the sun,
Wandering wayward from flower to flower,
      Sipping the honey from all, one by one;
So does the fanciful verse I've created
      Love 'mongst the experts in Science to roam,
Drinking their wisdom without being sated,
      Bringing the sweets of their intellect home.

"Bell" (Edward Newman)

This appeared as the Preface of Edward Newman's *The Insect Hunters; or Entomology in Verse* (1857), attributed to "Bell". In a second edition – actually a different version: *The Insect Hunters, and other Poems* (1861) – the lines were repeated, but not attributed. The first 80 pages or so of the 1st edition, apparently printed privately by Newman, contain a long description of various insect groups in the style of Longfellow's *Hiawatha*. The first section of the Preface to the 2nd edition (below), published by "John Van Voorst, 1, Paternoster Row, London", made it clear that Newman was concerned that his 1st edition might not be well received. It is likely that "Bell" was Edward Newman himself.

Little book! when I first launched thee
On the dark and dangerous waters
Of opinion, thinking judgement
Would for certain go against thee,
I withdrew from observation,
Hid myself from public notice;
I, thy parent, like a coward,
Launched thee on thy course unfathered.

Edward Newman (first verse)

THE ENTOMOLOGIST

The seeds of this anthology can be traced to the first poem in this section, Mark Isaak's parody of 'I am the very model of a modern Major General' from Gilbert & Sullivan's *The Pirates of Penzance*. It was pinned to the office door of an American entomologist who was working at that time at the British Museum (Natural History) – now the Natural History Museum – in London. In addition to being entomologically accurate (aside from the fact that it is cicadas rather than locusts that have the 17 year cycle), it is rather clever and has near-perfect metre. This was the first piece of paper in the first box file of 'insect' poems which swelled into unmanageable proportions, from which the content of the anthology was eventually selected. Many of the poems here – and in other sections – are parodies on well-known poetic works: the final poem in the section is a parody of Lewis Carroll's 'The Walrus and the Carpenter'.

The Modern Entomologist

I am the very model of a modern entomologist.
I've information useful to a tropical biologist.
I've studied which antennal parts of silverfish are muscular
And know quite well exactly which mosquitoes are crepuscular.
I scan the forest canopy in search of Lepidoptera
And burrow beneath rotting logs for certain Coleoptera.
I've mapped the complex passages that termites always
    scurry in
And studied insect evolution back to the Sulurian.
I know the economic consequences of herbivory
And all the different methods used for pesticide delivery.
In short, in matters vital to the tropical biologist,
I am the very model of a modern entomologist.

I watch as ants patrol the tunnels of their nests incessantly;
Some fireflies I have seen conversing bioluminescently.
I'll tell you gruesome stories of Mantodea ferocity
And quote you the statistics of Neuroptera velocity.
And then I've catalogued the major vectors of malaria
And listed all the earwigs in the Indonesian area.
I've analyzed the noises of the cricket and the katydid.
(The ones from Costa Rica sounded much like those from
    Haiti did.)
I've checked how mayfly populations vary with humidity
And double-checked all E. O. Wilson's theories for validity.
In short, in matters vital to the tropical biologist,
I am the very model of a modern entomologist.

In fact, when I know dragonflies from abdomen to mandible;
When I find aphids, fleas, and lice completely understandable;
When I have skill with killing jars and nets and other
    gimmickry;
And when I know minutiae of camouflage and mimicry;
When I have very detailed observations of a myriad
Of locusts reproducing in a seventeen-year period;
When I know how cockroaches grow from instar to maturity-
My papers (when I write them) won't be destined for
    obscurity.
Although I've studied insects, and in all their great diversity,
I've yet to get my tenure at a major university,
But still, in matters vital to the tropical biologist,
I am the very model of a modern entomologist.

                                                    Mark Isaak

The Strange Case Of The Entomologist's Heart

Consider the case of Mr. Suggs.

He was an eminent entomologist, which is to say he knew
    nothing but bugs.

He could tell the Coleoptera from the Lepidoptera,

And the Aphidae and the Katydididae from the
    Grasshoptera.

He didn't know whether to starve a cold or feed a fever, he
    was so untherapeutical,

But he knew that in 1737 J. Swammerdam's *Biblia Naturae*
    had upset the theories of Aristotle and Harvey by

demonstrating the presence of pupal structures under the
    larval cuticle.

His taste buds were such that he was always asking dining-
    car stewards for their recipe for French dressing and
    mayonnaise,

But he was familiar with Strauss-Durckheim's brilliant
    treatise (1828) on the cockchafer and that earlier
    (1760) but equally brilliant monograph on the goat-
    moth caterpillar of P. Lyonnet's

He was so unliterary that he never understood the different
    between *Ibid*. and *Anonymous*,

But he spoke of 1842 as the year in which Von Kölliker
    first described the formation of blastoderm in the egg of
    the midge *Chironomus*.

Mr. Suggs' speciality was fireflies, which he knew inside
    out and from stem to stern,

And he was on the track of why they blaze and don't burn,

And then one day he met a girl as fragrant as jessamine,

And he found her more fascinating than the rarest eleven-
    legged specimen,

But being a diffident swain he wished to learn how the land
   lay before burning his bridges,
So he bashfully asked her mother what she thought of his
   chances, and she encouragingly said, At sight of you my
   daughter lights up like a firefly, and Mr. Suggs
   stammered, Good gracious, what a strange place for a
   girl to light up! and rapidly returned to his goat-moth
   caterpillars, blastoderms and midges.

                                                    Ogden Nash

The Hunting Of The Moth

"Just the place for a moth," said the F.E.S.,
      As he daintily handled his net,
Supporting the ring on the tip of his nose,
      To keep the bag out of the wet.

Just the place for a moth. I have said it twice,
      As told me by one who knew;
Just the place for a Moth, which we'll catch in a thrice,
      If what I have stated is true!

F.E.S. was the name of this hunter bold –
      He had sworn he would catch or die;
He had bottles and pins his captures to hold,
      And a microscope stuck in his eye.

His kit was complete. It included a cork
      And a large pair of cotton-wool socks,
A net and a forceps, some sugar and rum,
      And last, but not least, came the box.

10

The cork is most useful in crossing a stream,
    When the Moth has flown over before:
With one foot on the cork you float over like steam,
    By using your net as an oar.

Now a moth, as you know, is a timorous bird,
    Which lives upon sugar and rum;
To catch it your footstep must never be heard,
    So in cotton-wool socks you must come.

His net went by clockwork, wound up by a spring
    Concealed in a handle of cane;
The top was of steel, which bent round in a ring,
    And was used as a shelter from rain.

The bag was of spiders' web, bound with red tape,
    Attached to the ring by a hook,
Of a parallel-octagon-circular shape;
    When full it shut up like a book.

Then the box, which he bore, was a wonderful sight,
    Compounded of paper and wool;
With chains and a padlock to keep it shut tight,
    And always half empty when full.

His comrade, the Buggist, was equally fine,
    And equally fully equipped;
His net was a vision, his pins were divine,
    Of oyster-beard, platinum tipped.

On their bikes they had ridden for many a mile,
    With many a check by the way;
For the Buggist would try to ride over each stile,
    Thus causing much needless delay.

But now all was over: their troubles were passed:
  To the Haunt of the Moth they had come!
Their nets and their boxes were ready at last,
  With the sugar, the pins and the rum.

Now a brush in each hand these bold hunters took,
  (Their excitement was awful to see),
As they read the instructions out of a book,
  Ere they carefully sugared each tree.

When the sugar was on, said the F.E.S.:
  "It is time for a speech from me:
For I know nothing but you know less,
  Of the Moths we may hope to see.

"We have cycled round, we have cycled across,
  And cross we have both of us been;
We have travelled for hours, each hour a loss,
  Since never a Moth we have seen.

"Now listen again while I tell you, my friend" –
  But the Buggist was strolling around –
"I cannot go on if you will not attend
  To the marks which on Moths must be found.

"I will first take the wings. They are large, they are small,
  They even are absent in some:
They are coloured or not, but the best thing of all
  Is – they make a bee-line for the rum.

"By easy gradations we come to the flight,
  About which there is nothing to say;
Since you cannot observe it when hunting at night,
  And they seldom are met with by day.

12

"The next is their speech, which is cheerful and bright –
    As far as we ever can hear;
Some squeak if you scratch them, some buzz round a light,
    But rather from pleasure than fear.

"The last is the feathers, which fall, sure as fate,
    If ever they're handled too rough;
But, though strips of paper will keep them on straight,
    One pin in each wing is enough.

"We next must divide them in sections and tribes,
    Defining each separate lot;
For those which eat sugar will always take bribes,
    But those which drink whiskey will not.

"Now, although common Moths can be easily set,
    Yet I think it but proper to say,
Some are bees." —Here the speaker broke off in a pet,
    For the Buggist was running away.

The F.E.S. chased him with anger and pride;
    He chased him with brickbats and will;
It seemed that for hours they raced side by side,
    Ere the Buggist thought fit to stand still.

He was red in the face, but you scarcely could trace
    A sign of repentance or fear,
As, holding his comrade in closest embrace,
    He whispered this tale in his ear:—

"Ere I started this trip I consulted a friend,
    Who often my fortune has told;
He bade me beware of the terrible end
    That awaits the unwary and bold.

13

"He said to me, then, did that wisest of men,
    If your Moth be a Moth that is well;
Bring it home in a box, it will wind up the clocks,
    Though the hour it never can tell.

"You may pin it with needles, preserve it with glue;
    (You may wrap it in paper with care),
You will find it is handy for mending a shoe,
    Or for ladies to wear in their hair:

"You may seek it with camphor and seek it with care;
    You may hunt it with broomsticks and bread;
You may threaten to kill it with country air;
    You may charm it with knocks on the head.

"But Oh, noble Hunter! Beware of the night
    When your Moth is a Bee, in which case
You must softly and swiftly arrange for your flight,
    Or you'll surely be stung in the face.

"It was this, it was this, which excited my fears;
    To be stung in the eye is no fun;
As you spoke I perceived quite a buzz in the ears,
    And instantly started to run."

"What rot," said the other, "you cannot mistake
    Two such totally different things;
Unless you are dreaming, but if you're awake,
    You must simply examine their wings.

"You have nothing to fear! With your F.E.S. near,
    On the hunt you may boldly proceed;
If you should be in doubt of the insects about,
    You will find him a true friend indeed.

14

"Just bear that in mind and you'll certainly find,
    If your eye and your lamp you keep bright,
With the ring of my net to keep out the wet,
    A moth will be taken to-night.

"With your forceps in hand, near each tree take your stand,
    And watch the peculiar flight
Of each bug which arrives—they won't come from the hives,
    For those are all closed for the night!

"We must seek them with camphor and seek them with care,
    We must hunt them with broomsticks and bread;
We must threaten to kill them with country air,
    We must charm them with knocks on the head."

But while they were seeking with camphor and care,
    A rat-trap stood silently by
And grabbed at the Buggist, who sprang in the air
    (Tho' he knew that he never could fly).

He offered some sugar, he offered his net—
    Not a gift, of course, merely a loan;
But the trap just continued compressing its jaws,
    And nipped the poor chap to the bone.

Down he sank on the mound, looking wildly around,
    While the ants it belonged to awoke;
He felt them bite in like the pricks of a pin
    And remarked "This thing passes a joke."

The F.E.S. rushed to the poor Buggist's side
    But, not being used to such things,
When implored to release him, he gently replied,
    That he "first must examine its wings."

He helped him at length with the whole of his strength,
　　And having with toil set him free,
Remarked that he thought, when the Buggist was caught,
　　He had merely been stung by a Bee!

"Now start we once more. I will go on before,
　　And avoid all the traps that are laid;
But see that you mind, as you limp on behind,
　　All the rules for your guidance I've made.

"You must look high and low, you must try all you know,
　　For a Moth is quite easily lost;
But when it is caught, all your toil seems as naught,
　　And you little reck what it has cost."

They sought it on sugar, they sought it on trees,
　　They sought it with broomsticks and bread;
They looked for it standing, they searched on their knees—
　　The Buggist twice stood on his head!

The F.E.S. suddenly sprang in the air,
　　With a scream like the squeak of a bat:—
"'Tis a Moth! I can swear I have taken a pair,
　　And have them safe under my hat."

"Be careful—be cautious!" The Buggist implored;
　　"Beware how you handle the things:
Your own sage advice must not now be ignored –
　　You have got to examine their wings!

"Let me lift up the hat, while the brim is kept flat,
　　And a small ray of sunshine creeps in:
The Moths will run round till that sunshine is found,
　　And be caught on the point of a pin."

Said the F.E.S.:—"Now! do not make such a row!
    For a row and a blunder are one—
The rule in this case, by the laws of the chase,
    Is simply to keep out the sun."

So saying, he took the hat into the crook
    Of his net with a vigorous twist;
Remarking he knew the correct thing to do,
    Was a delicate turn of the wrist.

The Buggist observed that the net-ring had swerved,
    And swiftly drew back in a fright:
He perceived in the law a most obvious flaw,
    And wished to preserve his full sight.

The insect flew out, and went buzzing about,
    He first flew down low, then flew high;
He flew this way and that, still avoiding the hat,
    Till he hit F.E.S. in the eye.

"'Tis a Moth! 'Tis a Fly! I am stung— 'tis a Bee!"
    Thus the F.E.S. aimlessly cried;
And hit at the creature, which injured his feature,
    Till it fell on the greensward and died.

The Buggist examined the mangled remains,
    With broomsticks and sugar and care,
And remarked as he did so:— "This amply explains
    The buzz that I heard in the air!

"Our hunting is over! Your rules are no good!
    All our pins are no use—for you see
You are stung in the eye. Let us flee from this wood,
    Lest every Moth turn to a Bee!"

So they trundled off home. But that Bee from the comb,
  Never more to the hive would it fly.
And the F.E.S. said a mass for the dead—
  With his microscope still in his eye.

"Ellnest Eriott" and "Maude Clorley"
(Ernest Elliot and Claude Morley)

This poem is a parody on Lewis Carroll's 'The Hunting of the Snark'. The term "buggist" – to describe someone interested in 'bugs' – is a horrible word, but may be marginally better than the anticipated "bugger". Reference to sugar and rum in the 4th verse is not as out of place as it might seem. "Sugaring" has been a recognised method for attracting moths at night since the mid-19th century, when well known entomologists of the day, Henry and Edward Doubleday, discovered that discarded empty sugar hogsheads (casks) attracted moths at night. It was soon found that a mixture of molasses, sugar and rum (or beer) painted onto gate posts or tree trunks, not only attracted nocturnal moths, but also rendered them drunk, so they could be more easily collected. The question of bees flying at night is quite unlikely in this country (although hornets sometimes do), but I well remember occasions in Borneo, collecting moths in the rainforest with a mercury vapour light, when particularly vicious black bees were attracted to the light in large numbers, and needed to be treated with great respect.

Tut, Tutt

Mr Tutt, who tells no lies,
Tells us that the butterflies
Are alas, what do you think?
Let me whisper, fond of drink!

He has watched them on the flow'rs,
Where they'll sit and suck for hours,
Quite devoid of any motion
Save absorption of the lotion.

Thus they spend the summer's day
While the females work away,
For this craving to regale
Is restricted to the male.

Lost illusion of our youth
In a scientific truth,
Tear drops gather in our eyes
When we think of butterflies.

Anonymous

This poem was published by the editor of Punch magazine following a public lecture by a well known entomologist of the time, James William Tutt (1858-1911), which included details of the Lepidoptera penchant for intoxicants.

The Buggist And The F.E.S.

The lamps were shining on the road,
    Shining with furtive ray;
They did their little best to light
    The rough and stony way—
And this was odd because it was
    The middle of the day.

The moon was shining sulkily,
    Because she thought the light
Had got no business to be there
    Just when the sun was bright—
"If it were not so hot," she said,
    "I would go down and fight."

The sun was hot as hot could be,
    The flask was dry and dry;
There was no shade upon the road
    To cool the cloudless sky;
The pupae groaned beneath the sod
    Because they could not fly.

The Buggist and the F.E.S.
    Were looking for the wood;
They wept like anything to see
    A clearing where it stood:
"Now that's all carried off," they said,
    "Our sugar is no good."

"If seven bugs, with seven broods,
    Had gnawed for half a year,
Do you suppose," the Buggist said,
    "They would have got it clear?"
"I doubt it," said the F.E.S.,
    And dropped a saline tear.

"O, bugglings, come and walk with us,"
    The Buggist did beseech—
"A pleasant walk: you've much to learn
    And we have much to teach;
We cannot do with more than ten,
    To give a box to each."

An ancient Beetle buzzed away,
    But ne'er a word he said;
That wary Insect winked his eye,
    And shook his hoary head—
To indicate, he would not choose
    A pill-box for his bed.

But ten young mothlings hurried up,
    All eager for the fun:
Their coats were brushed, their elytra
    Were shining in the sun—
And this was very odd because
    You know that moths have none.

Ten other mothlings followed them,
    And beetles many score:
Till thick and fast they came at last—
    The crowd grew ever more:
All hurrying through the wood to taste
    The luscious rummy store.

The Buggist and the F.E.S.
    Walked on a mile or so,
Then sat them down upon a stump
    Conveniently low;
While all the hungry insects stood
    And feasted in a row.

"The time is come," the Buggist said,
    "To talk of many things:
Of butterflies and *Cossus*-trees
    And shining beetles wings:
How many toes a Weevil has,
    And whether fleas have stings."

"But wait a bit," the bugglings cried,
    "Before we have our chat;
For some of us are very lean,
    And here we'll soon grow fat."
"No hurry," said the F.E.S.:
    They thanked him much for that.

"A lot of pins," the Buggist said,
    "Is what we chiefly need;
These modern killing-bottles too
    Are very good indeed …
Now, we are ready, bugglings dear,
    Have you enjoyed your feed?"

"Oh! Don't kill *us*," the buglets cried,
    Turning a little blue:
"After such kindness, that would be
    A horrid thing to do!"
"A well corked box," the Buggist said,
    "Is just the thing for you:

"It was so kind of you to come—
    And some of you are rare."
The F.E.S. said nothing but
    "I'd like to take a pair –
Now there's another one gone off:
    I really want to swear!"

"You are too slow," the Buggist said,
    "Your forceps are too long—
They see the light and off they go—
    That sugar was too strong."
The F.E.S. said nothing but
    "Now there, I think you're wrong."

"I grieve for you," the Buggist said,
    "I deeply sympathize."
With sobs and tears he stuck them through
    With pins of smallest size—
Blowing a cloud of smoke the while
    To drive away the flies.

"O, bugglings," said the F.E.S.,
    "You've had a lot of fun.
Shall we be getting home again?"
    But answer there was none—
And this was scarcely odd because
    They'd taken every one.

                    "Ellnest Eriott" and "Maude Clorley"

COLLECTING AND COLLECTORS

The father of modern taxonomy, Carl Linnaeus, wrote in *Glory of the Scientist* (1737): "I am tempted to ask whether men are in their right mind who so desperately risk life and everything else through the love of collecting". Linnaeus was referring to plant collectors, but the sentiment applies equally to collectors of other natural history objects.

The poems in this section refer almost exclusively to the collection of butterflies, whose beauty and diversity are obvious to anyone who lives in the countryside or visits it regularly.

Butterfly collecting (and collection of other creatures) is anathema to many people in these conservation-orientated days where habitats are being destroyed at such an alarming rate. Yet it has its place: professional entomologists almost all learned their trade, and certainly acquired appreciation and knowledge of nature in general, from making collections in their youth. Some grow out of it – but modern political correctness largely removes the choice for young people to 'learn' through this sort of experience. Collectively, this is our loss. Many so-called conservationists today show a depressing lack of knowledge of the creatures they claim to want to conserve, partly because they have not had the benefit of the understanding that comes with close observation of collecting and rearing them as children. Most butterflies and moths lay many hundreds of eggs, sometimes thousands, and the vast majority fall prey to predators of one kind or another – if they didn't, we would soon be knee deep in Cabbage Whites! Most individual butterflies will have mated and laid their eggs when they are collected, and to do so has little or no effect on local populations.

The "fond, useless toys" mentioned in the first poem are a basis of memories of long summers spent in the hills and mountains, in some of the most beautiful countryside on Earth. It is the habitats butterflies occupy that are in desperate need of protection, and one cannot help but think that this is appreciated more by those who have grown up in the country collecting butterflies (and engaged in other harmless country pursuits) than by the politically correct 'do-gooder' who has it firmly fixed in his or her mind that such activity is unacceptable.

My Butterflies

A cabinet of butterflies-
"Fond, useless toys", you say,
But, every one to me a prize
Made dearer day by day
As the years go by, and summer hours
Vanish with brief delay:
For each, "a thing of beauty rare
Is a joy for ever and aye."

So sang divine Euripides,
And true are his words of gold:
And every butterfly sleeping here
Can a dream of delight unfold.
Visions of alpine solitudes,
And cataracts pouring cold
Through glacier gardens aster-starred
These dark *Erebias*[1] hold.

Chrysophanus[2] with wings of flame
The marshlands of Garonne
Brings back, where I have wandered far
Contented, and alone
With Nature; or where, day and night
Broods from his golden throne
The arctic sun on silent meres
Where never a sail is blown.

---

[1] *Erebia*: a large circumpolar genus containing more than 100 species of mostly dull brown butterflies. Their larvae feed on species of grass and they occur from arctic Canada and Siberia to the high mountains of northern and central Europe.

[2] *Chrysophanus*: a genus with several 'copper' butterflies (none occur in the UK) which are brilliant orange and red.

This line of shimmering 'Azure Blues'
My heart with rapture thrills;
Silver on blue, as the clouds themselves,
And edged with ermine frills.
Boon memories of pensive hours
Among the gentle hills,
And billowy downs of England
When Spring her balm distils.

These are the pied "Half-Mourners"[3],
No mourners sad for me;
For they conjure up the olive yards
And the blue Aegean sea,
Where Vardar comes down singing
To the dusty plains, and free
The winds of Heaven make music
On the heights of Basilic.

Right Royal on bright vermilion
And orange pinions borne
"Aurora of Provence" reflects
The saffron-tinted morn,
Where the wine-dark Mediterranean
Sighs ever a song folorn,
And high in the scented pine trees
The zephyrs wind their horn.

---

[3] Half-Mourner: an old English name for the Marbled White butterfly,
Melanargia galathea which is one of several species to have extended
their range in the UK in recent years.

Or I gaze on the "Emperor"[4] laid in state
In his iris robes, and clear
A vista of green oak-forest breaks
On my sense, and far and near
The fairy flutes, and violins
Of the insect choir I hear...
The voice of Summer among the leaves
Made one with the perfect year.

The leaves must fall, the roses fade:
The daffodils will not stay;
The flashing diadem of the Dawn
Dims into twi-light gray;
But you, my butterflies, as of old
Your glory still display,
Though long the little spark of life
Has burnt itself away.

Oliver Grey

[4] The Purple Emperor, *Apatura iris*; common but rather local species of
well established oak woods in the UK. It is not seen often, since the
adults spend much of their time in the tops of the trees.

Of The Boy And Butterfly

Behold, how eager this our little boy
Is for a butterfly, as if all joy,
All profits, honours, yea, and lasting pleasures,
Were wrapped up in her, or the richest treasures
Found in her would be bundled up together,
When all her all is lighter than a feather.

He halloos, runs, and cries out, 'Here, boys, here!'
Nor doth he brambles or the nettles fear:
He stumbles at the molehills, up he gets,
And runs again, as one bereft of wits;
And all his labour and his large outcry
Is only for a silly butterfly.

Comparison

This little boy an emblem is of those
Whose hearts are wholly at the world's dispose.
The butterfly doth represent to me
The world's best things at best but fading be.
All are but painted nothings and false joys,
Like this poor butterfly to these our boys.

His running through nettles, thorns, and briers,
To gratify his boyish fond desires,
His tumbling over molehills to attain
His end, namely, his butterfly to gain,
Doth plainly show what hazards some men run
To get what will be lost as soon as won.

John Bunyan

The Boy And The Butterfly

Roving butterfly
Is flitting to and fro,
Now rapidly and high,
Now tardily and low,
In errant passage over
A blooming field of clover.

A boy, with longing gaze,
The roving insect views,
And through its devious ways
He hastily pursues,
Till, on a bloom reposing,
The butterfly seems dozing.

Then softly, silently,
To it the boy draws near;
His heart beats hurriedly
With mingled hope and fear;
His cheeks the rose resemble,
His feet beneath him tremble.

With eager hand the bloom
He grasps impetuously,
And with its sweet perfume
The heedless butterfly:
So tightly he enfolds it,
'Tis dying as he holds it.

Fill'd with a thousand joys,
He loudly from their play
Summons the other boys
Immediately away,

To share with him the pleasure
Of gazing on his treasure.

The lovely majesty
And beauty of his prize
He wishes all to see:
There with expectant eyes
They stand; but still he lingers,
Nor yet unlocks his fingers.

Meanwhile each lustrous hue,
The purple and the gold,
The wings that lightly flew,
And o'er the meadows stroll'd,
Untiringly he praises
In many sounding phrases.

At length he can decide
The captive to display:
His hand he opens wide –
Lo! there, to his dismay,
A little dust is lying-
A worthless grub is dying!

Soon from the butterfly had fled
The beauty so much coveted,
When in the boy's hand press'd,:
So what we eagerly desire,
Alas! leaves nothing to admire
Oft times, when once possess'd.

Peter Parley

The virtuoso thus, at noon,
Broiling beneath a July sun,
The gilded butterfly pursues
O'er hedge and ditch, through gaps and mews;
And, after many a vain essay
To captivate the tempting prey,
Gives him at length the lucky pat,
And has him safe beneath his hat;
Then lifts it gently from the ground;
But, ah! 'tis lost as soon as found.
Culprit his liberty regains,
Flies out of sight, and mocks his pains.

William Cowper

Retribution

"Send me some lines," said the F.E.S.[5],
As he drowsily swayed in his chair,
For his mind was blank and his fingers shrank
From the pen he had wiped in his hair.

"Send me some lines," he cried again,
As the swaying chair stood still,
"For the book is new and I look to you
First ink on the pages to spill."

[5] "F.E.S." refers to a Fellow of the Entomological Society of London. In
1933 the Society received royal patronage and became the Royal
Entomological Society of London and Fellows became F.R.E.S.

31

"Send me some lines," he whispered low,
As he sank from his chair to the floor—
He had named the last bug and lay on the rug,
Till the next post should bring him some more.

First he sank down in a slumber profound,
Then, sudden, sprang up in alarm,
For a grand old *Lucanus*[6] stood close by his side
With its mandibles fixed in his arm.

"You are wanted," it cried; and a warrant displayed
By the Marquis of *Carabus*[7] signed:
It charged him with treason and murder most foul,
Of the laurel-leaf, hot-water kind.

A court was soon formed with a Bug on the Bench,
A jury of beetles and fleas;
All insects in England appeared as his foes:
His sole friends were the mites from a cheese.

His accusers all clamoured and shouted for blood—
"He has poisoned us, boiled us," they cry:
"He has pierced us with pins, he has gummed us on card,
He has left us in bottles to die."

His advocate, Mites, could find nothing to say
(Except that he didn't eat cheese).
So the Judge found him guilty, and gently remarked:
"Your sentence, now, Gentlemen, please."

[6] *Lucanus* is the generic name of the stag beetle, *L. cervus*.
[7] *Carabus* is the generic name of several beetles in the large beetle family Carabidae.

32

And this was the terrible sentence they gave
In proof of their hearty goodwill:—
"That the lines he has asked for be ruled on his back,
And he swallow one Byrrhian pill[8]"

The poor F.E.S. said he wished to appeal,
But was angrily told to be still;
A sheet of instructions was placed in his hand
On the subject of Taking a Pill.

With a start, he awoke—Judge and Jury were gone
But the paper remained; and he smiled,
As in it he read, with a thrill of delight,
These lines which The Bard had compiled.

"Ellnest Eriott" and "Maude Clorley"

One can imagine the two old gentlemen sitting around their collecting light until late in the evening. Many of the poems of Eriott and Clorley are clever parodies of well-known works. Whilst not a parody, the poem above is reminiscent of Coleridge's *Khubla Khan*, said to have been constructed in its entirety following a vivid dream.

---

[8] The term Byrrhian refers to a beetle, *Byrrhus pilula*.

The lepidopterist with happy cries,
devotes his days to catching butterflies.
The leopard, through some feline mental twist,
would rather hunt the lepidopterist.
That's why I never adopted lepidoptery:
I do not wish to live in jeopardoptery.

Ogden Nash

In addition to Ogden Nash's humorous connection between butterfly collector and leopard, there is another. Butterflies (particularly males of some butterfly families which habitually 'patrol' large areas in search of a mate and may therefore benefit from the additional energy provided) have what some might regard as rather unpleasant habits, being partial to the juices of overripe fruit, rotting meat and animal faeces which they probe with their long proboscises. The most attractive faeces are those of meat-eaters, which of course include the big cats. If the leopard really did choose to hunt a lepidopterist, as Ogden Nash imagined, it might do worse than to leave its scats in a suitably prominent position, and wait behind a tree for the butterfly collector!

Butterflies are also attracted to urine, from which they appear able to obtain useful salts (particularly sodium) and minerals by imbibing the liquid. A French nursery rhyme places this in a convenient nutshell: *"Faites pipi sur le gazon / Pour embêter les papillons"*, translated as "Make weewee on the grass / It makes the butterflies excited". The BBC made a 'Wildlife On One' film on the Indonesian island of Sulawesi in 1985, which included a section with clouds of butterflies obtaining salts at the side of the Tumpah River (referred to as 'mud-puddling'). What is not obvious from the film is that cameraman Martin Saunders and I urinated on a suitable spot on the bank, returning two hours later for him to film the footage that was eventually shown on television. The content of our outpourings probably had more alcohol (of a particularly vicious local variety, referred to as 'screech') than meat, but it still worked a treat!

Sir Joseph Banks And
The Emperor Of Morocco

Pharaoh had not one grain of taste,
The flies on him were thrown to waste,
Nay, met, with strong objection:
But had Thy Servant, Lord, been there,
I should have made, or much I err,
A wonderful collection.

Then Sir Joseph began to trot round the fields—

When from a dab of dung, or some such thing,
An Emperor of Morocco rear'd his wing!
Lightly with winnowing wing amid the land,
His Moorish Majesty in circles flew!
With sturdy striding legs and outstretched hand
The Virtuoso did his game pursue.
He strikes – he misses – strikes again – he grins,
And sees in thought the monarch fixed with pins;
Sees him on paper giving up the ghost,
Nail'd like a hawk or martyr to a post.

Sir Joseph fell several times in the course of his pursuit, to
the amazement of a countryman standing near a hedge.

Now through the hedge, exactly like a horse,
Wild plunged the President with all his force,
His brow in sweat, his soul in perturbation,
Mindless of trees and bushes and the brambles,
Head over heels into the lane he scrambles,
Where Hob stood lost in wide-mouth'd speculation.

'Speak,' roared the President, 'this instant say
Hast seen, hast seen, my lad, this way,
The Emp'ror of Morocco pass?'
Hob to the insect-hunter naught reply'd,
But shook his head, and sympathising sigh'd, 'Alas,
And pity much your upper story!'

Sir Joseph raced down the lane, and presently saw The butterfly
fly over a garden wall. He rushed through the door, knocking
down the gardener, the bell-glasses and the scarecrow, and
trampling down hyacinths, tulips, anemones and carnations by

the score and by the hundred in his mad pursuit. Next he overturned a hive of bees, but in his excitement he Was impervious to their attacks, and rushed on in pursuit of the butterfly pursued in his turn by the furious gardener.

'At length the gard'ner swelled with grief and dolour,
O'ertaking, grasps Sir Joseph by the collar,
And blest with favourite oaths, abundance showers,
'Villain,' he cry'd, 'beyond example!
Just like a cart-horse on my beds to trample!
More than your soul is worth to kill my flowers!
See how your two vile hoofs have made a wreck.
Look, rascal, at each beauty's broken neck!'

Sir Joseph broke out into lamentations over the loss of the butterfly.

'Gone is my soul's desire, for ever gone!'
'Who's gone ?' the gard'ner strait reply'd.
'The Emperor, Sir,' with tears Sir Joseph cry'd,
"The Emp'ror of Morocco, thought my own!
To unknown fields behold the monarch fly,
Zounds, not to catch him what an ass was I!'
His eyes the Gard'ner full of horror stretch'd,
And then a groan, a monstrous groan he fetch'd,
Contemplating around his ruined wares;
And now he let Sir Joseph's collar go:
And now he bray'd aloud with bitterest woe,
'Mad, madder than the maddest of March hares!'

Peter Pindar

British explorer, naturalist and science patron Sir Joseph Banks (1743-1820) maintained (amongst many other interests), an interest in entomology, and his collection of insects remains intact at the Natural History Museum, London. It is one of the principal sources on which J. C. Fabricius, a pupil of Linnaeus, the founder of modern taxonomy, based many descriptions. Banks appears to have been ridiculed in certain quarters for his attraction to the natural world, and John Wolcot, a doctor and satirical writer of the period, who wrote under the pseudonym "Peter Pindar," seemingly never tired of poking fun at him. This is an extract from a satirical account of Banks' expedition to capture a butterfly: 'The Emperor of Morocco'. Wolcot tells the story in verse, first offering a prayer that the 'plague of flies' might be repeated for the benefit of allowing Banks to collect them. 'The President' refers to the fact that Banks was President of the Royal Society, the oldest and most prestigious scientific society in the world. History does not record what Banks thought of this shabby treatment!

The Sage

"You are old, Father Beaumont," the young Buggist said,
    "And your hair is uncommonly thin;
Yet you carry your net the whole summer through,
    And gather your specimens in."—

"In the days of my youth," old Alfred replied,
    "I enjoyed much the pleasures of life;
And the mounting of insects, I freely confess,
    Was the greatest (excepting my wife).

It is hardly too much to say to you now:
    Entomology long I have found
The first, most enduring, untiring research
    With which can one's labours be crowned."—

"I find it so irksome, collecting small things,
    One can't see without a strong lens,"
The Buggist went on, with a tear in his eye,
    "And I really don't see where it wends."—

"It wends," said the vet'ran, "to something quite new,
    That the world never heard of before:
Which is better, I ask you, great Science to aid
    Or of lucre to lay up a store?

Be a Darwin, my lad, and all humans assist,
    Through the ages and ages to come.
Did I give all my energies money to earn,
    Ephemeral must be the sum."

                    "Ellnest Eriott" and "Maude Clorley"

This is a loose parody of Lewis Carroll's poem 'You are Old, Father William …' from *Alice's Adventures in Wonderland*. Alfred Beaumont (1832-1905) was an entomological contemporary of the authors.

Then we gather, as we travel,
Bits of moss and dirty gravel,
    And we chip off little specimens of stone;
And we carry home as prizes
Funny bugs of handy sizes,
    Just to give the day a scientific tone.

                    Charles Edward Carryl

The Dream Of Betty

Beguiling Betty, lush but lonely
would often sigh and say "If only
some Charming Prince would come and woo me,
impress and pamper and pursue me—
perhaps a poet—an anthologist—
or better still, an entomologist,
or, best of all, a bit of both:
to him I'd surely plight my troth;
an insect-man both tough and tender
would spell immediate surrender.
Because you see," continued Betty,
"my heart is like the Serengeti,
a place of forces dark and raw,
of nature red in tooth and claw,
a place where wild and hornèd hopes
stampede about like antelopes."

One night to soothe an aching molar
she chewed a piece of gorgonzola,
and then she slept both long and deep,
but oh what dreams assailed her sleep!
Before her wide astonished eyes
appeared a moth of giant size—
a wondrous moth all smooth and white
that glowed and glistened in the night,
a silvery moth with blackish freckles,
a moth with countless crimson speckles,
a moth of might and masculinity
to which she felt a strange affinity.

"How do you do?" the Moth began,
and as it spoke it slowly ran

one soft antenna down her cheek,
which made her feel distinctly weak:
her knees began to shake like jelly;
butterflies fluttered in her belly;
she thought she was about to drown—
thank goodness she was lying down.
"My word," she said, "you *are* a charmer—
are you my Moth in Shining Armour?"
"It's possible," the Moth replied
and snuggled closer to her side,
"I have two names: my friends, you see,
refer to me as Triple G
(which stands for Gorgeous Gaudy Geezer)
but you may call me *Utetheisa*."

"I'm Betty," said the bashful maid,
"be nice to me or I'm afraid
I may withhold my full affection
and add you to my moth collection—
(and every moth that I impale
is, by the way, a perfect male)."
The Moth replied "O beauteous Betty,
your hair is thicker than spaghetti:
you clearly have a fertile scalp—"
he brushed it with his labial palp—
"your skin is smooth as vermicelli,
and oh what lovely dark ocelli!"

With admiration and surprise
she gazed into his compound eyes,
and though it seemed forbidden fruiticle
she longed to touch his lustrous cuticle.
The tension was extreme, exhaustin',
but then, as though he'd read Jane Austen

the Moth, as suave as Mr Darcy,
entwined her in his manly tarsi
and swept her off her feet and flew
away with her to pastures new.
He found a place no-one would notice
with lots of fragrant *Myosotis*
and there, amongst the ferns and mosses,
he kissed her with his long proboscis.

But then at once poor luckless Betty
awoke all feverish and sweaty—
and now her lepidopteran saviour
who'd shown such laudable behaviour
had vanished, nowhere to be seen—
alas the gorgeous Moth had been
(she realized with consternation)
a cheese-induced hallucination.

Robert Hoare

Utetheisa is a widespread genus of the family Arctiidae. They are
beautiful white moths with black and red spots on their forewings;
their larvae feed on various plants in the forget-me-not family,
including forget-me-nots (*Myosotis*). They also occur in Europe (and
rarely in the UK, where *Utetheisa pulchella* is known as the Crimson-
speckled Footman). The end of this poem has something of Wallace
& Gromit about it! See also 'Across The Stubble', by PBM Allan.

Uncle Jotham's Boarder

"I've kep' summer boarders for years, and allowed
  I knowed all the sorts that there be;
But there come an old feller this season along,
  That turned out a beater for me.
Whatever that feller was arter, I vow
  I hain't got the slightest idee.

"He had an old bait-net of thin, rotten stuff
  That a minner could bite his way through;
But he never went fishin'- at least, in the way
  That fishermen gen'ally do;
But he carried that bait-net wherever he went;
  The handle was j'inted in two.

"And the bottles and boxes that chap fetched along!
  Why, a doctor could never want more;
If they held pills and physic, he'd got full enough
  To fit out a medicine-store.
And he'd got heaps of pins, dreffle lengthy and slim,
  Allers droppin' about on the floor.

"Well, true as I live, that old feller just spent
  His hull days in loafin' about
And pickin' up hoppers and roaches and flies –
  Not to use for his bait to ketch trout,
But to kill and stick pins in and squint at and all.
  He was crazy 's a coot, th' ain't no doubt.

"He'd see a poor miller a-flyin' along,-
  The commonest, every-day kind,-
And he'd waddle on arter it, fat as he was,
  And follower up softly behind,

43

Till he'd flop that-air bait-net right over its head,
    And I'd laugh till nigh out of my mind.

"Why, he'd lay on the ground for an hour at a stretch
    And scratch in the dirt like a hen;
He'd scrape all the bark off the bushes and trees,
    And turn the stones over; and then
He'd peek under logs, or he'd pry into holes.
    I'm glad there ain't no more sech men.

"My wife see a box in his bedroom, one day,
    Jest swarmin' with live caterpillars;
He fed 'em on leaves off all kinds of trees –
    The ellums and birches and willers;
And he'd got piles of boxes, chock-full to the top
    With crickets and bees and moth-millers.

"I asked him, one time, what his business might be.
    Of course, I fust made some apology.
He tried to explain, but such awful big words!
    Sorto' forren, outlandish, and collegey,
'S near 's I can tell, 'stead of enterin' a trade,
    he was tryin' to jest enter *mology*.

"And Hannah, my wife, says she's heerd o' sech things;
    She guesses his brain warn't so meller.
There's a thing they call Nat'ral Histerry, she says,
    And, whatever the folks there may tell her,
Till it's settled she's wrong she'll jest hold that-air man
    Was a nat'ral Histerrical feller."

Annie Trumbull Slosson

This splendid poem contains sentiments familiar to many naturalists. There is an odd lack of understanding amongst non-natural historians who observe entomologists and others "acting strangely". I have lost count of the number of times I have been asked, when carrying an insect net in the forest or on a mountain many miles from the nearest stream, if I am fishing – and in the Solomon Islands, although local people were always polite, I knew that my collecting butterflies was completely beyond the comprehension of most people. If these tiny insects had no value, and couldn't be eaten, why on earth would the white man spend so much of his time and expend so much energy in the midday heat? A fair question, perhaps.

Occasionally however, one gets the opportunity to get one's own back. On the large island of San Cristobal, in the eastern Solomons Archipelago, I remember meeting a middle-aged American tourist (her presence there was much more unusual than mine, for I have never seen any other tourist in several visits to that island). She said "You must be the Butterfly Man". Word gets around. I agreed I was and she asked how I caught butterflies. Considering I was standing there with a very large net to which was attached a 3 metre long pole, this seemed a moderately foolish question. At that precise moment, I spotted movement from the corner of my eye, and reached out to snatch from the air a large butterfly which had been about to fly lazily past. Both butterfly and I were equally surprised at this unlikely success, but neither more so than the American tourist. Her jaw dropped. "How on earth did you do that?" I explained that I had been doing this for some years and that I always caught butterflies with my hands. With practice, it wasn't difficult, although I occasionally missed the small and very fast-flying ones. Since she had just seen me do it with her own eyes, and in an apparently relaxed manner, whilst I was casually talking to her, she swallowed it hook, line and sinker. Before going our separate ways, she asked what the net was for. Innocently, I told her that it was for when I got bored with collecting butterflies, and fancied a bit of fishing instead.

The Insects In Council,
A Fable

Thro' all the vast nations, that creep, float or fly,
In the boundless domains of earth, water, and sky,
The terrors of war spread distress and alarms,
For the BIPEDS, for conquest, were all under arms.
Not a nook of a bank—not a chink of a tree,
From these daily and nightly invaders was free;
In habit of sportsman, with net, bag, and knife;—
With poison and pins for destruction of life,
And portable prisons, in which to ensnare
The captives they seize in the water or air;—
They come forth by day,— then in gloom of the eve,
With nets all illumin'd, steal out to deceive;
An art, to which modern invention's no stranger,
By *light artificial* to lure into danger;
For men are like moths, and will heedlessly run,
To the glare of a taper and think it the sun.

     In emergence thus dire, each confederate State,
Agreed on a council for solemn debate.
The HUMMINGBIRD SPHINX[9] on her soft-sounding wings,
Like notes that sweep sweet o'er Eolian strings,
Was despatch'd to convene from their airy dominions,
The nations innumerous that float upon pinions,
The GRASSHOPPER—sacred to music of yore,
Whom the fam'd Grecian poets profess'd to adore,
And plac'd on the harp as an emblem renown'd,
Of the science that teaches the knowledge of sound;

[9] Hummingbird Sphinx: Hummingbird Hawkmoth, *Macroglossum stellatarum*

And now, as distinguish'd for fleetness and mirth,
Invited the states that inhabit the earth,
The GNAT, o'er the stream that so lightly can dart,
And in buzzing incessant so well play his part,
Was deputed the nations aquatic to wake,
That dwell in the regions of stream, fen, or lake,

The place of assembly was chosen with care,
As far as might be, from observance or snare;
In the heart of a forest, where open'd the shade,
Disclosing to daylight a sunshiny glade;
Young saplings around spread their tenderest green,
The lords of the wood overtopping the scene,
The bay of a brook, with its mirror of glass,
Stealing in thro' the bushes, enlighten'd the grass.
Boast monarchs and statesmen, or all of their race,
A chamber of council adorn'd with such grace?

In crowds to the spot all the nations repair,
And, save the small Midge, every insect was there;
He, (happy distinction! which greatness ne'er knows,)
Alike was unheeded by friends or by foes.

The *Butterfly* tribe first advanc'd thro' the air,
PURPLE EMPEROR[10] led them in splendor most rare;
A race blest by nature with privilege high,
To burst from the tomb and ascend to the sky,
Here came the gay PEACOCK[11] with eyes on his back,
And rich ATALANTA[12], in crimson and black

---

[10] Purple Emperor: a butterfly, *Apatura iris*
[11] Peacock: Peacock butterfly, *Inachis io*
[12] Atalanta: *Vanessa atalanta*, the Red Admiral butterfly

Light GAMMA[13], adorn'd with his elegant crest,
A Grecian inscription design'd on his vest,
And lovely VANESSA[14], so meek and serene,
Array'd like spring leaves, in a robe of pale green;
Beside her, (a contrast that oft strikes the sight),
Came the gay PAINTED LADY[15], in orange all bright.
In robes green and sable came PRIAM[16], grave sire,
With ADONIS[17] the beau, in his azure attire—
And SWALLOW-TAIL, graceful and ample of wing,
In yellow, imperial, like China's great king.
The lovely assemblage, in colors so bright,
Red, orange, and purple, blue, yellow, and white,
O'erspread all the trees, and, enchanting to view,
Mingled soft with the verdure each delicate hue;
While fine pencil'd lines their gay plumage bedeck,
In graceful design of streak, atom, or speck;
The motion of life and the richness of bloom
United, a wond'rous appearance assume,
As if, by the touch of some magical pow'rs,
The thicket was peopled with animate flow'rs.

Next, light as the ether, and almost as rare,
The GNATS and EPHEMERA[18] dance thro' the air;
Now riding on sunbeams, half-melting in light,
Now rapid as lightning, escaping from sight;
Interweaving gay movements in intricate play,
And enjoying with rapture their life of a day.—

[13] Gamma: *Plusia gamma*, the Silver-Y moth
[14] *Vanessa*: a genus of nymphalid butterflies
[15] Painted Lady: a butterfly, *Vanessa cardui*
[16] Priam: in Greek mythology, the king of Troy during the Trojan War
[17] Adonis: the Adonis Blue butterfly, *Lysandra bellargus*
[18] Ephemera: the Mayfly, *Ephemera vulgata*

Next arriv'd the light tribes, who so buoyant of limb—
Can walk on the water, can dive, or can swim;
And, foremost in rank, from his crystal retreat,
NOTO-NECTA[19], the Admiral, led on his fleet.

And lastly, the tribes of the earth o'er the lawn,
In ample and beauteous arrangement were drawn;
Here came DI'MOND BEETLE, so spendidly gay,
Like a Sultan of Ind, in his jewel'd array;
And with him a train all refulgent he brings,
In targets that close o'er their nice-folded wings,
Where colors of metals resplendent are set,
The burnish of gold and the polish of jet,—
The emerald's rich green and the amethyst bright,
Intermingling their hues with the changes of light.
It seem'd, that forsaking the caves of their birth,
The gems of the mines were emerging to earth.

Loud humming and buzzing now shook ev'ry leaf
With mingled emotions of terror and grief;—
The tribes, which by Nature's kind hand were prepar'd
With weapons offensive, for battle declar'd. –
When forth came the DRAGON-FLY, bright to behold,
in his mantle all checquer'd with black, green, and gold;
And wheeling in air on his gossamer wings,
Like a knight, who careers ere to combat he springs,
With his keen spacious eyes the assembly survey'd,
And thus his oration indignantly made,—

[19] Noto-necta: the water boatman, *Notonecta glauca*

"Free tribes of the earth! Here conven'd in debate,
"Not small in renown and in multitude great!
"Twere right in a cause so momentous as ours,
"To estimate fairly our merits and pow'rs;
"And poise in just balance (for surely we can)
"The *instinct* of Insects—the *reason* of Man.
"That attribute boasted by him as so strong,
"Directs him to actions now right and now wrong;
"Nay, often his logic bewilders him quite,
"And he fights to maintain that the *black* is the *white*!
"But we, by a wonderful effort of skill,
"Are endow'd with such perfect obedience of will,
"That since the first day when our being began,
"And in Eden we all were presented to man,
"Our instinct, ordain'd for the guide of our way,
"Was never yet known to conduct us astray;
"Our talents, our manners, our habits produce
"Unerring effects for our comfort and use.
"Then shew the superior gifts you inherit,
"And stand forth, demonstrated, Insects of merit!

    "In such an assembly, 'twere vain to retrace
"The injuries suffer'd, too long, by our race;
"And if we endure them and tamely submit,
"We are either deficient in *courage* or *wit*!
"With regard to our intellect, prove it we can,
"We possess a large portion as well as king MAN:
"He boasts of inventions are newly devin'd,
"Which to us were familiar from time out of mind!
"Friend GNAT!—'tis well known that, your offspring to save,
"You invented the life-boat to float on the wave;
"And the SPIDERS, who love an aerial station,
"Have used air-balloons ever since the creation.
"While Man, slow in arts, fram'd his dwelling of mud,

"With a bundle of straw, and rough rafters of wood;
"The architect ANT, noble cities outlaid,
"With street geometric, and long colonnade!—
"With regard to inventions, which moderns assume,
"Of wonderful pow'rs in the arts of the loom;
"Our weaver, the SILKWORM, e'er since the beginning,
"Has shewn far superior machin'ry in spinning.
"To pomp, fashion, commerce, what wonderful boons
"She confers on mankind by her precious cocoons!
"For, like the fam'd goose, in the fable of old,
"The eggs that she lays are indeed *eggs of gold*!
"Then as to our trades, we can show, if you will,
"Mechanics, whose industry rivals their skill;
"We have *Carpenters*, *Tailors*, and *Grave-diggers* too,
"And sempstresses neat, who can cleverly sew.
"Cousin BEE! I shall give you no more than your due,
"If I say Man is no better *builder* than you!
"And for chemical skill, all his genius and money
"Have not yet instructed him how to make honey!
"Then as to the point of *political science*,
"'Tis very well *known*, you may bind *him* defiance,
"Let him traverse his earth, and he cannot produce
"A state, like your hive, for art, labour, and use.
"Friend EMMET[20], renown'd mid the labouring kind,
"I beg you will not undervalue *your mind*;
"You are very sagacious, and though it is said,
"You imitate man in a certain base trade,
"Making slaves of your Negroes—in that you're *his* debtor,
"*He* gives the example—you *ought* to know better!
"Come, free all your slaves, and deserve our applause,
"And nobly unite in our patriot cause!

[20] emmet: an old-fashioned word for ant

"Come then, my brave friends! let us view our resources,
"Examine our arms, and arrange all our forces.
"Prepare for defence! we have weapons in store,
"That our tyrant at length may be brought to deplore.—
"We have lances and darts of a temper so fine,
"As mere human artists must fail to design.
"—Sir HORNET! you're arm'd, like the heroes of old,
"With a lance of keep point—and I know you are bold.
"STAG BEETLE! your antlers, though small be their span,
"May very soon cripple the fingers of Man!
"Cousin WASP!—for light archers, we fix upon you,
"For *your* poison'd arrows much mischief may do.
"And as to myself, you will own, without doubt,
"I shall make for our army an excellent *scout*!
"Still ready to fly, at the slightest alarms,
"A sentinel faithful, who sleeps on his arms.

"Behold! what vast forces!—unite, Insect pow'rs.
"Fight, steady and dauntless—and vict'ry is ours!"

The orator ceas'd—and from myriads of wings,
The tribes who had *not*, and the tribes who *had* stings,
Re-echo'd applause in continuous roar,
Like the winds on the forest or waves on the shore;
When, foremost the valiant suggestion to seize,
In dignified grace, rose the QUEEN of the Bees.
Aloft on an elm stood her majesty sweet,
With her subjects obedient in swarms at her feet.
In a moment, with chivalrous homage profound,
Each pinion is folded, and hush'd ev'ry sound;
All tribes and all parties unanimous own,
Such honor is due to the *feminine Throne*.

Her thanks with a grace, the fair sov'reign express'd,
And thus, in firm tone, the assembly address'd.
"Most honor'd Allies!—*I* shall firmly unite
"In the plan thus propos'd in defence of our right.
"We here are assembled, confed'rate in zeal,
"To consult and or act for the general weal;
"And, added to wrongs that have troubled of late
"The welfare and peace of each separate state,
"*My* nation of old from the proud human race,
"Had suffer'd oppression most cruel and base!

"'Tis very well known, that since time first began,
"My subjects all toil for the lux'ry of man;
"Collect and condense all the essences fine,
"His table to grace with confections and wine—
"They labor all summer—when, savagely rude,
"In winter he slays them to feast on their food!
"Too long have I witness'd, with terror and pain,
"My citadels storm'd, and my children all slain!

"'Tis time that I rouse me, such subjects to save,
"So faithful, industrious, skilful, and brave!—
"For never, since Man from *his* duty first fell,
"Have *my* loyal people been known to rebel.
"They shew to mankind an example most strange—
"A well-order'd government, never to change!
"Thus deeply impress'd by their virtues and wrongs,
"I feel that redress to their sov'reign belongs;
"And happy to execute duty so high,
"I'll lead them to combat—avenge them—or die!"

She spake—and stood ready to marshal her train,
Like her brave sister sov'reign on Tilbury's plain.
Here plaudits redoubled reverb'rate around,

And the circuit of air seems a chaos of sound;
Wasps, Hornets, and Bees, war and victory breath'd,
Each trunk was extended—each sting was unsheath'd.

In this critical space, like a counsellor, sage,
Uniting to valor the caution of age,
Who thinks ere he speaks, and who speaks what he thinks,
Grave, manly, and calm, rose the ATROPOS SPHINX[21],
In rich velvet vesture of orange and brown,
And, emblem of wisdom, a skull on his crown;
His station he took on the leaf of an oak,
And thus with deliberate eloquence spoke.

"Permit me, my friends, 'ere you rashly engage,
"'Gainst Man's mighty forces fierce combat to wage,
"With deference and friendly advice, if I can,
"To propose a more prudent and dignified plan.
"—I honor that zeal, which so fearless I see,
"In the valiant Sir Dragon and heroine Bee,
"'Tis a true British feeling, thus bravely to fight,
"In defence of our offspring, our friends, and our right.
"For though, from my conscience, I battle oppose,
"Yet deeply I mourn the extent of our woes.
"Yes, friends!—be assur'd that I feel with keen pain,
"The myraids of victims thus tortur'd and slain;
"And think not your counsellor tremblingly shrinks,
("No—far be such shame from a true-hearted sphinx!)
"From danger or death—but a way I'll devise,
"More just, constitutional, worthy, and wise,
"To save all our nations,—and this is my plan,
"That instead of *resisting*, we *reason* with Man,
"Explaining our wrongs and our rights with submission;—
"I therefore propose that we *send a petition*."—

[21] Atropos Sphinx: Death's Head Hawkmoth, *Acherontia atropos*

54

He spake—and the tribes of the butterfly kind,
To virtues pacific and gentle inclin'd,
Supported their leader with loud acclamations,
But murmurs were heard from the warrior nations.
At length, by majority, able and true,
The motion was carried with victory due;
The Petition was voted—applauses were warm,
And counsellor ATROPOS drew up the form;
PRAYING MANTIS was call'd, who by nature was meant
A supplicant gentle, the same to present,
And in posture persuasive, with grace of his own,
To lay it in form at the *foot of the throne*.

The Petition

To his Majesty MAN, lawful Sov'reign, by birth,
Of all Beasts, Birds, Fish, Insects, that dwell on the earth;
In whom, with their trust, their allegiance unites,—
PROTECTOR in chief of lives, properties, rights,
The nations of INSECTS, convok'd in debate,
In humble petition, respectfully state—

That your Majesty's subjects, for time out of mind,
Have liv'd midst the blessings by HEAVEN design'd;
Whose wisdom and goodness, which shine forth the same,
In *our* structure minute, and *your* wonderful frame,
To *life* gave *enjoyment*, a *general* dower,
From *your* throne in the world, to *our* house in a flower.
In the rapture of freedom, we glanc'd 'mid the bow'rs,
And sipp'd without danger, the nectar of flow'rs;
Then curl'd our proboscis, and slept on a leaf,
Nor dreamt of awaking to slav'ry and grief!—

Unmolested we liv'd, except now and then chas'd
And embalm'd to adorn some museum of taste;
Or enclos'd in the hat of the mischievous boy,
Who sees in a Butterfly only a toy.
But times are all alter'd.—Permit us to state
In your Majesty's ear, a reverse in our fate!—
For *now*—if fatigued with our frolics, we close
Our pinions to rest on the lap of a rose,
The Fowler's keen eye spreads his muslin device,
And the terrible clappers are clos'd in a trice!
Then closely confin'd, in the box or the glass,
How sick'ning!—how ling'ring the moments we pass!
Some captives, impatient for freedom and air,
Beat the walls of their prison in restless despair;
Some motionless wait till death's pang shall begin
In the dread boiling water or poisonous pin!
Should we suffer for science—to teach *you* to find,
In the works of Creation the governing MIND;
To admire how omnipotent skill could condense
In our form of a *point, beauty, usefulness, sense*;
Should we suffer to lead you of knowledge so high,
We should deem it our duty in silence to die.
By *Charter Divine* we are subject to you,
And if we can *serve* you, our *life* is your due;
But should *that* be claim'd on a *lawful* pretence,
To take it by torture is, sure, an offence.
Your SOV'REIGN SUPREME who that charter has lent,
Annex'd to the bounty no right to *torment*.

Of late has arisen, our race to o'erwhelm,
A practice that fashion has spread through the realm,

A species of slave-trade!—New merchants arise,
In this kingdom of commerce, who traffic in *Flies*;

56

And send out their agents abroad and at home,
For cargoes of Insects, industrious to roam,
Put quite out of question our rank in creation,
And make us mere objects of base speculation.
Among all the tribes that acknowledge your right,
From Giant Rhinoceros down to the Mite,
Say, have you a colony, 'mid all your pow'rs
Upheld and supported so cheaply as ours?
Independent and frugal, ourselves we maintain,
Nor tax your Exchequer—no, not for a grain.

We steal not *your* honey[22], you first have your due,
For our friends of the Hive labour solely for *you*.
For invisible food, we industriously roam,
And the curl of a leaf is our shelter and home;
Your store-house of viands, your treasuries of Grain,
And all the vast wealth of your boundless domain,
To us no vain thirst of ambition can give—
We crave but one favour—*permission to live*!
And we feel you will grant a petition so just,
(Your Majesty's *character* warrants the trust,)
For fame has describ'd you possessing a mind,
Enlighten'd, benevolent, lib'ral, and *kind.*—

That your reign may be blest, and your subjects true, all,
From the fly on your hand to the horse in your stall;
While with gen'rous protection their rights you defend,
Not merely their sov'reign – their *father*, their *friend*;
Enjoying that godlike delight in your breast,
Of loving your subjects and seeing them blest;

[22] This is not strictly true. As I have remarked elsewhere, the Death's
Head Hawkmoth, *Acherontia atropos* (who happens to be the voice of
caution here) has been known to steal honey from bee hives.

57

Supplying their wants, and their inj'ries re-dressing,
And using your pow'r for the purpose of *blessing*.
And that JUSTICE and MERCY may govern your sway,
We, your dutiful subjects, shall faithfully pray, &c. &c.
Signed—

For the nation of Lepidoptera—ATROPOS SPHINX.—
Death's-Head Moth.
—————————Neuroptera—LIBELLULA—Dragon-Fly.
—————————Coleoptera—LUCANUS CERVUS.—Stag-Beetle.
—————————Hymenoptera—APIS.—Bee.
&c. &c. &c.

Susannah Watts

This curious poem comprises the main content of a small book
entitled *The Insects in Council, addressed to Entomologists, with other
poems*, published in 1828. The first paragraph of the book's preface
explains: "The following little fable is not presented to the public
as a mere bagatelle of amusement suggested by the fashionable
popularity of entomology, but under a serious, anxious, and most
sincere desire to inculcate respect and tenderness towards all the
inferior creatures. Men, in theory, (if not in practice), have fully
explained and established a beautiful and perfect system of their
social duties towards each other;— but they have never thought of
admitting into their code as *a principle*, their own duty towards the
animals."

This is the first plate of Thomas Martyn's *English Entomologist*, published in 1793. It depicts stag beetles (Lucanidae) and includes *Lucanus cervus*, the largest terrestrial insect in Europe; figure 1, at the top, depicts a male stag beetle in flight, with wings extended (© Royal Entomological Society).

The Butterflies' Fad

"I happened one night in my travels
      To stray into Butterfly Vale,
Where my wondering eyes beheld butterflies
      With wings that were wide as a sail.
They lived in such houses of grandeur,
      Their days were a succession of joys,
And the very last fad these butterflies had
      Was making collections of boys.

"There were boys of all sizes and ages
      Pinned up on their walls. – When I said
'Twas a terrible sight to see boys in that plight,
      I was answered: '*Oh, well, they are dead*.
We catch them alive, but we kill them
      With ether—a very nice way:
Just look at this fellow—his hair is so yellow,
      And his eyes such a beautiful grey.

"Then there is a droll little darky,
      As black as the clay at our feet;
He sets off that blond that is pinned just beyond
      In a way most artistic and neat.
And now let me show you the latest,—
      A specimen really select,
A boy with a head that is carroty-red
      And a face that is funnily specked

"We cannot decide where to place him;
      Those spots bar him out of each class;
We think him a treasure to study at leisure
      And analyse under a glass.'
I seemed to grow cold as I listened

60

To the words that these butterflies spoke;
With fear overcome, I was speechless and dumb,
And then with a start — I awoke!"

Ella Wheeler Wilcox

BUTTERFLIES

Many poets have made at least a passing mention of butterflies. Together with moths, butterflies belong to the Order Lepidoptera, derived from the Greek words "lepis" and "pteron" meaning scale-winged. Colours on the wings of most butterflies comes from pigmented scales which cover the wings and overlap like house tiles; others have scales with iridescence derived from refracted light.

Metamorphosis of butterflies has received much attention – adult butterflies usually lay eggs on the stem, buds or leaves of the host-plant on which their caterpillars will feed. When fully fed, the caterpillar skin splits, revealing a pupa or chrysalis which after a period of time from weeks to years (at least one desert species has recently been recorded as remaining in the pupal state for up to 15 years) also splits and an adult butterfly emerges. Its wings are at first shapeless bags, but fluid is quickly pumped through the veins, causing the wings to expand, and when they have dried the butterfly is ready to take flight. The early writers liked nothing better than to make comparisons between man and the rest of nature. It has been observed that the chrysalis is the cradle of the butterfly, at the very moment it becomes the tomb of the caterpillar.

There is a widespread misconception that butterflies only live for a day. Some butterflies may live for only a matter of a few days, but most live considerably longer, and some survive for several months. In the UK there are several species that hibernate throughout the winter as adults, emerging from the chrysalis in mid or late summer and laying their eggs the following spring. Early writers sometimes struggled with the fact that whilst ants and other insects were perceived to be industrious, butterflies served no obvious purpose. They are in fact an important part of the food chain; adult butterflies lay many more eggs than are ever going to produce butterflies, and their caterpillars feed a large number of small birds in the spring and summer. Wordsworth's assumption that a butterfly motionless on a flower might be enjoying a period of relaxation is typical of the anthropomorphic assumptions of his day. Although butterflies do rest in dull weather, the reality for a butterfly is probably rather different: a limited time to find a mate, lay eggs and at the same time avoid a host of predators.

The Large White Butterfly, *Pieris brassicae*, was known to Aleazar Albin as "The great white Butterfly" in 1720, when his book *A Natural History of English Insects. Illuftrated with A Hundred Copper Plates, curioufly Engraven from the Life* ... was published. This is Plate One in the book and depicts the upper and under surfaces of a male (top) and female (bottom) Large White (see several poems in the anthology, notably Robert Graves' 'Flying Crooked'). Each book plate was dedicated to a notable person of the time; this one was dedicated to the Princess of Wales, Caroline of Brandenburg-Ansbach, whose husband became George II. (© Royal Entomological Society).

'Flying Crooked'

The butterfly, a cabbage-white,
(his honest idiocy of flight)
Will never now, it is too late,
Master the art of flying straight,
Yet has – who knows so well as I? –
A just sense of how not to fly;
He lurches here and here by guess
And God and hope and hopelessness.
Even the aerobatic swift
Has not his flying-crooked gift.

Robert Graves

Graves' "honest idiocy of flight" refers to the apparently aimless flight of the Cabbage White butterfly (the name 'Cabbage' White covers several species, including the Large White butterfly *Pieris brassicae*, which gains its scientific name from the generic name for the cabbage, *Brassica*, on which the larvae feed), which is probably a mechanism for evading avian predators. In fact, *P. brassicae* has the ability to fly long distances. It has a distribution across the palaearctic, from the north Atlantic islands (Canaries, Azores) to Japan and Taiwan, and has recently spread to Chile, though probably through accidental introduction rather than any recently discovered ability to fly in a straight line. In the UK, numbers are swelled by spring migrations from continental Europe – its numbers are held in check by a tiny parasitoid wasp, *Cotesia glomeratus*, which lays its eggs through the skin of the *brassicae* larva without killing it. When the parasitoid eggs hatch, the larvae feed on live tissue for some time, until the butterfly larva is eventually killed. The parasitoid larvae then pupate next to the dead butterfly larva, until the tiny wasps emerge and the cycle begins again.

Butterfly

Butterfly, the wind blows sea-ward, strong beyond the
    garden wall!
Butterfly, why do you settle on my shoe, and sip the dirt on
    my shoe,
Lifting your veined wings, lifting them? Big white butterfly!

Already it is October, and the wind blows strong to the sea
from the hills where snow must have fallen, the wind is
    polished with snow.
Here in the garden, with red geraniums, it is warm it is warm
but the wind blows strong to sea-ward, white butterfly,
    content on my shoe!

Will you go, will you go from my warm house?
Will you climb on your big soft wings, black-dotted,
as up an invisible rainbow, an arch
till the wind slides you sheer from the arch-crest
and in a strange level fluttering you go out to sea-ward,
    white speck!

Farewell, farewell, lost soul!
you have melted in the crystalline distance,
it is enough! I saw you vanish into air.

D H Lawrence

On Discovering A Butterfly

I found it in a legendary land
all rocks and lavender and tufted grass,
where it was settled on some sodden sand
hard by the torrent of a mountain pass.

The features it combines mark it as new
to science: shape and shade – the special tinge,
akin to moonlight, tempering its blue,
the dingy underside, the chequered fringe.

My needles have teased out its sculptured sex;
corroded tissues could no longer hide
that priceless mote now dimpling the convex
and limpid teardrop on a lighted slide

Smoothly a screw is turned; out of the mist
two ambered hooks symmetrically slope,
or scales like battledores of amethyst
cross the charmed circle of the microscope.

I found it and I named it, being versed
in taxonomic Latin; thus became
godfather to an insect and its first
describer – and I want no other fame.

Wide open on its pin (though past asleep),
and safe from creeping relatives and rust,
in the secluded stronghold where we keep
type specimens it will transcend its dust.

Dark pictures, thrones, the stones that pilgrims kiss
poems that take a thousand years to die
but ape the immortality of this
red label on a little butterfly.

Vladimir Nabokov

This rather nice poem by the author of *Lolita* comes to life with an understanding of the process of describing a butterfly new to science – in this case a lycaenid butterfly: blue on the upper surface, with chequered fringes and a dingy underside, which serves to make it less obvious to potential predators when sitting at rest with wings closed. Many small butterflies present difficulties in identification, and it is customary to examine the shape – often diagnostic – of the genitalia of the male butterfly by soaking the abdomen in corrosive chemical for a period in order to remove the soft tissue, before teasing out the chitinous sexual parts very carefully under a microscope using fine needles.

The first of its kind to be examined and named becomes the unique "name-bearing" specimen, against which difficult or undescribed specimens may be compared in the future. This is the holotype; the convention is that holotype specimens are identified in many of the major museums of the world, including the Natural History Museum, London, with a red-coloured label. When properly preserved, butterfly (and other invertebrate) specimens are indeed immortal – there are pinned butterflies in a special storeroom in the Linnean Society of London that were in the possession of Carl Linnaeus more than 250 years ago.

Fly, white butterflies, out to sea,
Frail pale wings for the winds to try;
Small white wings that we scarce can see,
    Fly.
Here and there may a chance-caught eye
Note, in a score of you, twain or three
Brighter or darker of tinge or dye;
Some fly light as a laugh of glee,
Some fly soft as a long, low sigh:
All to the haven where each would be,—
    Fly.

Algernon Charles Swinburne

To A Butterfly Near A Tomb

I stood where the lip of Song lay low,
Where the dust was heavy on Beauty's brow;
Where stillness hung on the heart of Love,
And a marble weeper kept watch above;

I stood in the silence of lonely thought,
While Song and Love in my own soul wrought;
Though each unwhisper'd, each dimm'd with fear,
Each but a banish'd spirit here.

Then didst though pass me in radiance by,
Child of the Sunshine, young Butterfly!
Thou that dost bear, on thy fairy wing,
No burden of inborn suffering.

Thou went flitting past that solemn tomb,
Over a bright world of joy and bloom;
And strangely I felt, as I saw thee shine,
The all that sever'd thy life and mine.

Mine, with its hidden mysterious things
Of Love and Grief, its unsounded springs,
And quick thoughts, wandering o'er earth and sky,
With voices to question Eternity!

Thine, on its reckless and glancing way,
Like an embodied breeze at play!
Child of the Sunshine, thou wing's and free,
One moment – *one* moment – I envied thee.

Thou art not lonely, though born to roam,
Thou hast no longings that pine for home!

Thou seek'st not the haunts of the bee and bird
To fly from the sickness of Hope deferr'd.

In thy brief being no strife of mind,
No boundless passion, is deeply shrined;
But I – as I gazed on thy swift flight by,
One hour of *my* soul seem'd infinity!

Yet, ere I turn'd from that silent place,
Or ceased from watching thy joyous race,
Thou, even *thou*, on those airy wings,
Didst waft me visions of brighter things!

Thou that dost image the free soul's birth,
And its flight away o'er the mists of earth,
Oh! Fitly *thou* shinest mid flowers that rise
Round the dark chamber where Genius lies.

Mrs Hemans

To A Butterfly
(partim)

I've watched you now a full half-hour,
Self-poised upon that yellow flower;
And, little Butterfly! indeed
I know not if you sleep or feed,
How motionless! – not frozen seas
More motionless! and then
What joy awaits you, when the breeze
Hath found you out among the trees,
And calls you forth again!

This plot of Orchard-ground is ours;
My trees they are, my Sister's flowers;
Here rest your wings when they are weary;
Here lodge as in a sanctuary!
Come often to us, fear no wrong;
Sit near us on the bough!
We'll talk of sunshine and of song,
And summer days, when we were young;
Sweet childish days, that were as long
As twenty days are now.

William Wordsworth

The Dead Butterfly

I
Now I see its whiteness
is not white but green, traced with green,
and resembles the stones
of which the city is built,
quarried high in the mountains.

II
Everywhere among the marigolds
the rainblown roses and the hedges
of tamarisk are white
butterflies this morning, in constant
tremulous movement, only those
that lie dead revealing
their rockgreen colour and the bold
cut of the wings.

Denise Levertov

Butterflies Of Lulworth

Shy fairies live on Bindon Hill
And gather nectar where they will.
Fluttering, fragile pinion hue
Brush yellow trefoil, scabious blue,
To sprinkle stardust as they fly,

Bewitching curious, watchful eye.
Adonis Blue and Lulworth Skipper
Weave a spell on casual tripper,
In sun and flowers, drift to sleep
On ancient soil, round and steep,
Above the shimmering, secret cove,
This magic place where fairies rove.

Kathryn L. Garrod

The Butterfly

The Butterfly, an idle thing,
Not honey makes, nor yet can sing,
As does it, like the prudent ant,
Lay up the grain for times of want,
A wise and cautious hoard.

Well were it for the world, if all
Who creep about this earthly ball,
Though shorter lived than most he be,
Were useful in their kind as he.

Vincent Bourne
(translated from the original Latin by William Cowper)

I'd be a Butterfly

I'd be a Butterfly born in a bower,
　　Where roses and lilies and violets meet;
Roving for ever from flower to flower,
　　And kissing all buds that are pretty and sweet!
I'd never languish for wealth and power;
　　I'd never sigh to see slaves at my feet:
I'd be a Butterfly born in a bower,
　　Kissing all buds that are pretty and sweet.

O could I pilfer the wand of a fairy,
　　I'd have a pair of those beautiful wings:
Their summer-day's ramble is sportive and airy,
　　They sleep in a rose when the nightingale sings.
Those, who have wealth, must be watchful and wary;
　　Power, alas! nought but misery brings!
I'd be a Butterfly sportive and airy,
　　Rock'd in a rose when the nightingale sings!

What, though you tell me each gay little rover
　　Shrinks from the breath of the first autumn day!
Sure it is better, when summer is over,
　　To die when all fair things are fading away.
Some in life's winter may toil to discover
　　Means of procuring a weary delay-
I'd be a Butterfly: living a rover,
　　Dying when fair things are fading away!

Thomas Haynes Bayly

To The Butterfly

Child of the sun! pursue thy rapturous flight,
Mingling with her thou lovest, in fields of light;
And, where the flowers of Paradise unfold,
Quaff fragrant nectar from their cups of gold.
There shall thy wings, rich as an evening sky,
Expand and shut with silent ecstasy!
—Yet wert thou once a worm; a thing, that crept
On the bare earth, then wrought a tomb, and slept!
And such is man; soon from his cell of clay
To burst a seraph, in the blaze of day.

Samuel Rogers

from Muiopotmos:
or The Fate of the Butterflie

There he arriving, round about doth flie,
From bed to bed, from one to other border;
And takes survey with curious busie eye,
Of every flowre and herbe there set in order;
Now this, now that, he tasteth tenderly,
Yet none of them he rudely doth disorder.
Ne with his feete their silken leaves deface
But pastures on the pleasures of each place.

And evermore, with most varietie
And change of sweetnesse (for all change is sweete),
He casts his glutton sense to satisfie,
Now sucking of the sap of herbe most meet
Or of the deaw, which yet on them doth lie

Now in the same bathing his tender feete:
And then he pearcheth on some braunch thereby,
To weather him, and his moyst wings to dry.

And whatso else of vertue good or ill
Grewe in this gardin, fetcht from farre away
Of every one he takes and tastes at will;
That when he hath both plaied and fed his fill
In the warme sunne he doth himselfe embay,
And there him rests in riotous suffisaunce
Of all his gladfulnes and kingly joyaunce.

What more felicitie can fall to creature
Than to enjoy delight with libertie,
And to be lord of all the workes of Nature?
To raigne in th' aire from th' earth to highest skie,
To feed on flowres and weedes of glorious feature?
To take whatever thing doth please the eie,
Who rests not pleased with such happines,
Well worthy he to taste of wretchednes.

                                        Edmund Spenser

To the Right Honorable
Sarah Bodville Countess Dow.r of Radnor
this plate is humbly Dedicated by Eleazar Albin .

Back of dust jacket: Plate 2 of Aleazar Albin's *A Natural History of English Insects*, 1720. The Brimstone may be the source of the word "butterfly" – a shortened version of 'butter-coloured fly'. The butterfly at the top of this plate is the Black-veined White, *Aporia crataegi*, which was very common in Albin's day, but became extinct in England in the early years of the 20th century, for reasons that are not known. It remains a common species in parts of continental Europe (© Royal Entomological Society).

A Brimstone Butterfly

The autumn sun that rose at seven,
Has risen again at noon,
Where the hill makes a later heaven,
And fringing with bright rainbow hair
The boughs that lace the sky
Has wakened half a year too soon
This brimstone butterfly,
That fluttering every way at once
Searches in vain the moss and stones, -
Itself the only primrose there.

Andrew Young

The Brimstone butterfly, *Gonepteryx rhamni* is one of several butterfly species in the UK which spends the winter hibernating as an adult in a semi-torpid state. It is one of the first butterflies to be seen flying in the spring, when the weather begins to get warmer. The butterflies feed from early spring flowers, and females lay their eggs on young, fresh leaves of Buckthorn, which the caterpillars eat on hatching. Our winters are becoming milder, and it is true that an unseasonal period of warm weather may rouse hibernating butterflies, which are then unable to find nectar if there are no suitable flowering plants available. As a matter of interest, the brilliant yellow male Brimstone may have given us the word butterfly – originating at a time when all insects were referred to as "flies", it may be a corruption of "butter-coloured fly". At least this is the view of some – others believe that the name Brimstone (there is also a yellow coloured Brimstone moth: *Phalaena luteolata*) is derived from the colour of sulphur. Perhaps both are true.

from March

The butterflies, by eager hopes undone,
Glad as a child, come out to greet the sun,
Beneath the shadow of a sudden shower
Are lost – nor see tomorrow's April flower

John Clare

The Song Of
The Michaelmas Daisy Fairy

"Red Admiral, Red Admiral
I'm glad to see you here,
Alighting on my daisies one by one!
I hope you like their flavour
And although the autumn's near,
Are you happy as you sit there in the sun?"

"I thank you very kindly, sir!
Your daises are so nice,
So pretty and so plentiful are they;
The flavour of their honey, sir,
It really does entice;
I'd like to bring my brothers, if I may!"

"Friend butterfly, friend butterfly,
Go fetch them one and all!
I'm waiting here to welcome every guest;
And tell them it is Michaelmas,
And soon the leaves will fall,
But I think autumn sunshine is the best!"

Cicely Mary Barker

The Michaelmas daisy is an important autumn nectar source for many insects. The Red Admiral, *Vanessa atalanta* is one of many butterfly species attracted to the flowers. Until recently, it might sadly have been a pointless exercise, since the Red Admiral, which might otherwise survive our winters by hibernating as an adult, was unable to cope with the cold, and individuals that did not take part in a return autumn migration (there is recent evidence for a high elevation return migration, taking advantage of synoptic wind conditions) died at the onset of or during the winter. Indeed, the butterfly was primarily 'British' as a result of spring migrants from continental Europe, which produced a summer brood. But since the advent of milder winters, there have been increased sightings of Red Admirals in early spring, indicating that at least some individuals have been able to withstand the winter period. Global climate change based on increasing carbon dioxide levels in the atmosphere is a reality. So far, it seems to have benefited the Red Admiral butterfly.

He said "I look for butterflies
That sleep among the wheat:
And make them into mutton-pies,
And sell them in the street."

Lewis Carroll

—Immortality

A butterfly basked on a baby's grave,
  Where a lily had chanced to grow:
"Why art thou here with thy gaudy dye,
When she of the blue and sparkling eye
  Must sleep in the churchyard low?"

Then it lightly soared thro' the sunny air,
  And spoke from its shining track:
"I was a worm till I won my wings,
And she, whom thou mourn'st, like a seraph sings:
  Would'st thou call the blest one back?"

Lydia Huntley Sigourney

Do you not perceive that we are worms
Born to form the angelic butterfly
Which flies to judgement without defence?

Dante

The metamorphosis of butterflies, from crawling 'worm' or 'reptile' to relatively fragile, gaudy butterfly, has long been a source of wonder. This is from Dante's *Inferno* (worms and defence do rhyme in Italian: *vermi* and *schermi*!). The well known last few lines of the following neatly turns the tables:

79

The Butterfly And The Snail

As in the sunshine of the morn,
A butterfly, but newly born,
Sat proudly perking on a rose,
With pert conceit his bosom glows;
His wings, all glorious to behold,
Bedropt with azure, jet and gold,
Wide he displays; the spangled dew
Reflects his eyes and various hue.

His now-forgotten friend, a snail,
Beneath his house, with slimy trail,
Crawls o'er the grass, whom when he spies,
In wrath he to the gardener cries:
"What means yon peasant's daily toil,
From choking weeds to rid the soil?
Why wake you to the morning's care?
Why with new arts correct the year?

Why glows the peach with crimson hue?
And why the plum's inviting blue?
Were they to feast his taste designed,
That vermin of voracious kind?
Crush then the slow, the pilfering race;
So purge the garden from disgrace!"
"What arrogance!" the snail replied;
"How insolent is upstart pride!

Hadst thou not thus, with insult vain,
Provoked my patience to complain,
I had concealed thy meaner birth,
Nor traced thee to the scum of earth,
For scarce nine suns have waked the hours,

To swell the fruit and paint the flowers,
Since I thy humbler life surveyed,
In base and sordid guise arrayed:

A hideous insect, vile, unclean,
You dragged a slow and noisome train;
And from your spider bowels drew
Foul film, and spun the dirty clue.
I own my humble life, good friend;
Snail I was born, and snail shall end.
And what's a butterfly? At best
He's but a caterpillar drest;
And all thy race (a numerous seed)
Shall prove of caterpillar breed."

John Gay

from The Giaour

As rising on its purple wing
The insect-queen of eastern Spring,
O'er emerald meadows of Kashmeer
Invites the young pursuer near,
And leads him on from flower to flower,
A weary chase and wasted hour,
Then leaves him, as it soars on high,
With panting heart and tearful eye:
So Beauty lures the full-grown child,
With hue as bright, and wing as wild,
A chase of idle hopes and fears,
Begun in folly, clos'd in tears.
If won, to equal ills betray'd,

Woe waits the insect and the maid;
A life of pain, the loss of peace.
From infant's play, and man's caprice:
The lovely toy so fiercely sought
Hath lost its charm by being caught,
For every touch that woo'd its stay,
Hath brush'd its brightest hues away,
Till charm, and hue, and beauty gone,
'Tis left to fly or fall alone.
With wounded wing and bleeding breast,
Ah! where shall either victim rest?
Can this with faded pinion soar
From rose to tulip as before ?
Or Beauty, blighted in an hour,
Find joy within her broken bower?
No: gayer insects fluttering by
Ne'er droop the wing o'er those that die,
And lovelier things have mercy shown
To every failing but their own.

George Gordon, Lord Byron

Hidden Virtues

The weedy nettle, with its deep jagg'd leaves,
All clothed in bristles, each a venom'd sting,
Hath yet its virtues, and its beauties too,
Like many another, seemingly worthless, thing.

Its want of colour'd flowers appears supplied
By the bright herd of glittering butterflies
Who hover round its foliage dusk and dark,
Lighting its shades like lamps of many dies.

Among its leaves (it has no sting for them)
The fluttering creatures store their teeming brood,
Who find in its rank juices, sweet to them,
Their genial, natural, delicious food.

Virtues, and powers, and uses often lie
Securely hid from our brief human view;
Yet, like the nettle, form some latent link
In the vast edifice of earth and sky,
To impose dark secret cells the mystic key
Has ne'er been wrought by our philosophy

Anonymous

The larvae of some of our best known butterflies, including the Red Admiral, Peacock and Small Tortoiseshell, feed on the leaves of stinging nettles. The caterpillars have urticating spines (the generic name of the stinging nettle is *Urtica* … and the scientific name of the Small Tortoiseshell is *Aglais urticae*) and form silken webs in which they live communally for part of their lives. A patch of nettles left in the corner of the garden helps support these butterflies and other wildlife. Small Tortoiseshell numbers were under pressure in the UK for several years; a circumstance presumed to be largely due to the activities of a parasitoid tachinid fly recently arrived from continental Europe. But perhaps the numbers have recovered – at the time of writing this note, in late August 2014, there are more than 40 tortoiseshells on my garden buddleia.

83

The Red Admiral

The Nettle, prickly, tingly, and despised,
Forms thy sole feasting till thou takest wing.
From many things by man but little prized,
The richest, fairest beauty oft will spring.

When Winter from his icy trumpet blows
His first chill blast, in Autumn's brilliant train
Thy gaudy wings, like flaunting banners, close
In homage o'er the Summer beauty slain.

Joseph Merrin

The Speckled Wood

Sombre tenant of the glade,
Lover of the cooling shade;
In nooks retiring wilt thou hide,
Afraid to show thy "speckled" pride
To the bright searching sun of day.
A lesson to the gaudy flirt,
Or pompous fop, with pride begirt,-
For thou hast beauty which would bear display.

Joseph Merrin

The Speckled Wood butterfly, *Pararge aegeria*, is a common woodland butterfly throughout much of Europe. Its pale yellow markings (darker orange in southern Europe) on brown wings offer excellent camouflage in a woodland glade dappled with sunlight. In his book *Doctor Zhivago* Boris Pasternak tells how Yuri Zhivago was hiding in a forest and learned a lesson in cryptic colouration from observation of a butterfly: "Folding and unfolding like a scrap of coloured stuff, a brown speckled butterfly flew across the sunny side of the clearing ... choosing a background colour nearest to its own, it settled on the brown speckled bark of a pine tree and disappeared into it, vanishing as completely as Yuri, hidden by the play of light and shadow". This was almost certainly a Speckled Wood butterfly, which occurs from North Africa, across Europe to the Caucasus and the Ural Mountains. Having said that, the Speckled Wood is perhaps more likely to rest on the upperside of a leaf in dappled sunlight than on the trunk of a tree, and is more likely to occur in deciduous woodland than pine forests.

This is Plate 6 from the third part of Jan Christiaan Sepp's *Beschouwing der Wonderen Gods, in de minstgeachte Schepzelen of Nederlandische Insecten & Co*, published in 1762. The butterfly is the Speckled Wood butterfly, *Pararge aegeria* (© Royal Entomological Society)

The Butterfly's Birth-Day

The shades of night were scarcely fled;
    The air was mild, the winds were still;
And slow the slanting sunbeams spread,
    O'er wood and lawn, o'er heath and hill:

From fleecy clouds of pearly hue
    Had dropp'd a short but balmy shower,
That hung like gems of morning dew,
    On every tree and every flower:

And from the blackbird's mellow throat,
    Was pour'd so loud and long a swell,
As echoed with responsive note
    From mountain side and shadowy dell!

When bursting forth to life and light,
    The offspring of enraptured May,
The butterfly, on pinions bright,
    Launch'd in full splendour on the day.

Unconscious of a mother's care,
    No infant wretchedness she knew;
But as she felt the vernal air,
    At once to full perfection grew.

Her slender form, ethereal light,
    Her velvet-textured wings unfold;
With all the rainbow's colours bright,
    And dropt with spots of burnished gold.

Trembling with joy awhile she stood,
    And felt the sun's enlivening ray;

Drank from the skies the vital flood,
    And wonder'd at her plumage gay;

And balanced oft her broider'd wings,
    Through fields of air prepared to sail:
Then on her vent'rous journey springs,
    And floats along the rising gale.

Go, child of pleasure, range the fields,
    Taste all the joys that spring can give,
Partake what bounteous summer yields,
    And live, whilst yet 'tis thine to live.

Go sip the rose's fragrant dew,
    The lily's honeyed cup explore,
From flower to flower the search renew,
    And rifle all the woodbine's store:

And let me trace thy vagrant flight,
    Thy moments, too, of short repose,
And mark thee, when, with fresh delight,
    Thy golden pinions ope and close.

But hark! while thus I musing stand,
    Pours on the gale an airy note,
And breathing from a viewless band
    Soft silvery tones around me float!

—They cease—but still a voice I hear,
    A whisper'd voice of hope and joy:—
"Thy hour of rest approaches near,
    Prepare thee, mortal! thou must die!"

"Yet start not! — on thy closing eyes

Another day shall still unfold,
A sun of milder radiance rise,
   A happier age of joys untold."

"Shall the poor worm that shocks thy sight,
   The humblest form in nature's train,
Thus rise in new-born lustre bright,
   And yet the emblem teach in vain?"

"Ah! where were once her golden eyes
   Her glittering wings of purple pride?
Conceal'd beneath a rude disguise,
   A shapeless mass to earth allied."

"Like thee the hapless reptile lived,—
   Like thee he toiled,—like thee he spun,—
Like thine, her closing hour arrived
   Her labour ceased, his web was done."

"And shalt thou, number'd with the dead,
   No happier state of being know?
And shall no future morrow shed
   On thee a beam of brighter glow?"

"Is this the bound of power divine,
   To animate an insect frame?
Or shall not He who moulded thine,
   Wake, at his will, the vital flame?"

"Go, mortal! in thy reptile state,
   Enough to know to thee is given;
Go, and the joyful truth relate;—
   Frail child of earth! Bright heir of heaven!"

William Roscoe

89

The Butterfly

The last, the very last,
So richly, brightly, dazzlingly yellow.
Perhaps if the sun's tears would sing
against a white stone...

Such, such a yellow
Is carried lightly 'way up high.
It went away I'm sure because it wished
to kiss the world goodbye.

For seven weeks I've lived in here,
Penned up inside this ghetto
But I have found my people here.
The dandelions call to me
And the white chestnut candles in the court.
Only I never saw another butterfly.

That butterfly was the last one.
Butterflies don't live in here,
In the ghetto.

Pavel Friedmann

The moving poem presented here is preserved in typewritten copy on thin paper in a collection of poetry by Pavel Friedmann, which was donated to the Jewish Museum in Prague. The poem, dated the 4th of June 1942, speaks for itself. It was composed during the Second World War, in a concentration camp, where Friedmann was killed at the age of 21.

MOTHS

There is no single difference between a moth and a butterfly which applies in every case. But in general, butterflies fly by day (some are crepuscular) and most moths (though by no means all) at night; most butterflies have thickened "knobs" on the end of each antenna, whilst moths have a variety of antennal forms; butterflies generally rest with wings held closed vertically above the thorax, whilst most moths rest with wings flat, often with forewings covering the hindwings; moths have a frenulum (a spiny 'hook') which connects fore and hindwings in flight, which butterflies lack.

The question of why moths and other nocturnal insects fly towards a bright light has occupied poets (and scientists) for many years. Looking through the eyes of early writers, insects do seem to commit suicide by deliberately flying towards a candle flame and burning their wings ("Thus hath the candle sing'd the moth. O, these deliberate fools!" writes Shakespeare, in *The Merchant of Venice*). Discussion continues, with more far-fetched theories including mate location (moths fly to a light ... therefore that would be a good place to find another moth!), and that moths fly towards the darkest part of the sky in pursuit of safety and are thus naturally inclined to circle bright objects (*i.e.* the darkest place is between – furthest from – the lights). In fact, the moth is more likely to be merely a victim of circumstances.

An accepted theory is that moths navigate at night by using bright celestial objects, in particular the moon. The modern world is full of artificial lights from all manner of human sources, which confuses what was once (for the moth) a fairly straightforward matter. Celestial bodies are so far away that the rays of light from them are almost parallel when they reach the eye. Insects have compound eyes and a nervous system which, it is believed, allows them to keep the light at more-or-less the same angle, thereby travelling in more-or-less the same direction. Artificial lights confuse matters dramatically, since the angle between moth and light source changes significantly over short distances. The moon is also always in the upper part of the moth's visual field; terrestrial lights are clearly not! The moth is therefore not 'attracted' to the light in any meaningful sense, but is confounded by it. This is something which is used to good advantage by moth collectors, who attract moths to mercury vapour bulbs which have a high surface brightness and are difficult to look at directly. On cloudless nights, with a full moon, far fewer moths are attracted to these lights than are attracted on dull drizzly nights when there is no moon—and when light competition is lower, or non-existent.

Personally, I prefer walking in the countryside in the sunshine to skulking around a bright light at night, with the hum of a generator drowning out the noises of the night, but night collecting can sometimes be exciting. I spent several weeks over Christmas and New Year 1990-91 in Brunei and Sarawak carrying out a moth project; having been dropped off by helicopter on a remote hilltop in the Brunei rainforest. It soon became clear that something or someone was rooting through the contents of my rubbish before it was burned or buried – I occasionally heard rustling in the undergrowth, and since I knew there was a honey bear in the vicinity, slept with a machette beside me in my hammock. Eventually I caught the culprit by leaning over the edge of the hammock and taking a flash photograph. The civet cat was as surprised as I was. I was further rewarded on Christmas Eve by discovering a species of hawkmoth new to science attracted to the light.

I also carried out a survey of resident hawkmoth species in Hong Kong over a period of a year, when I was supposed to be working. One misty evening – perfect conditions for light trapping – I visited a country park in the New Territories known as the Three Walks. I had a key to fit all the country park barriers, but the barrier when I entered was unlocked, and I spent a very successful few hours running three generators along a mile or so of ridge. Since it was dark, and the noise of the generators drowned out any other noise, I had no inkling of the approaching storm that hit without warning, and had no choice but to throw my equipment into the back of the car in cold driving rain. My clothes were instantly sodden, and the ground was almost as instantly a quagmire. It was easier to take my clothes off and throw them in the car than to roll around in the mud. So far so good, except that when I returned to the barrier it was locked. I got out of the car to hunt for the keys in the pocket of my trousers, now under generators and a pile of electrical leads in the boot, and looked up to find an elderly Chinese gentleman with an umbrella who had come from the unlit (and usually unmanned) forestry hut with a key, and opened the padlock to raise the barrier. I have no idea what he thought of a shivering Caucasian dressed only in soaking underpants shouting obscenities at himself. He maintained an absolutely deadpan face as he let me out—Chinese inscrutability at its best.

The Moth

Isled in the midnight air,
Musked with the dark's faint bloom,
Out into glooming and secret haunts
The flame cries, 'Come!'

Lovely in dye and fan,
A-tremble in shimmering grace,
A moth from her winter swoon
Uplifts her face:

Stares from her glamorous eyes;
Wafts her on plumes like mist;
In ecstacy swirls and sways
To her strange tryst.

Walter de la Mare

The Lesson Of The Moth

I was talking to a moth
the other evening
he was trying to break into
an electric light bulb
and fry himself on the wires

why do you fellows
pull this stunt I asked him
because it is the conventional
thing for moths or why
if that had been an uncovered
candle instead of an electric

light bulb you would
now be a small unsightly cinder
have you no sense

plenty of it he answered
but at times we get tired
of using it
we get bored with the routine
and crave beauty
and excitement
fire is beautiful
and we know that if we get
too close it will kill us
but what does that matter
it is better to be happy
for a moment
and be burned up with beauty
than to live a long time
and be bored all the while
so we wad all our life up
into one little roll
and then we shoot the roll
that is what life is for
it is better to be a part of beauty
for one instant and then cease to
exist than to exist forever
and never to be a part of beauty
our attitude towards life
is come easy go easy
we are like human beings
used to be before they became
too civilized to enjoy themselves

and before I could argue with him
out of his philosophy
he went and immolated himself
on a patent cigar lighter
I do not agree with him
myself I would rather have
half the happiness and twice
the longevity

but at the same time I wish
there was something I wanted
as badly as he wanted to fry himself

Don Marquis

Self-Destruction

Round her flaming heart they hover,
Lured by loveliness they go
Moth-like, every man a lover,
Captive to its gleam and glow.

Old and young, the blind and blinking,—
Fascinated, frenzied things,—
How they flutter, never thinking
What a doom awaits their wings!

It is all the same old story,—
Pleasure hung upon a breath:
Just a chance to taste of glory
Draws a legion down to death.

Fire is dangerous to handle;
Love is an uncertain flame;
But the game is worth the candle
When the candle's worth the game!

Author unknown

Lepidoptera
"moths"

Moths dart and dive in evening flight,
Attracted to a burning light.
What is the force that beckons strong?
It's not for food or sex they long.
It calls to each, the bold and shy –
Fly to me, come to die.

Al Grigarick

The Moth

When dew rolls fast, and rosy day
Fades slowly in the west away,
While evening breezes bend the future sheaves,
Votary of Vesper's humid light,
The moth, a pale wanderer of the night,
From his green cradle comes, amid the whispering leaves.

The birds that on insect life feast,
Now in their woody covers nest;
The swallow slumbers in his dome of clay;

And of the numerous tribes who war
On the small denizens of air,
The shrieking bat alone is on the wing for prey.

Eluding him, on lacey plume
The silver moth enjoys the gloom;
Glancing on tremulous wing thro' twilight bow'rs,
Now flits where warm nasturtiums glow,
Now quivers on the jasmine bough,
And sucks with spiral tongue the balm of sleeping flowers.

Yet if from open casement stream
The taper's bright aspiring beam,
And strikes with comet-ray his dazzled sight;
Nor perfum'd leaf, nor honied flower,
To check his wild career have power,
But to the attracting flame he takes his rapid flight.

Round it he darts in dizzy rings,
And soon his soft and powder'd wings
Are singed; and dimmer grows his pearly eyes;
And now his struggling feet are foil'd,
And scorch'd, entangled, burnt, and soil'd,
His fragile form is lost – the wretched insect dies.

Emblem too just of one, whose way
Thro' the calm vale of life might lay,
Yet lured by vanity's illusive fires,
Far from that tranquil vale aside,
Like this poor insect suicide
Follows the fatal light, and in its flame expires!

Charlotte Turner Smith

From death their happier life derive,
And tho' apparently entomb'd, revive:
Chang'd, thro; amazing transmigration rise,
And wing the regions of unwonted skies;
So late depress'd, contemptible on earth,
Now elevate to heaven by second birth.

Henry Brooke

One summer night, says a legend old,
 A moth a Firefly sought to woo:
"Oh wed me, I pray, though bright star-child,
 To win thee there's nothing I'd dare not do."

"If thou art sincere," the Firefly cried,
 "Go—bring me a light that will equal my own;
Not until then will I deign be thy bride;"—
 Undaunted the Moth heard her mocking tone.

Afar he beheld a brilliant torch,
 Forward he dashed, on rapid wing,
Into the light to bear it hence;—
 When he fell a scorched and blighted thing.—

Still ever the Moths in hope to win,
 Unheeding the lesson, the gay Firefly,
Dash, reckless, the dazzling torch within,
 And, vainly striving, fall and die!

Amanda Ruter Dufour

The White Moth

If a leaf rustled, she would start:
And yet she died, a year ago.
How had so frail a thing the heart
To journey where she trembled so?
And do they turn and turn in fright,
Those little feet, in so much night?

The light above the poet's head
Streamed on the page and on the cloth,
And twice and thrice there buffeted
On the black pane a white-winged moth:
'T was Annie's soul that beat outside
And "Open, open, open!" cried:

But poets polishing a phrase
Show anger over trivial things;
And as she blundered in the blaze
Towards him, on ecstatic wings,
He raised a hand and smote her dead;
Then wrote *"That I had died instead!"*

Sir Arthur Thomas Quiller-Couch

Prayer For Moths

When
– At the mid of moon,
– At the end of day–
My lamp is lit,
Grant me a boon,
I pray,
And do
So order it

– That the small creatures,
Terrified and blind;
The gold and silvern moths
Of lovely kind,
Do not whirl to my taper,
Nor, therein,
Die, painfully,
And bring my light
To sin.

My light
is innocent!
Grant
– That it may be
Harmless,
And helpful,
And remarked
Of thee.

James Stephens

The Red Underwing Moth

All as the moth call'd Underwing alighted,
Turning and pacing, so by slips discloses
Her sober simple coverlid underplighted
To colour as smooth and fresh as cheeks of roses,
Her showy leaves with gentle watchet foiling
Even so my thought the rose and grey disposes.

Gerard Manley Hopkins

Nocturnal moths need to hide from predators during the day. Having forewings much the same colour as the bark of trees on which they rest is a great help; many species have brightly coloured hind wings, hidden when the moth is at rest, but when disturbed, a flash of brilliant colour may be enough to frighten away a predator, or at least to startle them sufficiently for the moth to escape. The Red Underwing (*Catocala nupta*) occurs in the UK and is one of several species with common names indicating a different shade of hindwing red: Red, Crimson, Light Crimson, Dark Crimson, Rosy. There are additional species in Europe, and the genus *Catocala* is even more diverse in North America where there are more than 100 species, making identification a specialist task.

Fig. 7.

Fig. 3.

Fig. 4.

Fig. 1.

Fig. 6.

Fig. 2.

Fig. 5.

C. Sepp ad viv. del. et sculpsit

This is plate 7 from the third part of Jan Christiaan Sepp's *Beschouwing der Wonderen Gods, in de minstgeachte Schepzelen of Nederlandische Insecten & Co*, published in 1762. The moth is the Red Underwing, *Catocala nupta* (© Royal Entomological Society).

Madagascan Robber Moth

When robin ruffles
up her breast,
and shuts her eyes
at dark to rest,
while rain falls through
the forest night,
he takes to flight.

From powdered wings
no sound is heard,
he beats a path
to sleeping bird,
and settles on
her feathered head
with weightless tread.

While robin dreams
of where she flies,
safe roost in trees,
of song filled skies,
her forest full of
hopes and fears,
he steals her tears.

Then lifts to air;
so softly goes,
she never knows.

                                         Liz Brownlee

For many years, certain moths in Africa, Asia and South America
have been known to visit large mammals (cattle, big cats etc.) in

order to obtain nutrients, in particular salts, from eye "tears". This moth behaviour was not reported to include birds until 2006. In 2004, an endemic noctuid moth, *Hemiceratoides hieroglyphica*, was found visiting a sleeping male Magpie Robin on the island of Madagascar with its proboscis inserted into the bird's closed eye. The behaviour was subsequently observed with different bird species; the moth has a two-pronged barbed proboscis which it uses, remarkably, to open the closed eyelids of a sleeping bird to access moisture.

The Galling Problem

On twigs of *Muehlenbeckia*[23]
I find a gall[24], or swelling:
"What lives inside?" (I hear you cry)—
There is no way of telling

"Oh yes there is—" (I hear you shout)—
"Before you put the spuds on
Just go into the library
And look it up in Hudson![25]"

I go; I look; I see that George
Declares it is *Morova*[26]

---

[23] *Muehlenbeckia*: a genus of diverse plants of the family Polygonaceae, native to the southern hemisphere
[24] gall: abnormal growths of plant tissue caused by parasites including insect larvae, which develop inside the gall
[25] Hudson: George Vernon Hudson (1867-1946), accomplished New Zealand entomologist and astronomer – author of many popular and specialist books
[26] *Morova*: a genus of moths, larvae of which are associated with *Muehlenbeckia*

That finds the humble native vine
Delicious as pavlova.

"Oh yes, oh yum," (I hear you squeal)—
"We all agree with Georgie,
And now you mention it, let's have
Our own pavlova orgy!"

"Hold on, hold off!" I interrupt,
"You greedy little creatures!
This *Muehlenbeckia* affair
Still has some curious features ..."

"For instance, though my mind is old
And slow as any loris,
I noticed that one gall I kept
Produced a *Hierodoris*!²⁷"

"Oh nay, oh no!" (I hear you groan)—
"You're forcing us to teeter
On disillusionment's dark brim:
Don't say it was *illita*!²⁸"

"Oh yes, oh yeah!" I proudly say,
"You've named the very species!"
You still demur: "But had it fed?
And was there frass²⁹ or faeces?

"We only ask," (you now explain)—
"Since in the Auckland area,

---

²⁷ *Hierodoris*: another moth genus
²⁸ *illita*: a species of the genus *Hierodoris*
²⁹ frass: the name given to larval faeces

illita lives exclusively
In stems of *Coriaria*[30]"

"Indeed," I hasten to agree,
"The thought is rather charmin':
Each larva in its tutu tube
Like Tutu-Tutenkhamen.

"But ah, what if-" I speculate
"That tutu were to tighten?
A lad'd leave a tube too tight
If that lad were a bright 'un.

"He'd leave his too tight tube behind,
His tutu tube-time over;
What choicer new non-tutu tube
Than one chewed by *Morova*?"

You turn away and huddle up,
"Let's go!" (I hear you mutter)—
"Our time is too too wasted here—
We're dealing with a nutter!"

Robert Hoare

This is a poem written by an entomologist for entomologists, and
illustrates some of the difficulties in identifying similar species of
all manner of insects. To a non-entomologist its attraction is its
humour and some clever rhyming (for example "charmin'" with
"Tutenkhamen").

---

[30] *Coriaria*: a widespread genus of shrubs and small trees; the only genus
in the family Coriariaceae

Close Encounter Of The *Calicotis* Kind

I saw her flit between the forest ferns—
A creature pale and winsome as a fairy—
Her wings more slender than the wings of terns,
Her legs remarkably robust and hairy.

I saw her sit in sunshine on a frond—
A thing as blonde and beauteous as a bimbo—
Her body straighter than a magic wand,
Her tarsi almost painfully akimbo.

Longtime I stared! (I hope she didn't notice),
And once I nearly lost control and grabbed her;
I wondered: was she curvy *Calicotis*
Or could she be precocious *Pachyrhabda*?

I took my lens and pressed it to my eye—
(It wasn't very subtle of me, was it?)—
But it afforded me the chance (oh my!)
At 20x to see her oviposit.

I watched her lay an egg amongst the spores;
I watched the larva hatch and set up camp—
I watched a million movements of its jaws;
Then I was rushed to hospital with cramp.

Robert Hoare

The Stathmopodinae are narrow-winged moths that have the peculiar habit of raising their hindlegs above their folded wings when at rest. These legs are usually ornamented with long bristles, hence the name 'featherfoots' (or should that be 'featherfeet'?). The New Zealand and Australian genus *Calicotis* is an extreme example, with extra-bristly hindlegs that are held out sideways from the body at 90 degrees. The larvae feed on fern sporangia. *Pachyrhabda* is a similar genus from the same region.

Ode to *Tatosoma*

O *Tatosoma* green and fragile
You are both angular and agile
But through the dry days and the wet
I chase you with expectant net.

O *Tatosoma* green and thin
When I have captured you I grin:
You are so shapely and so narrow
It moves me to the very marrow.

O *Tatosoma* green and flexy,
Your abdomen is long and sexy:
What gave you sexiness and flexion?
Was it Darwinian selection?

O *Tatosoma* green and cheerful
Ending your life I feel quite tearful;
Yet nonetheless I hope a lot'll
Wind up in my killing bottle.

O *Tatosoma* green and dead
I place you in your final bed,
Your wings still lovely, but disabled
Now that you have been pinned and labelled.

O *Tatosoma* green and slender
you are so delicate and tender
I wouldn't like to have to mend a
specimen of either gender.

Robert Hoare

Tatosoma is an endemic New Zealand genus of looper moths (Geometridae) in which the males have very long abdomens. Lepidopterist Mr C.E. Clarke, wrote in 1931: "An interesting and beautiful scene observed by the light of the petrol lamp one night was a flight of *Tatosoma*'s [sic], many hundreds strong, hovering about the blossoms of an expanse of *Dracophyllum*'s [sic], their extraordinarily elongated and sinuous bodies and greenish-shaded wings giving them a most charming and dainty appearance as they rose and fell in the air, gracefully alighting at times on the flowers with vibrant wings and again with aerial evolutions appearing to resemble falling leaves, their undulations exhibiting a most decorative and unusual effect."

Across The Stubble

Mark over! Cry the beaters–
I can hear the cock's *tchak, tchak*;
Mark over! There's a hare as well–
Yes–no, he's breaking back.
But what is that that flutters by
Across the yellow stubble?
Down goes my gun and, hat in hand,
I chase it at the double.

"Look out, you silly ass!" I hear;
"Look out! The drive's not done!"
"Good God, he's suddenly gone mad–
Don't shoot there, everyone!"
I care not though they call me every
Kind of crazy fella–
For what are hares and partridges
Compared with *U. pulchella*?

No longer now *pulchella* flits
Across her native heath:
Above, a canopy of glass,
A label underneath,
Admiring friends upon her gaze
While I recital make
And tell them how I courted death
For *U. pulchella*'s sake.

P B M Allan

These nights the dusk comes slow and late,
The moths fly glimmering past the gate.
Here, in the light, and then gone by,
Ghost-moths, now brown, now pallid, fly
With scarce a whir of widening wings;
The heavier moths make sudden rings
Circling the woods in covert flight,
Till all their forms fade into night.

Trevor Blakemore

The ghost moth (family Hepialidae) is aptly named. Female's wings are pale brown, but males of some species are chalky white, and they often congregate in numbers shortly after dusk. This looks very eerie, floating silently at the edge of a forest. I remember as a small boy in Yorkshire being mesmerized by these moths on a warm summer evening. Ghost moths are amongst the most primitive of moths, and are at their most diverse in Australia.

And on the wall, as chilly as a tomb,
The Death's-head moth was clinging,—
That mystic moth, which, with a sense profound
Of all unholy presence, augurs truly;
And with a grim significance flits around
The taper burning bluely.

Thomas Hood

The Death's Head Hawk moth, *Acherontia atropos* (there are two additional *Acherontia* species in the Orient) is a robust moth which is perhaps unlikely to 'flit around' a taper, and is more likely to be seen, as this poem suggests, clinging to a wall near the light. It carries a remarkable skull and crossbones design on the thorax, and is one of several moths that can squeak quite loudly when handled – a strategy for deterring predators. Add to this the fact that it has been known to enter bee hives in order to feed on honey with its short proboscis, and it can be seen why this harmless creature has been the source of much mysticism.

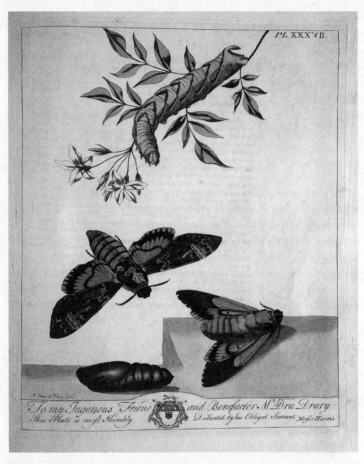

This is plate 37 of Moses Harris' 1766 book *The Aurelian: or Natural History of English Insects; namely. Moths and Butterflies: together with the Plants on which they feed*. It depicts the Death's Head hawk moth, *Acherontia atropos* which, in addition to the skull and crossbones on its thorax, which gives the moth its name, is a potential pest of cultivated potato, on which the larvae feeds. There are two other closely allied species in Asia: *Acherontia lachesis* and *A. styx*; all three scientific names are derived from Greek mythology, and are related to death. This plate was dedicated to Dru Drury (1725-1803), an early British entomologist (© Royal Entomological Society).

CATERPILLARS

Poets were – and are – fascinated by the metamorphosis of Lepidoptera. The caterpillar used to be quite commonly, but of course erroneously, referred to as a 'reptile'. Caterpillars, or larvae, are voracious eating machines, whose primary purpose is to eat as much as possible in the shortest time. This is the growing phase of an insect's life and, since the skin of a larva is only able to stretch a certain amount, they go through several "moults", during which the skin splits revealing a newly formed skin – slightly larger – underneath to accommodate further growth. When the final moult takes place, the new skin changes and hardens over a period of some hours into a chrysalis or pupa from which, eventually, the adult insect emerges. As John Gay pointed out (see 'The Butterfly and the Snail'), a butterfly is "but a caterpillar drest".

Most caterpillars are vegetarians, feeding on leaves, flowers and buds. Many insect species are able to feed on a wide variety of plants, whilst others are specific to only one kind of plant, distribution of which restricts distribution of the insect. Some larvae feed gregariously, whilst others are cannibalistic and lead solitary lives, and will happily eat their neighbours if population density is high or the host-plant is in short supply. Other species, notably larvae of blue butterflies of the family Lycaenidae, have a symbiotic relationship with species of ants, producing "honeydew" from a gland which ants find very attractive: in return, the ants provide protection from potential predators. Other lycaenids spend some or all of their lives in ants nests, feeding on ant larvae.

Some butterflies of the subfamily Pierinae, including the Cabbage White, sequester mustard oil glucosides from their host-plants which affords a certain amount of protection by making them unpalatable to predators. Part of the reason Cabbage White butterfly caterpillars are so destructive and hated by gardeners is that the adult female butterfly lays batches of up to 100 or more eggs on the under surface of cabbage leaves, and the larvae feed gregariously on hatching. Each caterpillar eats more than its own weight in food each day as it grows and they have the potential to destroy large quantities of cabbage (and other *Brassica*) leaves in a lifetime.

The Dream of the Cabbage Caterpillars

There was no magic spell:
    all of us, sleeping,
dreamt the same dream – a dream
    that's ours for the keeping.

In sunbeam or dripping rain,
    sister by brother,
we once roamed with glee
    the leaves that our mother

laid us and left us on,
    browsing our fill
of green cabbage, fresh cabbage,
    thick cabbage, until

in the hammocks we hung
    from the garden wall
came sleep, and the dream
    that changed us all –

we had left our soft bodies,
    the munching, the crawling,
to skim through the clear air
    like white petals falling!

Just so, so we woke –
    so to skip high as towers,
and dip now to sweet fuel
    from trembling bright flowers.

Libby Houston

The Dun-Bar

The rustle of a hundred small jaws
terrifies tall oaks. Here on their branches
a savage drive to kill overwhelms reason,
insidious shadows creep on each other
below, above, in a larval hell. They chomp,
metamorphose, gorge on their own kind,
each one a victim or a killer, combined
in a species that turns on itself in crowds.

Joyce Hodgson

The Dun-Bar, *Cosmia trapezina*, is a common night-flying moth with cannibalistic larvae. The Common or English Oak tree, *Quercus robur*, is attacked by a wide variety of herbivorous predators including butterfly and moth larvae. The tree attempts to overcome this predation by a complex series of chemical defences, including increasing the quantity of tannin and phenol produced in their leaves as a result of attack. This has the practical effect of inhibiting larval growth. A recent threat to native oaks is provided by the larvae of the Oak Processionary Moth, *Thaumetopea processionea*, so named because larvae form characteristic 'processions' as they move around the tree to feed. The moth is a native of southern and central Europe, where populations are held in check by natural predators. However, in recent years the species has spread to northern Europe, where a lack of predators has allowed numbers to increase rapidly. The species is thought to have reached the UK in 2006.

The Woolly Bear

Mary found a woolly bear
While gathering a posy,
She put it in a chocolate box
And kept it warm and cosy

It turned into a chrysalis,
Its face was like a mummy;
From time to time it wagged its tail,
And then it wagged its tummy

But one fine evening Mary's pet
Was seized with sudden rigor,
And split its waistcoat down the front
And turned into a tiger!

A tiger-moth, I really mean,
Of course it didn't eat her;
I couldn't get it in before,
It would have spoilt the metre

These startling facts distinctly prove,
Though experts may deride them,
That bears make nice domestic pets
And tigers grow inside them.

Harry Eltringham

Some of the hairy brown caterpillars ("woolly bears") seen crossing the road in late summer form part of childhood memories in the countryside, and – though they are perhaps seen less frequently nowadays – are the larvae of the Garden Tiger moth, *Arctia caja*. When ready to pupate, they wander (often some distance) from their host-plant before finding a suitable spot. If handled carefully, and kept in a dark, relatively warm environment, the result is quite likely to be an attractive Tiger moth the following spring. The following nursery rhyme (unattributed) is often sung in pre-school, to the tune of *Twinkle, twinkle, little star*.

Little Arabella Miller

Little Arabella Miller
Found a furry caterpillar
First it climbed upon her mother
Then upon her baby brother
"Ugh" said Arabella Miller
"Take away that caterpillar"

Author unknown (possibly Ann Elliot)

The Caterpillar

Brown and furry
Caterpillar in a hurry
Take your walk
To the shady leaf, or stalk,
Or what not,
Which may be the chosen spot.
No toad to spy you,
Hovering bird of prey pass by you;
Spin and die,
To live again a butterfly.

Christina Rossetti

I wish I was a woolly worm
With hairs upon my tummy
Then I could crawl through honey pots
And make my tummy gummy.

"The Unknown Lance Corporal in Sutton"

The Silk-Worm

The beams of April, ere it goes,
A worm, scarce visible, disclose;
All winter long content to dwell
The tenant of his native shell.
The same prolific season gives
The sustenance by which he lives,
The mulberry leaf, a simple store,
That serves him—till he needs no more!
For, his dimensions once complete,
Thenceforth none ever sees him eat;
Though till his growing time is past
Scarce ever is he seen to fast.
That hour arriv'd, his work begins:
He spins and weaves, and weaves and spins;
Till circle upon circle wound
Careless around him and around,
Conceals him with a veil, though slight,
Impervious to the keenest sight.
Thus self-inclosed as in a cask,
At length he finishes his task;
And, though a worm when he was lost,
Or caterpillar at the most,
When next we see him, wings he wears,
And in *Papilio*-pomp appears;
Becomes oviparous; supplies
With future worms and future flies
The next ensuing year; —and dies!
Well were it for the word, if all
Who creep about this earthly ball,
Though shorter lived than most he be,
Were useful in their kind as he.

Vincent Bourne
translated from the original Latin by William Cowper

There is an Oriental proverb that says "by patience and labour the mulberry-leaf becomes satin". The 'silk-worm' feeds exclusively on the leaves of Mulberry, and is the larvae of a bombycid moth, *Bombyx mori*, formerly native to various parts of Indo-China. It no longer occurs in the wild, and adults have become flightless and entirely dependent on human cultivation for continued reproduction. The larva spins a silken cocoon in which to pupate, prior to completing its metamorphosis into the adult moth. What is not perhaps so generally known is that cocoons are placed in boiling water to kill the pupa inside and to make unravelling the silken thread easier. Silk production has been practiced for at least 5,000 years in China.

The Caterpillar

The helpless crawling caterpillar trace,
From the first period of his reptile race.
Cloth'd in dishonour, on the leafy spray
Unseen he wears his silent hours away;
Till satiate grown of all that life supplies,
Self-taught, the voluntary martyr dies.
Deep under earth his darkening course he bends.
And to the tomb, a willing guest descends.
There, long secluded, in his lonely cell,
Forgets the sun, and bids the world farewell.
O'er the wide wastes the wintry tempests reign,
And driving snows usurp the frozen plain:
In vain the tempest beats, the whirlwind blows;
No storms can violate his grave's repose.
But when revolving months have won their way,
When smile the woods, and when the zephyrs play,
When laughs the vivid world in summer's bloom,
He bursts; and flies triumphant from the tomb;
And while his new-born beauties he displays,
With conscious joy his altered form surveys.

119

Mark, while he moves amid the sunny beam,
O'er his soft wings the varying lustres gleam.
Launched into air, on purple plumes he soars,
Gay nature's face with wanton glance explores;
Proud of his varying beauties wings his way,
And spoils the fairest flowers, himself more fair than they.

Adrian Hardy Haworth

Many butterflies pupate in the open – on the stem of the larval host-plant or under a leaf for example – and depend upon cryptic shape or colouration to escape the notice of predators that would consider them a tasty morsel. On the other hand, many moths pupate by burrowing into leaf litter under a tree, or into the soil – some species just under the surface; others deeper in the soil where there they spin a loose cocoon, or fashion a chamber, before pupating. Depending on the species, they spend anything from days to several months in this chamber, before completing metamorphosis and struggling to the surface as an adult moth.

The Caterpillar And The Ant

A pensy Ant, right trig and clean,
Came ae day whidding o'er the green,
Where, to advance her pride, she saw
A caterpillar, moving slaw.
'Good ev'n t'ye, Mistress Ant,' said he;
'How's a' at hame? I'm blyth to s' ye.'
The saucy Ant view'd him wi' scorn,
Nor wad civilities return;
But gecking up her head, quoth she,
'Poor animal! I pity thee;
wha scarce can claim to be a creature,
but some experiment o'Nature,

whase silly shape displeased her eye,
and thus unfinish'd was flung bye.
For me, I'm made wi' better grace,
wi' active limbs and lively face;
And cleverly can move wi' ease
Frae place to place where'er I please;
Can foot a minuet or jig,
And snoov't like ony whirly-gig;
Which gars my jo aft grip my hand,
Till his heart pitty-pattys, and-
But laigh my qualities I bring,
To stand up clashing wi' a thing.
A creeping thing the like o' thee,
Not worthy o' a farewell t' ye,'
The airy Ant syne turned awa,
And left him wi' a proud gaffa.
The caterpillar was struck dumb,
And never answered her a mum:
The humble reptile fand some pain,
Thus to be banter'd wi' disdain.
But tent neist time the Ant came by,
The worm was grown a butterfly;
Transparent were his wings and fair,
Which bare him flight'ring through the air.
Upon a flower he stapt his flight,
And thinking on his former slight,
Thus to the Ant himself addrest:
'Pray, Madam, will ye please to rest?
And notice what I now advise:
Inferiors ne'er too much despise,
For fortune may gie sic a turn,
To raise aboon ye what ye scorn:
For instance, now I spread my wing
In air, while you're a creeping thing.'

Allan Ramsay

121

The Ant And The Caterpillar

As an ant, of his talents superiorly vain,
Was trolling, with consequence, over the plain,
A worm, in his progress remarkably slow,
Cried— "Bless your good worship wherever you go!
I hope your great mightiness won't take it ill;
I pay my respects with a hearty good-will."
With a look of contempt and impertinent pride,
"Begone you vile reptile," his antship replied;
"Go – go, and lament your contemptible state,
But first, look at me, see my limbs how complete;
I guide all my motions with freedom and ease,
Run backward and forward, and turn when I please;
Of nature (grown weary) you shocking essay!
I spurn you thus from me—crawl out of my way."

The reptile insulted, and vexed to the soul,
Crept onwards, and hid himself close in his hole;
But nature, determined to end his distress,
Soon sent him abroad in a butterfly's dress.

Ere long, the proud ant, as repassing the road
(Fatigued from the harvest and tugging his load),
The beau on a violet bank he beheld,
Whose vesture in glory a monarch's excelled;
His plumage expanded, 'twas rare to behold
So lovely a mixture of purple and gold.

The ant, quite amazed at a figure so gay,
Bowed low with respect, and was trudging away;
"Stop friend," says the butterfly, "don't be surprised,
I once was the reptile you spurned and despised;
But now I can mount, in the sunbeams I play,
While you must for ever drudge on in your way."

MORAL

A wretch, though to-day he's o'erloaded with sorrow,
May soar above those that oppress'd him — tomorrow

John Cunningham

I wish I were a caterpillar
Life would be a farce.
I'd climb up all the tall green trees
And slide down on my – hands and knees!

Author unknown

The caterpillar on the leaf
Repeats to thee thy Mother's grief
Kill not the moth or butterfly
For the last judgement draweth nigh.

William Blake

The little caterpillar creeps
Awhile before in silk it sleeps.
It sleeps awhile before it flies,
And flies awhile before it dies,
And that's the end of three good tries.

David McCord

Only My Opinion

Is a caterpillar ticklish?
Well, its always my belief
That he giggles, as he wiggles
Across a hairy leaf

Monica Shannon

The Caterpillar

I find among the poems of Schiller
No mention of the caterpillar,
Nor can I find one anywhere
In Petrarch or in Baudelaire,
So here I sit in extra session
To give my personal impression.
The caterpillar, as it's called,
Is often hairy, seldom bald;
It looks as if it never shaves;
When as it walks, it walks in waves;
And from the cradle to the chrysalis
It's utterly speechless, songless, whistleless.

Ogden Nash

Ogden Nash's poetry is renowned for being entomologically accurate and he is, in a general sense, correct in saying that larvae are "speechless, songless and whistleless". However, there are examples of larvae (that of the Death's Head Hawk Moth is a notable example) which can make a noise by clicking their mandibles if threatened, probably as a means of deterring predators.

Up The Food Chain

Things aren't always what they aposeme:
The model monarch as a caterpillar eats
Milkweeds, stores their hearty poisons,
       and the butterfly defeats
Some portion of an avian predation team
By advertising—with show of color, lack of haste—
That those that dare to peck will find it in bad taste;
But the monarch straddles defence with another gimmick
When it feeds on milkweed species in which there are
No poisons and becomes an edible adult,
       the so-called "automimic."
(Or is that a chrysomelid beetle that recalls
       the German peoplescar?)

John M Burns

The Monarch butterfly (also known in the UK as the Milkweed, or Wanderer) is a migrant renowned for the astounding feat of flying from as far north as Canada to its overwintering sites in Mexico. The offspring return in the spring. This and many other butterfly species are able to sequester (usually at the larval stage) pyrrolizidine alkaloids (PAs) from 'poisonous' plant species. This has the effect of making them distasteful to predators; a bird, or other potential predator, will learn that prey with certain colours or form are not worth bothering with – and other species, which may not be distasteful, may gain protection from imitating them. Warning colouration, known as aposematic colouration, warns a potential prey species of unpalatability.

In butterflies, versions of mimicry were described by two 19th century travellers to Brasil: German naturalist Fritz Müller and English entomologist Henry Walter Bates. The first, mullerian mimicry, is the adaptation of distasteful species to appear similar (usually visually), in the hope that a predator will only have to learn one distasteful combination of colours; in batesian mimicry, a distasteful 'model' may be 'copied' in its appearance by a species that might actually taste pretty good, in the expectation that a predator will mistakenly reject it through its association with the 'model'.

Gum-Leaf Skeletonizer Blues

Uraba is a gruesome beast:
We do not like her in the least;
It makes us fly into a rage
To see this eucalyptophage
Devouring everything myrtaceous:
Has no-one taught her? Goodness gracious!
You'd learn from any decent Mum
The naughtiness of chewing gum.

And here's another thing: that stack
Of hollow heads upon her back:
It's like a little starved cadaver
Made from each earlier instar larva—
I think it shouldn't be allowed
(Though Ozzy Osbourne might be proud)—
One man alone can help *Uraba*:
A starved-cadaver-larva-barber.

Robert Hoare

Uraba lugens is an Australian moth that has recently become established in New Zealand. The larvae feed on gum trees (*Eucalyptus*), skeletonizing the leaves, hence the common name 'gum-leaf skeletonizer'. A curious feature of the larva is that each time it sheds its skin, the head-capsule is retained; thus the larger larvae end up with a little pile of old heads just behind their current one.

How does the little *Cossus*-grub
  Destroy the poplar-tree,
And makes therein his hollow home
  As gaily as can be.

How gallantly he gnaws his way,
  And makes his body swell,
And causes all the air around
  Most nastily to smell.

And when his work is almost done,
  He spins a little coat,
And, last, becomes a wondrous cross
  Between a moth and a goat!

"Ellnest Eriott" and "Maude Clorley"

The Goat moth, *Cossus cossus*, lays its eggs in bark crevices on fruit and other deciduous trees and the larva spends up to two years eating wood and making tunnels inside the tree as it feeds. The larva has an obnoxious smell, said to be reminiscent of a goat! The witchetty (or witchety) grub prized by Australian aboriginals is also a moth or beetle larva (the name applies to the edible larvae of several different insects), particularly the cossid moth *Endoxyla leucomochia*. I have no idea whether the larva smells of kangaroo, but can personally attest to the fact that it tastes rather like peanut butter.

Scribbly-gum

The cold spring falls from the stone.
I passed and heard
the mountain, palm and fern
spoken in one strange word.
The gum-tree stands by the spring.
I peeled its splitting bark
and found the written track
of a life I could not read.

Say the need's born within the tree,
and waits a trigger set for light;
say sap is tidal like the sea
and rises with the solistice-heat –
but wisdom shells the words away
to watch this fountain slowed in air
where sun joins earth – to watch the place
at which these silent rituals are.

Words are not meanings for a tree.
So it is truer not to say
"These rags look like humility,
Or this year's wreck of last year's love,
or wounds ripped by the summer's claw."
If it is possible to be wise
here, wisdom lies outside the word
in the earlier answer of the eyes.

Wisdom can see the red, the rose,
the stained and sculptured curve of grey,
the charcoal scars of fire, and see
around that living tower of tree
the hermit tatters of old bark

split down and strip to end the season;
and can be quiet and not look
for reasons past the edge of reason.

Judith Wright

The title and first verse of the above poem refer to damage caused to the trunks of some smooth-barked *Eucalyptus* (gum) trees in eastern Australia. The culprits are very small micro-moths, notably of the genus *Ogmograptis* (Bucculatricidae). Adult moths lay their eggs in depressions on the *Eucalyptus* bark; the resulting caterpillars bore into the bark to a precise level (the phellogen) and proceed to bore wide, arching tracks. As the larva grows, it continues to feed on the tree tissue, before emerging from the bark to pupate at the base of the tree, leaving an intricate series of heiroglyphics – mines that become visible when the outer bark falls away.

The scribbles were thought for a long time to be caused by beetle larvae, and the biology of the moths has only recently been fully researched and explained in a multi-authored paper in the journal *Invertebrate Systematics* in 2012. The authors, led by Marianne Horak, one of the top entomologists in Australia, included part of the first verse of this poem in the introduction to their paper. An interesting connection is that Julia Cooke, whose captivating poem *My Little World* appears in the 'Ragbag' section of this anthology, carried out statistical analysis on the characteristics of scribbly gum moth mining behaviour together with Ted Edwards – also one of the top entomologists in Australia and one of the authors referred to above.

BEES AND WASPS

Together with ants, bees and wasps belong to the insect Order Hymenoptera. Many people's early experience with them will be through having been stung, something which may appear unprovoked, but which is generally an aggressive defence of the nest, or a consequence of careless handling. Bee and wasp stings can be very painful, and cause an allergic reaction in some people. The actual 'sting' through which venom is delivered is a modified ovipositor – and therefore only females have them. The honey-bee sting has a series of backward-projecting barbs that leave behind the sting and venom sac, fatally damaging the bee when it struggles to retract its sting. Wasps on the other hand have smooth stings, capable of stinging repeatedly. Many groups of bees (eg. sweat bees and vulture bees) are stingless.

Most bees are adapted for feeding on nectar and pollen – the former for a source of energy, and the latter (mostly used as food for larvae) as a source of protein. They play a critical role in pollinating flowering plants, and a high proportion of human food supply depends on pollination by bees, especially the "domesticated" European honey bee, one of several bee species that produces honey. Both bees and wasps may be solitary or social, depending on the species. Many thousands of species have been described, and they occur in a wide variety of forms – the smallest bees are little more than 2mm in length; the largest almost 40mm. Some bee species, called cuckoo bees for obvious reasons (see the anonymous poem on *Apathus*), lack the structures for collecting pollen and lay their eggs in nest cells of pollen-collecting species provisioned by the host bee. On hatching, the larva helps itself to the host species pollen ball and kills the host larvae.

Bees are prominent in the writings of ancient and modern times, and despite their ability to sting, are rightly well regarded due to their usefulness as pollinators and producers of honey. Wasps are not so well regarded, as some poems in this section testify.

Against Idleness And Mischief

How doth the little busy bee
Improve each shining hour,
And gather honey all the day
From every opening flower!

How skilfully she builds her Cell!
How neat she spreads the Wax!
And labours hard to store it well
With the sweet Food she makes.

In Works of Labour or of Skill
I would be busy too:
For Satan finds some Mischief still
For idle Hands to do.

In Books, or Work, or healthful Play
Let my first Years be past,
That I may give for every Day
Some good Account at last.

                                        Isaac Watts

There's a whisper down the field where the year has shot
    her yield,
And the ricks stand grey to the sun,
Singing: "Over then, come over, for the bee has quit the
    clover,
And your English summer's done."

                                        Rudyard Kipling

131

The Plight Of The Humble Bee

A little bee named Elsie May, was working very hard one day,
Flying on from rose to rose, despite the pollen up her nose,
Doing what a bee does best, gathering nectar like the rest.
She tried the daisy, then the poppy, and wondered why she felt
so sloppy.

The opium poppy, there's no doubt, perked her up, but spaced
her out,
And made her think, that she was tough, topped up with the
funny stuff,
She met a great big dragon fly, so stung him twice as she passed
by,

And when a spider made a grab, he also got a stinging stab.
Then a wasp, who thought it funny, tried to steal the wee bee's
honey,
But in a flash, she drew her sting, and chopped a lump from off
his wing,
He spiralled downwards, mad and stinging, she flew off still
gaily singing
And made a beeline to the trees, where blossom waved in gentle
breeze.

And where the butterflies were dancing, wheeling, reeling and
romancing
So she thought she'd take a chance, and join them in the merry
dance,
But unbeknown to Elsie May, in a tree not far away,
A hornet watched, and wondered why, she acted like a
butterfly.

And then he thought he'd make a pass, at the pretty honey lass,
So keen and smart, this handsome fellow, in his suit of black
    and yellow,
Looped the loop up in the sky, then gave a wink as he passed by,
And Elsie May, to her surprise, saw the twinkle in his eyes,

Imagining, that one day, she might have a baby called Hornbee,
So, with a smile she gave a wave, ready just to misbehave,
But then the tears came to her eyes, it wasn't right to fraternise,
So wiping eyes and shaking head, she went off back to work
    instead,

She had a job that must be done, no time for frolicking and fun,
But with the thought still in her mind, despite the fact that love
    is blind,
And in her haste to fill the day, she shot off down the motorway,
Then finished up a messy scar, on the windscreen of a car.

So that's how little Elsie May, ended up and passed away,
And now she's higher up than high, in that big beehive in the
    sky,
Where the days are always sunny, making lots of heavenly
    honey,
And angels lick their lips and sing, with sticky lips and waxy
    wing.

The moral of this story goes, wipe your eyes and blow your
    nose,
A man should watch what he is doing, or Elsie May end up in
    ruin.

John Seville

The Bee Song

Oh, what a wonderful thing to be,
A healthy grown up busy busy bee;
Whiling away all the passing hours
Pinching all the pollen from the cauliflowers.
I'd like to be a busy little bee,
Being as busy as a bee can be.
Flying around the garden brightest ever seen,
Taking back the honey to the dear old queen.

(Chorus): Bz bz bz bz, honey bee, honey bee,
Bz if you like but don't sting me,
Bz bz bz bz, honey bee, honey bee,
Buzz if you like, but don't sting me!

Oh, what a wonderful thing to be,
A healthy grown up busy busy bee.
Toying with the tulips, tasting every type,
Building up the honey-comb that looks like tripe.
I'd like to be a busy little bee,
Being just as busy as a bee can be,
Flying all around in the wild hedgerows,
Stinging all the cows upon the parson's nose!
Oh, what a wonderful thing to be,
A healthy grown up busy busy bee,
Visiting the picnics quite a little tease,
Raising little lumps on the maiden's knees.
I'd like to be a busy little bee
Being with the butterfly strong upon the wing.
Whooppee! O death, where is thy sting?

(Chorus)

Oh, what a wonderful thing to be,
A nice obedient busy busy bee,
To be a good bee one must contrive,
For bees in a beehive must behive.
But maybe I wouldn't be a bee,
Bees are allright when alive you see,
But when bees die you really should see 'em
Pinned on a card in a dirty museum.

Bz bz bz bz, honey bee, honey bee,
Bz if you like but don't sting me,
Bz bz bz bz, honey bee, honey bee,
Bz if you like but if you sting me I'll wack ye
With this dirty great newspaper!

Arthur Askey

Vespa vulgaris

The season of wasps is upon us, or nearly,
I know you'll agree,
Brave men will faint, as wasps stick to their paint,
Or fall in their coffee or tea.

Women will worry and panic,
Or rush round the house in despair,
Or can in their hand, courageously stand,
And spray funny stuff in the air.

Children will find their jam sandwich,
Attractive as never before,

And if a big hornet, should land on their cornet,
They'll throw their ice cream on the floor.

Bakers will pull down the shutters,
Hoping they'll all go away,
Then open at night, when there isn't much light,
'Cos wasps only work in the day.

Greengrocers care for their workers,
By showing a measure of love,
And do the right thing, before there's a sting,
And issue their staff with a glove.

Animals start to get itchy,
Cats and dogs tails start to whip,
They all try their best, to snap at the pest,
And probably get a fat lip.

Picknickers having a party,
Decide to pack up and depart,
As wasps make a play, for the cake on the tray,
Or powerdive into the tart.

Arms start to wave like a windmill,
As everyone's trying to swot,
The wasps dive and duck, keep trying their luck,
As we try to murder the lot.

But just take a moment to ponder,
Before you lash out at the pest,
Why did god make them, I wonder?
For surely the maker knows best.

John Seville

A selection of Hymenoptera From James Barbut's 1781 *Les Genres des Insectes de Linné constatés par divers échantillons d'insectes D'Angleterre, copies d'apres Nature* (© Royal Entomological Society).

There was an Old Man in a tree,
Who was horribly bored by a bee;
When they said "Does it buzz?"
He replied "Yes, it does!"
It's a regular brute of a bee

Edward Lear

There was an old person of Dover,
Who rushed through a field of blue clover;
But some very large bees,
Stung his nose and his knees,
So he very soon went back to Dover

Edward Lear

I could hear the faint buzz of a bee,
As it buried its sting deep in me.
Her arse it was fine,
But you should have seen mine,
In the shade of the old apple tree.

Stephen Cordwell

The Wasp

The wasp and all his numerous family
I look upon as a major calamily.
He throws open his nest with prodigality,
But I distrust his waspitality.

Ogden Nash

The careful insect midst his works I view,
Now from the flowers exhaust the fragrant dew,
With golden treasures load his little thighs,
And steer his distant journey through the skies.

John Gay

The Bumble Bee

You know the conundrum both ancient and trite,
Why millers are prone to wear hats that are white
It's a puzzle that seems, when you think of it, rummer,
Why a bumble bee wears a fur coat in the summer

Perhaps it prevents him contracting the flu
When sleeping in places exposed to the dew;
But a problem so deep may be left for solution
To the London Ent. Soc. or some like institution

Though you'll find that in general good temper prevails,
Don't place much reliance in bumble bee tails;
Very few, and especially the large black and red ones
Should be thoughtlessly handled, unless they are dead ones

If you must have a bumble bee, treat it with care,
And remember to stroke the right way of its hair;
Be most tactful, bee circles don't think it a bit nice
To hear mentioned in company, lime trees and titmice

Harry Eltringham

The Wasp

If a wasp were as big as a bunny,
And you asked for his *carte de visite*,
You would probably get something like the vignette
Roughly shown on the opposite sheet [31]

It is true you can't call him good-looking,
But of course you must bear it in mind,
That his principal claim to the popular fame
Is not carried in front but behind

And perhaps his unhappy expression
Misanthropical thoughts may suggest,
Since his efforts for good are so misunderstood,
Causing grief in his chitinous breast

So permit me to say just a trifle
In defence of the wasp and his ways,
He destroys many flies, in the Autumn he dies,
If he eats a few plums, well, he pays

Harry Eltringham

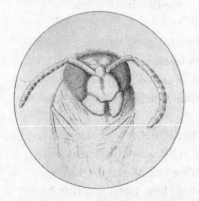

---

[31] This poem is part of a short, hand-written booklet. 'The opposite sheet'
refers to a line drawing shown below this poem

The Rose And The Bee

"Well, what tidings today?" said the bee
    To the burgeoning rose.
"You are young, yet already you see
    Much of life, I suppose."
Said the rose, "Oh, this life is so filled
    With astonishing things
That I think I could not be more thrilled
    E'en if roses had wings.

Three lupins have bloomed by the pond
    Since last you were here;
In the nest of the blue-wrens beyond
    Three nestlings appear.
A gay butterfly slept by my side
    All yesternight thro'
Till dawn, when a thrush hymned his pride.
    But how goes it with you?"

"There are great things at hand," said the bee.
    "Change comes to my life.
In my hive in the woollybutt tree
    Strange rumors are rife.
The old queen grows restless, I fear,
    She is planning to roam;
And I must adventure this year
    From the old, safe home.

"Old Black Wallaby's limping, I see,
    Trap again, I suppose.
Life is full of mischance," said the bee.
    "Ah, no," sighed the rose.
"Despite all the folly and sin

And the gala and the strife,
It's a wonderful world we live in,
    It's a wonderful life."

C. J. Dennis

Bee! I'm Expecting You!

Bee! I'm expecting you!
Was saying Yesterday
To Somebody you know
That you were due –

The Frogs got Home last Week –
Are settled, and at work –
Birds, mostly back –
The Clover warm and thick –

You'll get my Letter by
The seventeenth; Reply
Or better, be with me –
Yours, Fly

Emily Dickinson

Opportunity

When Mrs. Gorm (Aunt Eloise)
Was stung to death by savage bees,
Her husband (Prebendary Gorm)

Put on the veil, and took the swarm.
He's publishing a book next May
On "How to make Bee-keeping pay"

Harry Graham

The Wasp

When the ripe pears droop heavily,
The yellow wasp hums loud and long
His hot and drowsy autumn song.
A yellow flame he seems to be,
When darting suddenly from on high
He lights where fallen peaches lie;

Yellow and black – this tiny thing's
A tiger-soul on elfin wings.

William Sharp

Wasps

If I could rhyme your name with asps
it would be more appropriate, wasps,
or if I could, when something rarsps,
invoke your tribe, how useful, warsps,
or, when the dentist plies his forcps,
how natural to think of worsps.
Instead of which, in general osps
I lie, and curse the sound of wasps.

You small striped tiger burning bright,
you jerseyed champion of spite,
was I to blame that when I bit
a plum you were asleep in it,
or is it any fault of mine,
sot, that you cannot carry wine,
so that disturbed by me you stung
of those you saw the middle tongue?
O what a warning against drink!
Yes! I am better, nurse, I think.
I'm thirsty though. No water handy?
Don't bother! I'll make do with brandy.

Humbert Wolfe

Bumble-bees

Under the hot August sun
Ruling a cloudless sky,
Bumble-bees, both big and small,
Fly from their nests
To the Lavender bush
Grown by a south-facing wall.
Here, upward the scented
Spikes they climb,
Clambering madly in the rush,
Or with a low-pitched hum,
Buzzing from flower to flower
As they eagerly gather
Nectar and pollen
Until fully loaded,
Their tiny brains are overcome

With the prime notion
To return home;
An ancient power
Driving them back, then forth –
They know not why –
Beyond the immediacy of their chores;
Round, furry, clockwork creatures
Working every daylight hour
For the common cause.
Never goaded.
A thing they do most willingly,
Without teachers,
Emotion,
Profit,
Or applause.

Hugh Llewelyn

The Wasp He Is A Nasty One

The wasp he is a nasty one
He scavenges and thrives,
Unlike the honest honey bee
He doesn't care for hives.
He builds his waxy nest
Then brings his mates from near and far
To sneak in your house
When you have left the door ajar.

Then sniffing round for jam he goes
In every pot and packet,
Buzzing round the kitchen

In his black and yellow jacket.
If with a rolled-up paper
He should spot you creeping near
He will do a backward somersault
And sting you on the ear!

You never know with wasps,
You can't relax, not for a minute.
Whatever you pick up – Look Out!
A wasp might still be in it.
You never even know
If there's a wasp against your chest,
For wasps are very fond
Of getting folded in your vest.

And he *always* comes in summer.
In the wintertime he's gone
When you never go on picnics
And you've put a jersey on.
I mean what other single comment
Causes panic and despair
Like someone saying, "Keep still!
There's a wasp caught in your hair!"

But in a speeding car
He finds his favourite abode.
He likes poor Dad to swat like mad
And veer across the road.
He likes to watch Dad's face
As all the kids begin to shout,
"Dad! I don't like wasps!
Oh where's he gone, Dad? Get him *out*!"

And I'd like to make a reference
To all the men who say,
"Don't antagonise it
And the wasp will fly away,"
For I've done a little survey
To see if it will or won't,
And they sting you if you hit them
And they sting you if you don't.

As we step into the sunshine
Through the summers and the springs,
Carrying our cardigans
And nursing all our stings,
I often wonder, reaching for the blue bag
Just once more,
If all things have a purpose
What on earth can *wasps* be for?

Pam Ayres

It is impossible to read the above poem without hearing Pam Ayre's voice! For the record, wasps' nests are constructed from chewed wood and are papery rather than waxy.

The Humble-Bee

Burly, dozing humble-bee,
where thou art is clime for me.
Let them sail for Porto Rique,
Far-off heats through seas to seek;
I will follow thee alone,

147

Thou animated torrid-zone!
Zigzag steerer, desert cheerer,
Let me chase thy waving lines;
Keep me nearer, me thy hearer,
Singing over shrubs and vines.

Insect lover of the sun,
Joy of thy dominion!
Sailor of the atmosphere;
Swimmer through the waves of air;
Voyager of light and noon;
Epicurean of June;
Wait, I prithee, till I come
Within earshot of thy hum,
– all without is martyrdom.

When the south wind, in May days,
With a net of shining haze
Silvers the horizon wall,
And with softness touching all,
Tints the human countenance
With a colour of romance,
And infusing subtle heats,
Turns the sod to violets,
Thou, in sunny solitudes,
Rover of the underwoods,
The green silence dost displace
With thy mellow, breezy bass.

Hot midsummer's petted crone,
Sweet to me thy drowsy tone
Tells of countless sunny hours,
Long days, and solid banks of flowers;
Of gulfs of sweetness without bound

In Indian wilderness found;
Of Syrian peace, immortal leisure,
Firmest cheer, and bird-like pleasure.

Aught unsavoury or unclean
Hath my insect never seen;
But violets and bilberry bells,
Maple-sap and daffodils,
Grass with green flag half-mast high,
Succory to match the sky,
Columbine with horn of honey,
Scented fern, and agrimony,
Clover, catchfly, adder's-tongue
And brier-roses, dwelt among;
All beside was unknown waste,
All was picture as he passed.

Wiser far than human seer,
Yellow-breeched philosopher!
Seeing only what is fair,
Sipping only what is sweet,
Thou dost mock at fate and care,
Leave the chaff, and take the wheat.
When the fierce northwestern blast
Cools sea and land so far and fast,
Thou already slumberest deep;
Woe and want thou canst outsleep;
Want and woe, which torture us,
Thy sleep makes ridiculous.

Ralph Waldo Emerson

The Bees

   Their Government
Of all the race of animals, alone
The bees have common cities of their own,
And, common sons; beneath one law they live,
And with one common stock their traffic drive:
Each has a certain home, a sev'ral stall:
All is the State's, the State provides for all.

   Their economy
Mindful of coming cold, they share the pain,
And hoard, for winter's use, the summer's gain.
Some o'er the public magazines preside;
And some are sent new forage to provide.
These drudge in fields abroad, and those at home
Lay deep foundations for the labor'd comb,
With dew, *Narcissus* leaves, and clammy gum.
To pitch the waxen flooring some contrive;
Some nurse the future nation of the hive.
Sweet honey some condense; some purge the grout;
The rest in cells the liquid nectar shut:
All, with united force, combine to drive
The lazy drones from the laborious hive:
With envy stung, they view each other's deeds;
With diligence the fragrant work proceeds.
As when the Cyclops, at th' almighty nod,
New thunder hasten for their angry god,
Subdued in fire the stubborn metal lies;
One brawny smith the puffing bellows plies
And draws and blows reciprocating air:
Others to quench the hissing mass prepare;
With lifted arms they order ev'ry blow,
And chime their sounding hammers in a row;

With labor'd anvils Etna groans below:
Strongly they strike; huge flakes of flames expire;
With tongs they turn the steel, and vex it in the fire.
If little things with great we may compare,
Such are the bees, and such their busy care;
Studious of honey, each in his degree,
The youthful swain, the grave experienc'd bee:
That in the field; this, in affairs of state
Employ'd at home, abides within the gate,
To fortify the combs, to build the wall,
To prop the ruins, lest the fabric fall:

Their return from labour
But late at night, with weary pinions, come
The lab'ring youth, and heavy laden home.
Plains, meads, and meadows, all the day he plies;
The gleans of yellow thyme distend his thighs:
He spoils the saffron flow'rs; he sips the blues
Of violets, wilding-bloom, and willow-dews.
Their toil is common; common is their sleep;
They shake their wings when morn begins to peep,
Rush through the city-gates without delay,
Nor ends their work, but with declining day.

Their repose
Thus having spent the last remains of light,
They give their bodies due repose at night,
When hollow murmurs of their ev'ning bells
Dismiss the sleepy swains, and toll them to their cells;
When once in beds their weary limbs they steep,
No buzzing sounds disturb their golden sleep.
'Tis sacred silence all.

Virgil's Georgics (partim), translated by John Dryden

Wild Bees

These children of the sun which summer brings
As pastoral minstrels in her merry train
Pipe rustic ballads upon busy wings
And glad the cotters' quiet toils again.
The white nosed bee that bores its little hole
In mortared walls and pipes its symphonies,
And never absent couzen, black as coal,
That Indian-like bepaints its little thighs,
With white and red bedight for holiday,
Right earlily a-morn do pipe and play
And with their legs stroke slumbers from their eyes.
And aye so fond they of their singing seem
That in their holes abed at close of day
They still keep piping in their honey dreams,
And larger ones that thrum on ruder pipe
Round the sweet smelling closen and rich woods
Where tawny white and red flushed clover buds
Shine bonnily and bean fields blossom ripe,
Shed dainty perfumes and give honey food
To these sweet poets of the summer field,
Me much delighting as I stroll along
The narrow path that hay laid meadow yields,
Catching the windings of their wandering song.
The black and yellow bumble first on wing
To buzz among the sallow's early flowers,
Hiding its nest in holes from fickle spring
Who stints his rambles with her frequent showers;
And one that may for wiser piper pass,
In livery dress half sables and half red,
Who laps a moss ball in the meadow grass
And hoards her stores when April showers have fled;
And russet commoner who knows the face

Of every blossom that the meadow brings,
Starting the traveller to a quicker pace
By threatening round his head in many rings:
These sweeten summer in their happy glee
By giving for her honey melody.

John Clare

Prone to revenge, the bees, a wrathful race,
When once provok'd, assaults th' aggressor's face;
And through the purple veins a passage find,
There fix their stings, and leave their souls behind

Virgil
(Dryad)

The Wasp, or Vanity's Ruin

The Wasp was a very fine gentleman;
    Such was his silly pride,
He wore his coat laced over with gold,
    And his hat cocked on one side.

One morning he rose betimes from his bed,
    And called to the drone to bring
His cowslip boots, with spurs of steel,
    And his sword with pointed sting.

Said he "I'll fly from east to west,
    And none shall dare dispute
My right o'er the sweetest blossoms around,
    Or claim to the ripest fruit.

And if a vile bee cross my path,
    I'll soon despatch his life,
Then fly to his hive and eat all his honey,
    And drink his wine with his wife.

What care I for a paltry tribe
    Of insects mean and vile?
Such low mechanics as worms and ants,
    I scornful on them smile.

And as for moth and beetle, they
    My contempt are quite beneath;
'Tis very hard that I'm condemned
    the self-same air to breathe.

On the cricket, who dares of knowledge boast,
    I most indignant frown:
What signifies learning to such as I?
    The world *is* all my own.

I'll get me a golden sceptre bright—
    I'll brandish it over all—
I'll crush beneath my royal foot
    The reptiles, great and small.

And when I'm gone, o'er my honoured dust
    A diamond tomb shall rise;
Therein I'll sleep, while the insects wail,
    And never more dry their eyes.

Their tears shall fall so far and wide
    As dew-drops from the sky,
And thus shall be, on onyx wrought,
    My modest elegy:

154

Here lies the best, the noblest Wasp
    That ever waved a wing:
His virtues bloomed like the sweetest flowers
    In nature's fairest spring

Without conceit, and wise he was,
    And great, and grand of birth;
But could we write a thousand years,
    We could not write his worth."

Just here, in wo's vast pomp, Wasp threw
    His regal wing aside,
And tumbled into the mustard-pot,
    Wherein, alas! He died.

Author unknown

"Double, Double, Toil And Trouble."

An ant, a wasp and a bumble-bee
Were met one day beneath a tree;
"Alas" said the wasp, "the wood these days
Is so very tough I am nearly crazed,
And they have plastered the posts with creosote
It has given me a pain in my throat."

"Pooh, pooh!" quoth the ant, "your troubles are mean,
Why they've slaughtered my aphids with nicotine,
And filled my halls with a poisonous gas
So that even our workers cannot pass;
Such a horrible odour you never sniffed,
I've a racking cough and I'm terribly miffed!"

The bumble-bee hummed in his contra-bass,
As he wiped the pollen from his face,
"This farmer of mine is exceedingly rude,
He has cut his clover and starved my brood!"
Then they groaned in chorus, to disappear,
In the circumjacent atmosphere.

Anonymous

To A Bee

Thou wert out betimes, thou busy, busy bee!
As abroad I took my early way,
Before the cow from her resting-place
Had risen up and left her trace
On the meadow, with dew so grey,
Saw I thee, thou busy, busy bee.

Thou wert working late, thou busy, busy bee!
After the fall of the Cistus' flower;
When the Primrose of Evening was ready to burst,
I heard thee last, I saw thee first;
In the silence of the evening hour,
Heard I thee, thou busy, busy bee.

Thou art a miser, thou busy, busy bee!
Late and early at employ;
Still on thy golden stores intent,
Thy summer in heaping and hoarding is spent
What thy winter will never enjoy;
Wise lesson this for me, thou busy, busy bee.

Little dost thou think, thou busy, busy bee!
What is the end of thy toil;
When the latest flowers of the ivy are gone,
And all thy work for the year is done,
Thy master comes for the spoil:
Woe then for thee, thou busy, busy bee.

Robert Southey

The Bee's Winter Retreat

Go, while the summer suns are bright,
Take at large thy wandering flight,
Go, and load thy tiny feet
With every rich and various sweet;
Cling around the flowering thorn,
Dive in the woodbine's honeyed horn,
Seek the wild rose that shades the dell,
Explore the foxglove's freckled bell;
Or in the heath-flower's fairy cup,
Drink the fragrant spirit up.
But when the meadows shall be mown,
And summer's garlands overblown,
Then come, thou little busy bee,
And let thy homestead be with me:-
There, sheltered by the straw-built hive,
In my garden thou shalt live,
And that garden shall supply
Thy delicious alchemy;-
There, for thee, in autumn, blows
The Indian pink and latest rose,
The mignonette perfumes the air,
And stocks, unfading flowers, are there.

Yet fear not when the tempests come,
And drive thee to thy waxen home,
That I shall then, most treacherously,
For thy honey murder thee:-
Oh, no! – throughout the winter drear
I'll feed thee, that another year
Thou mayst renew thy industry
Among the flowers, thou busy bee

                              Charlotte Turner Smith

        Oh! Cruel is the heart of man
            To our industrious kind!
        No pity melts it, no remorse,
            No obligations bind.

    How have we rang'd the field and mead,
            The hill, the heath, the wood;
    And ransack'd every summer flow'r,
            To cull the golden food.

    How did we build our waxen cell,
            With ever-skilful care;
    To lodge our young, and hoard our stores
            Abundant for the year.

        For charity we never begg'd,
            Injustice never knew;
    Nor from the toil of other hands
            A mean subsistence drew.

But what avail'd our constant zeal
And labour for the state,
Since our protector was our foe,
And had decreed our fate?

And was it not enough for him
To snatch our wealth away;
But, for the favours he bestow'd
To cause our lives to pay?

Hence warn'd, dear youth! A lesson learn
Of tender gratitude;
And, while you have the pow'r, enjoy
The bliss of doing good.

Author unknown

The Harnet And The Bittle
(The Hornet And The Beetle [and the Woodpecker])

An harnet[32] zet[33] in a hollow tree –
A proper spiteful twoad[34] was he;
An merrily zung while a did zet
Er stinge as sharp as a baganet[35];
'Oh, who's so bowld and vierce[36] as I?
I vears[37] not bee, nor waspe, nor vly![38]'

A bittle[39] up thuck[40] tree did clim'[41],
And scarnvully[42] did luk at him;

[32] hornet; [33] sat; [34] toad; [35] bayonet; [36] fierce; [37] fear; [38] fly; [39] beetle; [40] that; [41] climb; [42] scornfully

159

Zays he, 'Zur harnet, who giv' thee
A right to zet in thuck there tree?
Although zings[43] so nation vine[44],
I tell 'e it's a house of mine!'

The harnet's conscience velt a twinge,
But growin' bowld[45] wi' his long stinge,
Zays he 'Possession's the best law,
Zo here th' shasn't put a claw,
Be off and leave the tree to me,
The mixen's[46] good enough for thee.'

Just then a yuccle[47], passin' by,
Was axed[48] by them their cause to try;
"Ha! ha! Its very plain!" zays he,
"They'll make a vamous nunch[49] for me!"
His bill was sharp, his stomach lear[50],
Zo up e snapped the caddlin'[51] pair

Moral

All you as be to law inclined,
This leetle story bear in mind;
Var if to law you ever gwo[52],
You'll vind they'll allus zarve'e zo;
You'll meet the vate[53] o' these ere two:
They'll take your cwoate[54] and carcass[55] too!

John Yonge Akerman

---

[43] sings; [44] fine; [45] bold; [46] midden or dung heap; [47] Green Woodpecker, known locally also as the Lawyer Bird; [48] asked; [49] lunch; [50] empty; [51] quarrelling; [52] go; [53] fate; [54] coat; [55] carcass (body)

This poem was sent to me (written out by hand) by Ernest Taylor, who claimed it as his 'party piece' of Gloucestershire dialect, to be recited on suitable occasions! It seems to occur in many similar forms, with claims made for the dialect of Wiltshire, Dorset and Somersetshire as well as Gloucestershire. This version is taken from Akerman's *Wiltshire Tales*, published in 1853, and is also a song with a chorus formed from the last two lines of each verse. The dialect is difficult to understand (unless, I suppose, you happen to be from the southwest of England), but with explanation the meaning is clear.

Waspish

On glossy wires artistically bent
He draws himself up to his full extent.
His natty wings with self-assurance perk.
His stinging quarters menacingly work.
Poor egotist, he has no way of knowing
But he's as good as anybody going.

Robert Frost

Oh! An *Apathus* sat on a chrysanthemum
A-cleaning her antennae,
And she little thought of the *Pyrethrum*
That would take her life away!

And there she sat, a-taking a rest,
And smiled in a satisfied way,
For she'd laid ten eggs in a *Bombus* nest
And there'd soon be the devil to pay.

For her offspring dear, her very first brood,
Would hatch in a very short time,

161

And no trouble she'd have storing up food,
    For she worked on the cuckoo line.

Her young would hatch 'ere the young bumblebees,
    And the young bumblebees would die,
While the young Apathi would live at their ease
    And fatten like pigs in a sty!

So she sat in the sun, this wicked old bee,
    And scratched her tibiae,
And chuckled inside in a lazy glee
    At the business she'd done that day.

Against Aphids and slugs, with a Buhach-gun
    Filled with Peter's and Milco's best,
And seeing the *Apathus*, just for fun,
    She dusted her yellow vest.

Lord! How the cheat kicked as she fell to the ground!
    And how she did buzz and hum!
But she never got well – she never "came round" –
    Her fraudulent life was done.

From this little tale can a moral be drawn –
    How the bumblebee loafs not a bit;
But works all day from the earliest dawn,
    And thus 'scaped the death-dealing hit?

This moral is good, but please don't forget
    Those eggs that the *Apathus* hid!
The *Bombus* is working and slaving yet,
    But it's all for the other one's kid!

Author unknown

162

The generic name *Apathus* should really be changed to *Psithyrus* in this poem if it is to remain abreast of modern taxonomy; *Apathus* is now a synonym of (it has been combined with) *Psithyrus*, which has itself been 'demoted' to a subgenus of *Bombus*! Although frequently associated with the subfamily Nomadinae, the term "cuckoo bees" or brood parasites includes a great many species placed in numerous genera in a number of subfamilies.

A swarm of bees in May
Is worth a load of hay.
A swarm of bees in June
Is worth a silver spoon.
A swarm of bees in July
Is not worth a fly.

Country fable

If hornets build low,
Winter storms and snow;
If hornets build high,
Winter mild and dry

Anonymous

The Bee-Boy's Song
("Dymchurch Flit")

BEES! Bees! Hark to your bees!
"Hide from your neighbours as much as you please,
But all that has happened, to us you must tell,
Or else we will give you no honey to sell!"

A maiden in her glory,
  Upon her wedding-day,
Must tell her Bees the story,
  Or else they'll fly away,
        Fly away – die away –
              Dwindle down and leave you!
        But if you don't deceive your Bees,
              Your Bees will not deceive you,

Marriage, birth or buryin',
  News across the seas,
All you're sad or merry in,
  You must tell the Bees.
        Tell 'em coming in an' out,
              Where the Fanners fan,
        'Cause the Bees are just about
              As curious as a man!

Don't you wait where trees are,
  When the lightnings play,
Nor don't you hate where Bees are,
  Or else they'll pine away.
        Pine away – dwine away –
              Anything to leave you!
        But if you never grieve your Bees,
              Your Bees'll never grieve you.

                                        Rudyard Kipling

ANTS

Ants belong to the family Formicidae, which is part of the insect Order Hymenoptera – meaning membranous wings – which includes bees and wasps. Ants are numerous both in individuals (ants and termites are said to constitute up to 15% of the terrestrial animal biomass) and in terms of species (some 12,000+ species are known). Some species form colonies ranging from several dozens to many millions of individuals, whilst others are nomadic and do not build permanent structures. The largest colonies are sometimes referred to as "superorganisms" because they appear to operate almost as a single entity, with all individuals working collectively for the common good. These massive colonies contain mainly sterile females working in specialised groups such as "workers" and "soldiers", and are able to exploit resources through communication between individuals and have the ability to overcome complex difficulties.

Herbivores, predators and scavengers, ants are sometimes referred to by the Old English name emmet. They are able to defend themselves, and to mount attacks by biting or stinging, or injecting or spraying chemicals such as formic acid. The Bullet ants of Central and South America are said to have the most painful sting of any insect: excruciatingly painful, though rarely fatal to humans.

Due no doubt in large part to their extremely organised social lives which might be seen to have some parallel with human societies, ants were viewed by most of the early writers and poets as industrious creatures to be respected and celebrated for perceived qualities of economy, foresight and industry. The likes of Virgil, Horace, Ovid and Pliny believed that ants laid up provisions for the winter ... "Go to the Ant, thou sluggard: consider her ways, and be wise: Which having no guide, overseer, or ruler, – Provideth her meat in the summer, and gathereth her food in the harvest" (Proverbs, vi, 6-8).

The little drudge doth trot about and sweat,
Nor will he strait devour all he can get;
But in his temp'rate mouth carries it home;
A stock for winter, which he knows must come.

Horace (translation)

The Ant

The ant has made himself illustrious
Through constant industry industrous.
So what?
Would you be calm and placid
If you were full of formic acid?

Ogden Nash

Tit For Tat

The Anteater has always fed
On ants, but when at last he's dead,
The Ants will feed on him instead.

Dick King-Smith

Ant Hill

Black ants have made a musty mound
My purple pine tree under
And I am often to be found,
Regarding it with wonder
Yet as I watch, somehow it's odd,
Above their busy striving
I feel like an ironic god
Surveying human striving

Then one day came my serving maid,
And just in time I caught her,
For on each lusty arm she weighed
A pan of boiling water.
Said she with glee: "When this I spill,
Of life they'll soon be lacking".
Said I, "If even one you kill,
You bitch! I'll send you packing".

Just think – ten thousand eager lives
In that toil-worn upcasting
Their homes, their babies and their wives
Destroyed in one fell blasting!
Imagine that swift-scalding hell! ...
And though, mayhap, it seem a
Fantastic, far-fetched parallel
Remember ... Hiroshima.

Robert William Service

This poem by Robert Service is my favourite of all the insect poems
in this anthology, and not just for daring to rhyme "seem a" with
"Hiroshima". I came across it in a bookshop in Dawson City, in the
Canadian arctic, not 500 metres from the tiny cottage where Robert
Service lived for many years and wrote some of his best known
work. It was a Sunday morning, and the staff in the shop had little
to do – I had been in the arctic for three months and was due to fly
back home shortly thereafter, with all the issues of excess baggage
that staying away from home for long periods brings with it. I'm
afraid I copied the poem longhand into my diary. It was a while
before I realised I was being casually watched with some
disapproval by two members of staff as I sniggered to myself and
scribbled. If it's not too late, I apologise to them – but the last thing
I needed was another book in my rucksack.

The Ant-Heap

High in the woodland, on the mountain-side,
I ponder, half a golden afternoon,
Storing deep strength to battle with the tide
I must encounter soon.

Absorbed, inquisitive, alert, irate,
The wiry wood-ants run beneath the pines,
And bustle if a careless footfall grate
Among their travelled lines.

With prey unwieldy, slain in alien lands,
When shadows fall aslant, laden they come,
Where, piled of red fir-needles, guarded stands
Their dry and rustling dome.

They toil for what they know not; rest they shun;
They nip the soft intruder; when they die
They grapple pain and fate, and ask from none
The pity they deny.

Arthur Christopher Benson

Starting From Scratch

Have you ever been bird-spotting
And observed a starling squatting
On an ants' nest, and you wonder
As you watch it, why in thunder
Is the silly creature doing
Something it must soon be rueing?
I'll explain.

168

Parasites that drive it frantic
Make the bird perform this antic,
Knowing ants will then infest it
And efficiently divest it
Of the pests, with formic acid,
Rendering the starling placid
Once again.

Dick King-Smith

Ants

Lo! In battalia march embodied ants,
Fearful of winter and of coming wants,
T' invade their corn, and to their cells convey
The plunder'd forage of their yellow prey.
The sable troops along the narrow tracks
Scarce bears the weighty burden on their backs.
Some set their shoulders to the pond'rous grain
Some guard the spoil, some lash the lagging
All ply their tasks, and equal toil sustain

Virgil (translation)

The Bee, The Ant, And The Sparrow

A Fable, Addressed to Phoebe and Kitty C. at Boarding School

My dears, 'tis said in days of old,
That beasts could talk, and birds could scold;
But now, it seems the human race
Alone engross the speaker's place.
Yet lately, if report be true
(And much the tale relates to you),
There met a Sparrow, Ant, and Bee,
Which reasoned and conversed as we.

Who reads my page will doubtless grant
That Phe's the wise industrious Ant;
And all with half an eye may see
That Kitty is the busy Bee.
Here then are two – but where's the third?
Go search the school, you'll find the bird.
Your school! I ask your pardon fair,
I'm sure you'll find no sparrow there.

Now to my tale – One summer's morn
A Bee ranged o'er the verdant lawn,
Studious to husband every hour,
And make the most of every flower.
Nimble from stalk to stalk she flies,
And loads with yellow wax her thighs,
With which the artist builds her comb,
And keeps all tight and warm at home;
Or from the cowslips' golden bells
Sucks honey, to enrich her cells;
Or every tempting rose pursues,
Or sips the lily's fragrant dews;
Yet never robs the shining bloom,

Or of its beauty or perfume.
Thus she discharged in every way
The various duties of the day.

It chanced a frugal Ant was near,
Whose brow was wrinkled o'er by care:
A great economist was she,
Nor less laborious than the Bee;
By pensive parents often taught
What ills arise from want of thought;
That poverty on sloth depends,
On poverty the loss of friends.
Hence every day the Ant is found
With anxious steps to trace the grain,
And drag the heavy load with pain.

The active Bee with pleasure saw
The Ant fulfil her parents' law.
'Ah! sister-labourer,' says she,
'How very fortunate are we!
Who, taught in infancy to know
The comforts which from labour flow,
Are independent of the great,
Nor know the wants of pride and state.
Why is our food so very sweet?
Because we earn before we eat.'

A wanton Sparrow longed to hear
Their sage discourse, and straight drew near.
The bird was talkative and loud,
And very pert and very proud;
As worthless and as vain a thing,
Perhaps, as ever wore a wing.
She found, as on a spray she sat,

The little friends were deep in chat;
That virtue was their favourite theme,
And toil and probity their scheme:
Such talk was hateful to her breast;
She thought them arrant prudes at best.

When, to display her naughty mind,
Hunger with cruelty combined,
She viewed the Ant with savage eyes,
And hopped and hopped to snatch her prize.
The Bee, who watched her opening bill,
And guessed her fell design to kill,
Asked her from what her anger rose,
And why she treated Ants as foes.

The Sparrow her reply began,
And thus the conversation ran:
'Whenever I'm disposed to dine,
I think the whole creation mine;
That I'm a bird of high degree,
And every insect made for me.
Hence oft I search the emmet-brood
(For emmets are delicious food),
And oft, in wantonness and play,
I slay ten thousand in a day.
For truth it is, without disguise,
That I love mischief as my eyes.'

'Oh fie!' the honest Bee replied,
'I fear you make base man your guide;
Of every creature sure the worst,
Though in creation's scale the first.
Ungrateful man! 'tis strange he thrives
Who burns the bees to rob their hives.

I hate his vile administration,
And so do all the emmet nation.
What fatal foes to birds are men,
Quite to the eagle from the wren!
Oh, do not men's example take,
Who mischief do for mischief's sake;
But spare the Ant – her worth demands
Esteem and friendship at your hands.
A mind with every virtue blest,
Must raise compassion in your breast.'

'Virtue!' rejoined the sneering bird,
'Where did you learn that Gothic word?
Since I was hatched, I never heard
That virtue was at all revered.
Trust me, Miss Bee – to speak the truth
I've copied man from earliest youth;
The same our taste, the same our school,
Passion and appetite our rule;
And call me bird, or call me sinner,
I'll ne'er forego my sport or dinner.'

A prowling cat the miscreant spies,
And wide expands her amber eyes:
Near and more near Grimalkin draws;
She wags her tail, extends her claws,
Then, springing on her thoughtless prey,
She bore the vicious bird away.

Nathaniel Cotton

The Ants

What wonder strikes the curious, while he views
The black ant's city, by a rotten tree,
Or woodland bank! In ignorance we muse:
Pausing, annoyed, – we know not what we see,
Such government and thought there seem to be;
Some looking on, and urging some to toil,
Dragging their loads of bent-stalks slavishly:
And what's more wonderful, when big loads foil
One ant or two to carry, quickly then
A swarm flock round to help their fellow-men.
Surely they speak a language whisperingly,
Too fine for us to hear, and sure their ways
Prove they have kings and laws, and that they be
Deformed remnants of the Fairy-days.

John Clare

The Ant

Thou little insect, infinitely small,
  What curious texture marks thy tiny frame!
How seeming large thy foresight, and withal,
 Thy labouring talents not unworthy fame,
To raise such monstrous hills among the plain,
 Larger than mountains, when compar'd with thee:
To drag the crumb dropp'd by the village swain,
 Huge size to thine, is strange indeed to me.
But that great instinct which foretels the cold,
 And bids to guard 'gainst winter's wasteful power,
Endues this mite with cheerfulness to hold

Its toiling labours through the sultry hour:
So that same soothing power, in misery,
Cheers the poor pilgrim to eternity.

John Clare

The busy ant works hard all day,
And never stops to rest or play.
He carries things ten times his size,
and never grumbles, whines or cries.
And even climbing flower stalks,
he always runs, he never walks.
He loves his work, he never tires,
And never puffs, pants or perspires.
Yet though I praise his boundless vim,
I am not really fond of him.

Mary Ann Hoberman

I too am not that keen on ants! I well remember my first visit to the jungle south of Jahore Bahru in Malaysia 40 years ago. I didn't know then that some ant species have the uncanny ability to climb aboard without being noticed and then, at some unseen signal, bite all at the same time. The pain can be excruciating! On that occasion, I jumped into a river in an effort to escape them.

On a later occasion, my wife and I left the house of a friend near Kuala Lumpur following a storm, and stopped the car to move some branches which had fallen across the narrow road. My wife hadn't spotted the nest of a Green Tree Ant woven into the branches ... and paid the price. But my worst 'ant experience' was over Christmas 1990, when I was dropped by helicopter into the Brunei rainforest. On the second day, I put down a cheese biscuit I was eating on a log – a remarkably stupid thing to do – whilst I tied a bootlace. Luckily, when I picked the biscuit up a few moments later I didn't put it straight in my mouth. It was covered with what seemed like thousands (it was certainly several dozens) of tiny fire ants which attacked viciously. I could hardly see the individual ants

175

because they were so small, but I had a badly swollen hand and a painful rash for well over a week.

More recently, in 2011, I travelled to the Laughlan Islands (also known as Budu Budi) in eastern Papua New Guinea, arriving bruised and battered after a 12 hour journey in an open dinghy over very rough seas. My tasks included collecting weaver ants for Harvard University, who were carrying out a molecular analysis in order to study the spread of this species. Weaver ants are so called because of their habit of building quite large colonial nests in trees by 'weaving' large leaves together. Their nests are easy to spot from a distance, and are viciously defended by the occupants, who rush to the site of any disturbance ready to sink their mandibles into … well … anything. Bites are non-venomous, but pretty painful. Sampling required putting five individuals ants from each nest into a small vial containing 80% alcohol, a process made mildly problematic by the fact that there are no ant volunteers. In order to prevent cross-contamination, it was also necessary to sterilize the end of my forceps with the flame from a cigarette lighter between each use. Since this is a rather fiddly process, it's better to do it in the open rather than in the forest, and I had got into the habit of getting a small boy to find a nest and bring it to the beach whenever I went ashore on an unsampled island.

A small crowd gathered on the beach, watching me take a gps reading, whilst we all awaited the return of the boy, who returned quickly with a nest. Rather cleverly, since he knew that ant bites were painful, he'd selected an empty nest, which caused a good deal of mirth and ridicule, and he was sent back to the bush to make amends. He returned eventually with a fresh nest seething with angry ants which he dropped on the sand in front of me. The task requires concentration and I had almost finished when I felt an ant bite my leg inside my trousers. What I'd failed to notice whilst engaged in 'sampling' some of their number, was that a military assault force of ants had left the nest and decided I was the cause of their home being completely wrecked. I had to excuse myself and dash along the beach with my hand down my trousers, pulling biting ants off parts of my anatomy which really should remain ant-free. He who laughs last, laughs longest. On this occasion I suspect it was the small boy.

The Ant

Turn on the prudent ant thy heedless eyes,
Observe her labours, sluggard, and be wise.
No stern command, no monitory voice,
Prescribes her duties, or directs her choice:
Yet timely provident she hastes away,
To snatch the blessings of a plenteous day:
When fruitful summer loads the teeming plain,
She crops the harvest, and she stores the grain.
How long shall sloth usurp thy useless hours,
Unnerve thy vigour, and unchain thy powers?
While artful solicitation courts repose,
Amidst the drowsy charms of dull delight,
Year chases year with unremitted flight,
Till want now following, fraudulent and slow,
Shall spring to seize thee like an ambush'd foe.

Samuel Johnson

The Ant Explorer

Once a little sugar ant made up his mind to roam –
To far away, far away, far away from home.
He had eaten all his breakfast, and he had his Ma's consent
To see what he should chance to see and here's the way he
    went –
Up and down a fern frond, round and round a stone,
Down a gloomy gully where he loathed to be alone,
Up a mighty mountain range, seven inches high,
Through the fearful forest grass that nearly hid the sky,
Out along a bracken bridge, bending in the moss,

Till he reached a dreadful desert that was feet and feet across.
'Twas a dry, deserted desert, and a trackless land to tread;
He wished that he was home again and tucked-up tight in bed.
His little legs were wobbly, his strength was nearly spent,
And so he turned around again and here's the way he went –
Back away from desert lands feet and feet across.
Back along the bracken bridge, bending in the moss,
Through the fearful forest grass, shutting out the sky,
Up a mighty mountain range, seven inches high,
Down a gloomy gully where he loathed to be alone,
Up and down a fern frond, and round and round a stone,
A dreary ant, a weary ant, resolved no more to roam,
He staggered up a garden path and popped back home.

C. J. Dennis

BEETLES

There are said to be more species of beetle than of any other insect, and more insects than any other kind of animal. This prompted British geneticist and evolutionary biologist J B S Haldane (1892-1964) to respond to a theological enquiry as to what might be concluded about The Creator from the study of creation, by observing that God, if He existed, must have had "an inordinate fondness for beetles". Almost 40% of described insects are beetles – some 350,000 species.

Many kinds of beetles will be familiar, from dung beetles to stag beetles, and ladybirds to death-watch beetles. Glow-worms and fireflies (these colloquial terms are interchangeable and refer generally to larvae or adults respectively) are also beetles, notably of the family Lampyridae and are most frequently encountered in the tropics, although some occur in Europe and there are many species in North America. The cold light emitted by living things is called bioluminescence, and ranges from white and red to yellow or green. It is extremely efficient, with almost 100% of energy output turned into visible light (a high proportion of energy used by a light bulb is lost in heat). The purpose of the glow varies: some adult males and females use the light to advertise or to attract a mate; some larvae are believed to indicate non-palatability to potential predators; yet other larvae (of the fly genus *Arachnocampa*) use the light to attract small insect prey to sticky snare lines suspended from the roof of a cave.

The first poem in this section, "Ladybird, Ladybird" ("Ladybug, Ladybug" in the USA), will be known to almost everyone. There are many versions of it. One of the commonest short versions invariably begins "Ladybird, ladybird, fly away home", and continues "Your house is on fire, your children are gone", or "Your house is on fire, your children will burn". Exactly where this couplet originated is not known, but it is probably based on the fact that ladybird larvae feed upon soft-bodied insect pests such as aphids, mealybugs, and scale insects infesting hop vines. After the hops were harvested it was customary to burn the vines, clearing the field for a subsequent planting and at the same time destroying the insect pests. Of course, the burning also destroyed the ladybird larvae. This version came from Blackwood's Magazine published in 1827, and probably arose from the fact that in the autumn of 1827, the ladybird was so abundant in many parts of the country, "as to alarm the farmer, who ignorantly fancied this favourite of our childhood to be detrimental to his crops".

Similar population explosions of ladybirds have been experienced recently, notably in 1976. Such events are due to a number of factors; in the case of 1976, the summer of that and the previous year were unusually warm and sunny, with the summer of 1975 having no significant periods of bad weather. Ladybirds, and aphids, on which ladybirds feed, both did rather well, and by the autumn of 1975 ladybird populations were much larger than usual. Ladybirds overwinter as adults, and usually suffer a significant mortality rate – but the mild winter reduced mortality with the result that in the spring of 1976 there were many more ladybirds than might usually be the case. A wet, warm spring assisted lush plant growth, providing optimum conditions for aphid development, and when ladybirds appeared in larger numbers than usual, they found ideal temperatures and plentiful food. From May, when it became unseasonally hot for an extended period, ladybirds were able to complete their development more quickly than is usual in the UK, but by August, conditions became difficult for them. The scorching summer resulted in deterioration of vegetation, with a corresponding fall in the number of aphids. The huge numbers of ladybirds had by then more or less eaten themselves out of house and home, and had little choice but to search for new food sources. They took to the air in billions. Press reports of people being 'stung' or 'bitten' by ladybirds were partly true, in the sense that the starving ladybirds were desperate enough to test the edibility of anything they came across, and the tiny amounts of pre-digestive enzyme they inject into their prey might have caused a mild chemical reaction in some people. Population explosions of any animal on this scale inevitably result in a population crash, whilst predator and prey recover. Perhaps there is a lesson here for humans!

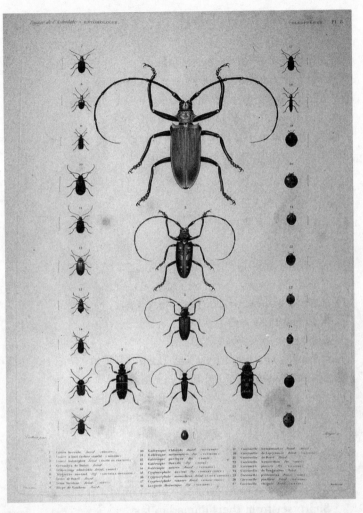

One of many plates from a series of volumes known to entomologists as *Voyage L'Astrolabe* published between 1826 and 1829; the insects were dealt with by Boisduval (full name: Jean-Baptiste Alphonse Déchauffor de Boisduval); the full title is *Voyage de la corvette L'Astrolabe exécuté pendant les années 1826-1827-1828-1829 sans le commandement de M. Jules Dumont D'Urville capitaine de Vaisseau ....* The plate depicts a variety of beetles, from the enormous Longicorn beetles of the tropics, to familiar ladybirds (© Royal Entomological Society).

Ladybird! Ladybird!

Ladybird! Ladybird! fly away home,
Night is approaching, and sunset is come;
The herons are flown to their trees by the Hall;
Felt, but unseen, the damp dewdrops fall.
This is the close of a still summer day;
Ladybird! Ladybird! haste! fly away!

To A Lady Bird

"Lady-bird! Lady-bird! fly away home,"
      The field-mouse has gone to her nest,
The daisies have shut up their sleepy red eyes,
      And the bees and the birds are at rest.

"Lady-bird! Lady-bird! fly away home,"
      The glow-worm is lighting her lamp,
The dew's falling fast, and your fine speckled wings
      Will flag with the close-clinging damp.

"Lady-bird! Lady-bird! fly away home,"—
      Good luck if you reach it at last,
the owl's come abroad, and the bat's on the roam,
      Sharp set from their Ramadan fast.

"Lady-bird! Lady-bird! fly away home,"—
      The fairy bells tinkle afar,
Make haste, or they'll catch ye and harness ye fast.
      With a cobweb to Oberon's car.

"Lady-bird! Lady-bird! fly away home,"—
　　But do as all serious people do, first
Clear your conscience, and settle your worldly affairs,
　　And so be prepar'd for the worst.

"Lady-bird! Lady-bird!" make a short shrift,
　　Here's a hair-shirted Palmer hard by,
And here's a lawyer earwig to draw up your will,
　　And we'll witness it, death-moth and I.

"Lady-bird! Lady-bird!" —don't make a fuss,—
　　You've mighty small matters to give,
your coral and jet, and ... there, there ... you can tack
　　A codicil on, if you live.

"Lady-bird! Lady-bird!" fly away now,
　　To your house, in the old willow-tree,
Where your children, so dear, have invited the ant,
　　And a few cozy neighbours to tea.

"Lady-bird! Lady-bird! fly away home,"—
　　And if not gobbled up on the way,
Nor yoked by the fairies to Oberon's car,
　　You're in luck—and that's all I've to say.

Author unknown

Ladybird

Ladybird, ladybird, fly away home!
Athens is burning, the Goth is in Rome,
Russia's gone Bolshevik, Germany's Nazi,
de Valera in Ireland has mesmerized Patsy.
The world is all jaundice in layers of chrome.
Ladybird, ladybird, for God's sake fly home!

Humbert Wolfe

This Lady-fly I take from off the grass,
Whose spotted back might scarlet red surpass.
Fly, Lady-bird, north, south, or east or west,
Fly where the man is found that I love best.
He leaves my hand, see to the west he's flown,
To call my true-love from the faithless town.

John Gay

There are many superstitions associated with the ladybird, which
was considered by most of the Christian world something of a good
luck charm: when it spreads its wings and flies away, a young girl
would note the direction it took, which was said to be the direction
from which her sweetheart would come. This doesn't seem to have
been a service available for young men.

The Eagle And The Beetle

A beetle loved a certain hare
And wandered with him everywhere:
They went to fairs and feasts together,
Took walks in any kind of weather,
Talked of the future and the past
On sunny days or overcast,
But, since their friendship was so pleasant,
Lived for the most part in the present.

One day, alas, an eagle flew
Above them, and before they knew
What cloud had shadowed them, the hare
Hung from her talons in mid-air.
'Please spare my friend,' the beetle cried.
But the great eagle sneered with pride:
'You puny, servile, cloddish bug –
Go off and hide your ugly mug.
How do you dare assume the right
To meddle with my appetite?
This hare's my snack. Have you not heard
I am the great god Zeus's bird?
Nothing can harm me, least of all
A slow, pathetic, droning ball.
Here, keep your friend's head –' And she tore
The hare's head off, and swiftly bore
His bleeding torso to her nest,
Ripped off his tail, and ate the rest.

The beetle stared at her friend's head,
And wished that she herself was dead.
She mixed her tears with his dark blood
And cloaked his face with clods of mud.
She swore that till her dying breath

She would avenge his cruel death,
That she would make the eagle pay
For what she had performed today.

Next day she slowly tracked the trail
From drop of blood to tuft of tail,
Till, high up on a mountain crest,
She found the huge unguarded nest,
And at the hour that yesterday
The bird had plunged towards her prey,
The beetle with her six short legs
Rolled out the mighty eagle's eggs.
She left at once, but she could hear
The eagle's screams of pain and fear
When later she returned and found
The broken eggshells on the ground.

Next day the eagle moved her nest
Ten miles or more towards the west,
But still the beetle's scrutiny
Followed her flight from rock to tree.
When finally the eagle laid
Another clutch, the beetle made
Straight for the nest in which they lay,
And, when the bird was hunting prey,
With much fatigue but little sound
Rolled the great eggs onto the ground.

When this had gone on for a year
The eagle, crazed with rage and fear,
Would turn back, screeching, in mid-air
Whenever she would sight a hare.
The far drone of the beetle's flight
Shattered her calm by day or night.
For weeks on end she scarcely slept.

She laid her eggs in grief, and wept
When what she'd feared had come to pass –
And her smashed brood lay on the grass.

At last she cried: 'What is the use
Of bearing your protection, Zeus –
When that small, evil clot of mud
Has massacred my flesh and blood?
King of the gods, where may I rest?
Where may I safely build my nest?
Where lay my eggs without mishap?'
'Here –' said the god. 'Here, in my lap.'

And so the eggs lay, more secure
Than they had ever lain before.
What in the universe could be
More safe than Zeus's custody?
So thought the eagle, till one day
The beetle saw them where they lay –
And, aiming with precision, flung
A microscopic ball of dung
Into the lap of mighty Zeus –
Who, rising, spewed divine abuse,
And, shaking dirt from off his legs,
Unthinkingly tipped out the eggs.

Past hope, the eagle pined away
And died of grief – and to this day
They say that eagles will not nest
In months when beetles fly their best;
But others, not so superstitious,
Merely assert that Fate's capricious,
And that the strong who crush the weak
May not be shown the other cheek.

Vikram Seth

Glow-Worms

With a yellow lantern
I take the road at night,
And chase the flying shadows
By its cheerful light.

From the banks and hedgerows
Other lanterns shine,
Tiny elfin glimmers,
Not so bright as mine.

Those are glow-worm lanterns,
Coloured green and blue,
Orange, red and purple,
Gaily winking through.

See the glow-worms hurry!
See them climb and crawl!
They go to light the dancers
At the fairy ball.

P. A. Ropes

I remember taking an expedition to the Mulu Caves in Sarawak, on the island of Borneo, about 25 years ago. We travelled up-river for several days and were pleased to reach a rather nice wooden hut on stilts which was to be our accommodation for a week and a base for climbing Gunung Mulu itself. There was a wooden balcony, and looking down at many thousands of extraordinary green lights blinking silently in the dusk between the hut and the river was a surreal experience. I have never seen so many together before or since – and when I stayed alone in the same place years later, saw none.

The Fire-fly flashes through the sky,
A meteor rich and bright;
And the wide space around, on high,
Gleams with its emerald light:
Though glory tracks that shooting star,
And bright its splendours shine,
The glow-worm's lamp is dearer far
To this sad heart of mine.

Emma Roberts

Fireflies

I like to chase the fireflies,
  Chase them to and fro'
I like to watch them dart about,
  Their little lamps aglow.
In the evening's twilight dim
  I follow them about,
I often think I have one caught,
  And then his light goes out.
I cannot tell just where he is
  Until he winks, you see,
Then far away I see his light,
  He's played a joke on me.

Grace Wilson Coplen

Fireflies In The Garden

Here come real stars to fill the upper skies,
And here on earth come emulating flies,
That though they never equal stars in size,
(And they were never really stars at heart)
Achieve at times a very star-like start.
Only, of course, they can't sustain the part.

Robert Frost

The Glow-Worm

There's a creature called a glow-worm
Which on point of fact is no worm
But a beetle in an unfamiliar light
She is usually a lady
Conduct anything but shady
Though inclined to be conspicuous at night

She is never very active
Or especially attractive
Wouldn't strike you in the daytime as being smart
She is nothing in a high light
But she lights up well at twilight
And owes everything to nature not to art

You would scarcely have suspected
That the war would have affected
Even glow-worms, but the law is quite succinct
And in view of lighting orders
Made to baffle Hun marauders
They will soon become undoubtedly extinct

Harry Eltringham

To A Glow-Worm

Little being of a day,
    Glowing in thy cell alone,
Shedding light, with mystic ray,
    On thy path, and on my own;

Dost thou whisper to my heart?
    'Though I grovel in the sod,
Still I mock man's boasted art
    With the workmanship of God'!

See! The fire-fly in his flight
    Scorning the terrene career;
He, the eccentric meteor bright,—
    Thou, the planet of thy sphere.

Why within thy cavern damp,
    Thus with trembling dost thou cower?
Fear'st thou I would quench thy lamp,—
    Luster of thy lonely bower?

No!—regain thy couch of clay,
    Sparkle brightly as before:
Man should dread to take away
    Gifts he never can restore.

Anonymous

The Fire-Fly

Tell us, O Guide! By what strange natural laws
This winged flower throws out, night by night,
Such lunar brightness? Why,—for what grave cause
Is this earth-insect crown'd with heavenly light?
Peace! Rest content! See where, by cliff and dell,
Past tangled forest paths and silent river,
The little lustrous creatures guide us well,
And where we fail, his little light aids us ever,—
Night's shining servant! Pretty star of earth!

Barry Cornwall

Yet mark! As fade the upper skies,
Each thicket opes ten thousand eyes:
Before, beside us, and above,
The fire-fly lights his lamp of love,
Retreating, chasing, sinking, soaring,
The darkness of the copse exploring.

Barry Cornwall

The Mower To The Glow-worms

Ye living lamps, by whose dear light
The nightingale does sit so late,
And studying all the summer-night,
Her matchless songs does meditate;

Ye country comets, that portend
No war, nor prince's funeral,
Shining unto no higher end
Than to presage the grass's fall;

Ye glow-worms, whose officious flame
To wand'ring mowers shows the way,
That in the night have lost their aim,
And after foolish fires do stray;

Your courteous lights in vain you waste,
Since Juliana here is come,
For she my mind hath so displac'd
That I shall never find my home.

Andrew Marvell

The Glow-Worm

Beneath the hedge, or near the stream,
A worm is known to stray,
That shows by night a lucid beam,
Which disappears by day.
Disputes have been, and still prevail,
From whence his rays proceed;
Some give that honour to his tail,
And others to his head.
But this is sure—the hand of Might,
That kindles up the skies,
Gives him a modicum of light
Proportioned to his size.
Perhaps indulgent Nature meant,
By such a lamp bestowed,
To bid the traveller, as he went,
Be careful where he trod.
Nor crush a worm, whose useful light
Might serve, however small,
To show a stumbling stone by night,
And save him from a fall.
Whate'er she meant, this truth divine
Is legible and plain—
'Tis power Almighty bids him shine,
Nor bids him shine in vain.
Ye proud and wealthy, let this theme
Teach humbler thoughts to you;
Since such a reptile has its gem,
And boasts its splendours too.

Vincent Bourne
Translated from the original Latin by William Cowper

Glow-Worm

When evening closes Nature's eye,
    The Glow-worm lights her little spark,
To captivate her favourite fly,
    And tempt the rover through the dark.

Conducted by a sweeter star,
    Than all that deck the fields above,
He fondly hastens from afar,
    To sooth her solitude with love.

Thus in this wilderness of tears
    Amid the world's perplexing gloom,
The transient torch of Hymen cheers
    The pilgrim journeying to the tomb.

Unhappy he, whose hopeless eye
    Turns to the light of love in vain;
Whose Cynosure[56] is in the sky,
    He, on the dark and lonely main.

James Montgomery

---

[56] The star, in the constellation of Ursa Minor, near the North Pole, used as a navigation aid by sailors. John Milton, in his Comus: A Masque, calls it the Tyrian Cynosure

A little worm whose lover flies
At twilight through the air,
Displays a light from where she lies
To guide the wanderer there.

When darkness veils the summer night,
And spreads her gloom around,
Her little light, will cheer the sight
And glimmer from the ground

And safely through nocturnal shade
Her lover's path 'twill lead,
And in his little breast pervade,
And hasten on his speed

So cheerly may your brighter ray
Ye Ladies lead our will,
Around us play where'er we stray
And be our safety still.

For surely Nature kindly meant
In giving us this fly
That unto the Phosphor lent
The moral should apply

But mostly ere experience gives
Her torch to light the way,
Whilst ev'ry youthful passion lives
So apt to lead astray;

'Tis then when all your power reigns
Supremely o'er the soul,
No other power so well restrains,
So sweetly can control.

As Cynthia sheds her radiance mild,
As gems in darkness shine,
So shine ye o'er the heart so wild,
Soft, lovely, and benign.

Oh! Then should darkness veil the sight
Should meteors lead aside,
'Tis then your light shall cheer the night,
And sweetly be the guide.

Whether for me its radiant beam
Shall e'er be taught to shine,
Full well do I its pow'r esteem,
And deem it all divine.

Then may it e'er be train'd to glow
With Virtue's hallow'd fire,
So where it shines it shall bestow
Each chaste and pure desire.

And may it o'er the paths of life,
So oft with clouds o'erspread,
With darkly lurking dangers rife
Where'er we chance to tread,

Diffuse in sweetly social joy,
In grace, in love, in truth,
And lead the man as erst the boy
Or love-imploring youth.

So be ye e'er the light, the guide
To cheer and aid our will;
In vestal robes or matron pride
Our polar star be still.

Author unknown

The Nightingale And Glow-Worm

A nightingale, that all day long
Had cheered the village with his song,
Nor yet at eve his note suspended,
Nor yet when eventide was ended,
Began to feel, as well he might,
The keen demands of appetite;
When, looking eagerly around,
He spied far off, upon the ground,
A something shining in the dark,
And knew the glow-worm by his spark;
So, stooping down from hawthorn top,
He thought to put him in his crop.

The worm, aware of his intent,
Harangued him thus, right eloquent:-
"Did you admire my lamp," quoth he,
"As much as I your minstrelsy,
You would abhor to do me wrong
As much as I to spoil your song;
For 'twas the self-same Power divine
Taught you to sing, and me to shine;
That you with music, I with light,
Might beautify and cheer the night."

The songster heard his short oration,
And warbling out his approbation,
Released him, as my story tells,
And found a supper somewhere else.

William Cowper

I wish I was a glow-worm,
a glow-worm's never glum,
'cos how could you be grumpy,
when the sun shines out your bum

Anonymous

The Glow-Worm

You with light gas the lamps nocturnal feed
That dance and glimmer on the marshy mead;
Shine round Calendula[57] at twilight hours,
And tip with silver all her saffron flowers;
Warm on her mossy couch the radiant worm,
Guard from cold dews her love-illumined form,
From leaf to leaf conduct the virgin light,
Star of the earth, and diamond of the night!

Erasmus Darwin

---

[57] *Calendula* is the plant genus that includes marigolds (Asteraceae).

Forgiven

I found a little beetle, so that beetle was his name,
And I called him Alexander and he answered just the same.
I put him in a matchbox, and I kept him all the day...
And Nanny let my beetle out
Yes, Nanny let my beetle out
She went and let my beetle out-
And beetle ran away.
She said she didn't mean it, and I never said she did,
She said she wanted matches, and she just took off the lid
She said that she was sorry, but it's difficult to catch
An excited sort of beetle you've mistaken for a match.
She said that she was sorry, and I really mustn't mind
As there's lots and lots of beetles which she's certain we
    could find
If we looked about the garden for the holes where beetles hid-
And we'd get another matchbox, and write BEETLE on the lid.
We went to all the places which a beetle might be near,
And we made the sort of noises which a beetle likes to hear,
And I saw a kind of something, and I gave a sort of shout:
"A beetle-house and Alexander Beetle coming out!"
It was Alexander Beetle I'm as certain as can be
And he had a sort of look as if he thought it might be ME,
And he had a kind of look as if he thought he ought to say:
"I'm very, very sorry that I tried to run away."
And Nanny's very sorry too, for you know what she did,
And she's writing ALEXANDER very blackly on the lid,
So Nan and me are friends, because it's difficult to catch
An excited Alexander you've mistaken for a match.

A. A. Milne

Nursery Rhymes For The Tender Hearted

I knew a black beetle, who lived down a drain,
And friendly he was, though his manners were plain;
When I took a bath he would come up the pipe,
And together we'd wash and together we'd wipe.

Though mother would sometimes protest with a sneer
That my choice of tub-mate was wanton and queer,
A nicer companion I never have seen:
He bathed every night, so he must have been clean.

Whenever he heard the tap splash in the tub
He'd dash up the drain-pipe and wait for a scrub,
And often, so fond of ablution was he,
I'd find him there floating and waiting for me.

Christopher Morley

The Waterbeetle

The waterbeetle here shall teach
A sermon far beyond your reach:
He flabbergasts the Human Race
By gliding on the water's face
With ease, celerity and grace;
But if he ever stopped to think
Of how he did it, he would sink.

Hilaire Belloc

Water beetles and water striders are able to 'glide' across the surface
of water by taking advantage of surface tension, but also by

'floating'. The water strider's superhydrophobic legs are covered with microscopic hairs that trap tiny air bubbles, which form an air cushion, preventing the legs from getting wet. Their legs are used like oars, allowing forward movement.

He – Tick, tick, tick! I'm waiting for thee
In the crevice the bookcase behind.
She – Tick, tick tick! I'm coming, my love,
Though not on the wings of the wind.

He – Tick, tick, tick! why don't you make haste?
I cannot wait here all night.
She – Tick, tick, tick! Well, do as you please,
It's the same to me, sir, quite.

He – Tick, tick, tick, tick, tick, tick! Good-bye!
I'm off to you know who,
She – she was squeezed in the hinge of the door last night;
Tick, tick, tick, tick! Adieu!

Henry Gardiner Adams

from Wood an Insect

A wood-worm
That lies in old wood, like a hare in her form:
With teeth or with claws it will bite or will scratch,
And chambermaids christen this worm a death-watch;
Because like a watch it always cries click;
Then woe be to those in the house who are sick!
For, sure as a gun, they will give up the ghost,
If the maggot cries click, when it scratches the post;

But a kettle of scalding hot water injected,
Infallibly cures the timber affected:
The omen is broken, the danger is over,
The maggot will die, and the sick will recover.

Jonathan Swift

The audible click of the woodboring Death Watch beetle, *Xestobium rufovillosum*, is a tapping or clicking sound made by the beetles to attract mates. Because they are most often heard on quiet nights in old wooden rafters, they became associated with the "watch" maintained beside the dying or the dead, and by extension were considered an omen of impending death. No doubt a kettle of scalding water would indeed stop the clicking.

Dung Beetle

It's a dirty job, I know it is,
But someone has to do it,
You can't leave a pile just steaming there,
'Cus someone might walk through it.
Some say that I'm the lowest of the low,
But I don't care what people think,
'Cus if stuff was left just where it fell,
The jungle would really stink.
So I roll it up into nice big balls
And shift it if I can,
I'm a dung beetle and always have
A big job on my hands.
As a career it may not seem like much,
But I do not really care,
That I've started at the bottom
And like as not, will always stay there.

I don't get the respect that I deserve,
Although the job I do is super,
It means folks can do things where they want,
And I'll be their pooper-scooper.
I'm one of nature's street cleaners,
As a job you cannot beat it,
'Cus I get to take my work home with me,
And then I get to eat it.

Most dung beetles belong to the family Scarabaeidae and feed partly or exclusively on faeces. Some species live in manure; others are renowned for rolling spherical balls of dung which they use as brood chambers and/or a food source; yet others bury the dung, often by burrowing underneath it. When crossing part of the Sahara Desert some years ago, it was interesting to watch the speed with which – and sensitive readers may want to skip this bit – dung beetles arrived, sometimes several dozen together, at fresh faeces and caused them to disappear under the sand. Within a matter of literally minutes there was nothing at all visible.

Step on a black beetle,
it will rain;
Pick it up and bury it,
the sun will shine again

Traditional proverb

Now fades the glimmering landscape on the sight,
And all the air a solemn stillness holds,
Save where the beetle wheels his droning flight,
And drowsy tinklings lull the distant folds

Thomas Gray

204

FLIES

Flies belong to the Order Diptera, meaning "two-winged". Many other insects include "flies" in their common names (eg. butterflies, mayflies, dragonflies, fireflies etc.), but the true flies have two wings (as opposed to four). They include house-flies, blue-bottles, gnats, midges, and mosquitoes. Mosquitoes in particular have important significance in carrying and transmitting diseases, including malaria.

The mosquito is aptly described as a 'ghoul on wings' by DH Lawrence, as anyone who has travelled in the arctic or tropics can confirm. In the arctic, the best one can hope for is a breeze, which can keep the numbers down, although they still harass the walker at every step. They are apparently less willing to fly over snow, and in early summer reindeer congregate in tight groups in the middle of remaining drifts, in order to avoid them. They bite through thick clothing, and I have spent weeks in the European, Russian and American/Canadian arctic dressed in a thick shirt and a woolly hat, sweating in the mid-summer sun, just to avoid being eaten alive. In the tropics, mosquitoes are fewer in number, but arguably more vicious. Beautiful photographs of idyllic tropical island beaches that adorn glossy magazines hide the fact that only a fool would sit on that beach without a plentiful supply of insect repellant. I have travelled extensively around Pacific islands in the last few years, often in an open fibre-glass boat with an outboard engine, and it is usually possible to tell whether an unihabited island or islet is going to be comfortable by the number, size and sometimes colour of the mosquitoes that glide out silently to greet the boat. Inhabited islands are often worse because copra production is widespread, and the number of upturned (and water-filled) empty coconut shells around villages harbour large mosquito populations. I also remember heading for the shore of a small cay off the coast of Belize in the Caribbean in a tiny dinghy; there were four of us and we must have been at least 50 metres off the shore when we were attacked by a cloud of massive black mosquitoes. Three of us jumped overboard to get away from them, leaving the poor chap who happened to have the helm at the time to get eaten alive in the few moments it took to do a swift U-turn. We never did make it to the cay.

In a windswept coastal locality on the east coast of Australia a few years ago, I told my wife that we could safely eat outside our camper vehicle for once with absolute impunity because there wouldn't be any mosquitoes associated with salt water, but within seconds of taking our lunch outside we were covered in the damn things (*Ochlerotatus australis*: the Saltwater Mosquito) – and my credibility, always fragile, had taken another dive!

Flies are able to 'stick' to vertical surfaces, or on ceilings, apparently defying gravity, because of specialised footpads equipped with tiny hairs with thickened tips. The hairs produce an adhesive substance which allows the fly to "stick" to the surface. Fly larvae – commonly known as "maggots" – can be of value to forensic scientists in indicating time elapsed since death through assessing natural succession and growth stage.

The Fly And The Poet

Dark were the cares of the poet's breast,
    Grand were the thoughts of his head,
But sad thoughts and grand ones must all be represt,
    For he had to write nonsense for bread.

Proud was the curl on the Poet's lip,
    And big was the tear in his eye;
Scarce he saw in the inkstand his pen to dip,
    But he saw on its summit a Fly.

There Blue-bottle sat, and stroked down his face
    With a twirl of his head, twice or thrice,
Then says he, "Brother bard – I pity your ease,
    And have brought you a bit of advice.

Nay, man, never wince! I heed not your scorn,
    'Tis a fact, and I'll presently show it,
That if not, as you think yourself, Poet born,
    I'm by place and by feeding a Poet.

I come from a spot where the fruit of the vine,
    And the oil of the olive abound;
Where Arabia and India their riches combine,
    And shed spiciest of odours around.

High over blue mountains with snowy white tips,
    I wonder —, but use your own eyes,
Only look round the shop where you go for your dips,
    And you'll see the Parnassus of Flies.

And now for my council – thus rich the domain,
    Whence I draw inspiration and bread;
But by lightness, not weight, I this empire maintain,
    And by emptiness stand on my head.

While others can't climb, using infinite pains,
    I, gravity turning to jest,
Ascend, with all ease, perpendicular planes,
    Rough or smooth, just as pleases me best.
So try lightness, friend Poet – I warrant you'll find
That as I rule matter, so you may rule mind!"

                                        Acheta domestica

To A Fly

Prithee, little buzzing fly,
Eddying round my taper, why
Is it that its quivering light
Dazzling captivates your sight?
Bright my taper is, 'tis true;
Trust me, 'tis too bright for you.

'Tis a flame, fond thing, beware-
'Tis a flame you cannot bear.

Touch it, and 'tis instant fate;
Take my counsel ere too late:
Buzz no longer round and round-
Settle on the wall or ground:
Sleep till morning: with the day
Rise, and use your wings you may:
Use them then of danger clear.
Wait till morning; do, my dear.

Lo! My counsel nought avails;
Round and round, and round it sails-
Sails with idle unconcern:
Prithee, trifler, canst thou burn?
Madly heedless as thou art,
Know thy danger, and depart.
Why persist? I plead in vain:
Singed it falls, and writhes in pain.

Is not this, deny who can-
Is not this a draught of man?
Like the fly, he rashly tries
Pleasure's burning sphere, and dies.
Vain the friendly caution; still
He rebels, alas! And will.
What I sing let pride apply:
Flies are weak, and man's a fly.

Anonymous

There was a Young Lady of Troy,
Whom several large flies did annoy;
Some she killed with a thunk
Some she drowned at the pump,
And some she took with her to Troy

Edward Lear

There was an old person of Skye,
Who waltz'd with a bluebottle fly:
They buzz'd a sweet tune,
To the light of the moon,
And entranced all the people of Skye

Edward Lear

God in his wisdom made the fly
And then forgot to tell us why.

Ogden Nash

A flea and a fly in a flue,
Were imprisoned, so what could they do?
Said the flea, "Let us fly"
"Let us flee," said the fly,
So they flew through a flaw in the flue

Ogden Nash

A flea and a fly flew up in a flue.
Said the flea to the fly, 'Oh what shall we do?'
'Let us flee,' said the fly;
'Let us fly,' said the flea;
So they fluttered and flew up a flaw in the flue

probably Ogden Nash

Ogden Nash did not consider his poetry to be static, and made constant revisions and versions of some of his poems; the second version of what is much the same poem, above, was unattributed, but is almost certainly a variant from his own hand.

Wish I Were A Fly On The Wall

There once was a fly on the wall
I wonder why didn't it fall
Because its feet stuck
Or was it just luck
Or does gravity miss things so small?

Robert D. Cowan

Song of the Fly

Straight from the rubbish heap I come
I never wash my feet.
And every single chance I get
I walk on what you eat.

Tom Crew

To a troublesome fly

"He came to make us merry with his humming"
(partim)

Off busy, curious torment! Hence
You little black impertinence!
Your tiny snout and suckered toes
Invade my hands and face and nose,
And "tickle slumber" from my eye;
While your eternal buzzings by
Annoy my ear with ceaseless hum,
Worse than recruiting serjeant's drum—
Go, sing to those who like your note,
I wish your trumpet down your throat!

J. C. Children

On A Fly Drinking Out Of His Cup

Busy, curious, thirsty fly!
Drink with me and drink as I:
Freely welcome to my cup,
Couldst thou sip and sip it up:
Make the most of life you may,
Life is short and wears away.

Both alike are mine and thine
Hastening quick to their decline:
Thine's a summer, mine's no more,
Though repeated to threescore.
Threescore summers, when they're gone,
Will appear as short as one!

William Oldys

Changing Perceptions

Oh thirsty fly, who sipped from cup
Of William Oldys long ago,
I wonder whether you were clean:
Or had you dined on turd of dog
Before you sought to quench your need?
And did you spring from larva raised
On rotting meat? Before the eye
Of microscope revealed this world
As home for microbe hordes one could
Delight in humble fly who shared
One's drink. But now we know the risk
Of germs that hitch a ride on feet
Of such as sampled William's wine,
We're wise to swat, as swift as can,
As soon as seen. The same applies
To outworn creeds our current facts
Repudiate. As knowledge grows
We shift our course, like lowland stream
That ever feels its way to sea
Whose boundless truth extends beyond
The line our gaze can hope to reach.

Henry Disney

In 1732, when Oldys welcomed a fly drinking from his cup, the consequences of poor hygiene were not understood as they are today, when the potential for flies to carry disease is clear. These two approaches to a fly drinking from a cup remind me of an occasion several years ago when I was marooned on the remote Pacific island of Tikopia for eight weeks due to a *coup d'etat* in the Solomon Islands capital, Honiara. Island culture decreed that no-one could turn their back on the chief, nor ever have their head higher than his, and this was facilitated by the door to his hut being only three feet high, necessitating entry and exit on hands and knees.

The current Chief, Edward, was well educated, and spoke pretty good English. His hut was a focal point for the village, and he was consulted every day on important matters of village life by a stream of visitors, who treated him with great deference, as befitted his status. I got into the habit of visiting him each morning and we became good friends. During my first week he offered me tea in a half pint beer mug (one of his treasured possessions from rare visits to Honiara), and apologised profusely when flies were attracted to the sweet tea, indicating to his wife that she should throw it away. I told him it didn't matter to me because I didn't think the flies would drink much. For some reason he thought this was hilarious, and repeated it to every one of his many visitors – unfortunately the novelty never wore off. He would engineer a situation with every visitor. *"Ae wanfela fly na insaet lo tea bilong iu ia? Hem set nomoa, bae hem no drink finisim"* ("Is that a fly inside your tea here? Don't worry. He won't finish the drink"), before rolling around in fits of laughter, with tears rolling down his face. The first hundred or so times were amusing, but it began to wear a little thin. He would do it to his family too, and at first his wife would raise her eyes to the heavens; latterly she glared at me, since I was clearly to blame. He's probably telling the same story now, a decade or so later, to anyone who will listen.

Basic Fly Control

I never bought a fly spray, I used to say I'm Green,
Although, I guess, I must confess, I'm probably too mean.

I thought I'd try a method that wouldn't be so dear,
I looked around, and then I found, it wasn't quite that clear.

I bought a Venus Fly trap, and this is what it did,
It never caught a single fly, but bit our little kid.

I tried the sticky paper, hanging from the light,
It caught my hair, and made me swear, I threw it out last
  night.

Someone mentioned fly swat, I thought I'd try it out,
But hit the fancy teapot, and broke the blooming spout.

I read about repellents, but all the ones I got
Just gave the flies red watery eyes and didn't help a lot.

I asked about the light trap, in the butcher's shop,
He flicked a fly from off a pie, and squashed it on a chop.

Then I thought of Granddad, who used to live down south,
He'd have a booze, and then a snooze, and catch 'em in his
  mouth.

But when I tried that method, it didn't work for me,
It makes you think, if you don't drink, it's not the same
  with tea.

I sat there in my armchair, reading Sunday news,
About the Pope, and Christian hope, and other people's views.

A fly came buzzing round me, I rolled the paper up,
It wasn't nice, I lashed out twice, and broke a coffee cup.

And that's when I admitted, I'd done my best and lost,
So in dismay, I bought a spray, and never mind the cost.

John Seville

The original creation and the powers of irritation
Of the common and infuriating fly,
Are things which neither churches nor zoological researches
Can possibly attempt to justify

Not the nicest of the features of these horrid little creatures
Is the way they get a fellow when he's down.
And with maddening persistence choose the point of least
　resistance
On which to run around and play the clown.

They drive one to profanity and nearly to insanity
Perambulating lightly on the nose,
In that necessary session – known to ev-ery profession
As the afternoon, or cogitating doze.

Now the Arabic variety, the bane of the society
Which settles in the delta of the Nile,
Cannot irritate the Sphinx and, as everybody thinks,
Accounts for his infuriating smile.

They're as prolific in their habits, as a colony of rabbits,
There's nothing in this world that they respect.
From Farouk upon his throne, to a dog without a bone
And there's nothing in between that they neglect.

With motives dark and sinister, they'll settle on a Minister
Or mar romantic evenings in the glade.
They can ruin the impression of a dignified expression
And the steadfastness of soldiers on parade.

I can say without compunction that there isn't any function
To be quoted to the credit of the fly.
Some people have a bias that such things are sent to try us –
But can anyone explain the reason why?

Author unknown

Where Do The Bloody Flies Come From?

Where do the bloody flies come from?
It's a dilemma quite perplexing
Scholars, cooks and scientists
Have found it rather vexing.

Where do the bloody flies come from?
It's a question often asked
An environmental problem
That's seen several studies tasked.

For when the weather's rain and cold
Without a ray of sun
You won't see sight nor sign of them
Not a single one.

But if you crack a coldie
And prepare to take a sip
You'll find a couple of the blighters
Camped on the stubbie's lip.

And should you light the barbie
As a bloke is wont to do
You'll find a fly, who will invite himself
With a thousand mates or two.

I'm sure there are members of their union
Who think it's just a hoot
That their cousins from the country
Have created a salute.

We buy flash screens and insect doors
We fit electronic, whizz bang zappers
For all the good they seem to do
You may as well shoo them with the wrappers.

You'll clean the yard and bath the pets
You're thinking "this will stop them sure"
But as you go to walk inside
A mob will beat you through the door.

So you set about with swat and spray
To create a cloud of toxic air
You choke and gag, you sweat and swoon
But they're still landing in your hair.

Where do the bloody flies come from?
I know not, nor do I care
But wherever the bloody hell it is
I wish they'd all "bugger off" back there!

Tony Sargeant

I saw this unattributed poem on a pub wall in the Australian
outback some years ago. Flies in Australia have to be experienced
to be believed. It is just impossible to get away from them. In stock
areas they are overwhelming – elsewhere they may be a major
nuisance in summer, especially as they are unwilling to fly off when
swatted and difficult to dislodge when they get behind your
spectacles or sunglasses. The author of this poem (subsequently
found to be bush poet Tony Sargeant) clearly had experience!

Mosquito

When did you start your tricks,
Monsieur?

What do you stand on such high legs for?
Why this length of shredded shank,
Your exaltation?

Is it so that you shall lift your centre of gravity upwards
And weigh no more than air as you alight upon me,
Stand upon me weightless, you phantom?

I heard a woman call you the Winged Victory
In sluggish Venice.
You turn your head towards your tail, and smile.

How can you put so much devilry
Into that translucent phantom shred
Of a frail corpus?

Queer, with your thin wings and your streaming legs,
How you sail like a heron, or a dull clot of air,
A nothingness.

Yet what an aura surrounds you;
Your evil little aura, prowling, and casting a numbness on
My mind.

That is your trick, your bit of filthy magic:
Invisibility, and the anaesthetic power
To deaden my attention in your direction.

But I know your game now, streaky sorcerer.

Queer, how you stalk and prowl the air
In circles and evasions, enveloping me,
Ghoul on wings
Winged Victory.

Settle, and stand on long thin shanks
Eyeing me sideways, and cunningly conscious that I am aware,
You speck.

I hate the way you lurch off sideways into air
Having read my thoughts against you.

Come then, let us play at unawares,
And see who wins in this sly game of bluff.
Man or mosquito.

You don't know that I exist, and I don't know that you exist.
Now then!

It is your trump,
It is your hateful little trump,
You pointed fiend,
Which shakes my sudden blood to hatred of you:
It is your small, high, hateful bugle in my ear.

Why do you do it?
Surely it is bad policy.

They say you can't help it.

If that is so, then I believe a little in Providence protecting
    the innocent.
But it sounds so amazingly like a slogan,
A yell of triumph as you snatch my scalp.

Blood, red blood
Super-magical
Forbidden liquor.

I behold you stand
For a second enspasmed in oblivion.
Obscenely ecstacied
Sucking live blood,
My blood.

Such silence, such suspended transport,
Such gorging,
Such obscenity of trespass.

You stagger
As well you may.
Only your accursed hairy frailty,
Your own imponderable weightlessness
Saves you, wafts you away on the very draught my anger
    makes in its snatching.

Away with a paean of derision,
You winged blood-drop.
Can I not overtake you?
Are you one too many for me,
Winged Victory?
Am I not mosquito enough to out-mosquito you?

Queer, what a big stain my sucked blood makes
Beside the infinitesimal faint smear of you!
Queer, what a dim dark smudge you have disappeared into!

D H Lawrence

Mosquito

O Mrs. Mosquito, quit biting me please!
I'm happy my blood type with your type agrees.
    I'm glad that my flavor
    Has met with your favor.
    I'm touched by your care,
    Yes, I'm touched everywhere.
On my arms and my legs, on my elbows and knees,
    Till I cannot tell which
    Is the itchiest itch
    Needs the scratchiest scratch.
Your taste for my taste is the reason for these,
So Mrs. Mosquito, quit biting me, please!

Mary Ann Hoberman

The Mosquito Knows

The mosquito knows full well, small as he is
he's a beast of prey.
But after all
he only takes his bellyful,
he doesn't put my blood in the bank.

D H Lawrence

Glossina morsitans or The Tsetse

A *Glossina morsitans* bit rich Aunt Betsy.
Tsk, tsk, tsetse.

Ogden Nash

Tsetse flies (several species of the genus *Glossina*) are natives of Africa
and are vectors of various trypanosomes between vertebrate hosts.
In humans, this includes sleeping sickness, or trypanosomiasis.

Gnats

As when a swarm of gnats at eventide
    Out of the fens of Allean do arise,
    Their murmuring small trumpets sounden wide,
    Whiles in the air their clustering army flies,
    That as a cloud doth seem to dim the skies;
    Ne man nor beast may rest, or take repast,
    For their sharp wounds, and noyous injuries,
    Till the fierce northern wind with blustring blast
Doth blow them quite away, and in the ocean cast.

Edmund Spenser

Epitaph On A Gnat
Found Crushed On The Leaf Of A Lady's Album

Lie there, embalm'd from age to age! –
This is the album's noblest page.
Though every glowing leaf be fraught

With painting, poesy, and thought;
Where tracts of mortal hands are seen,
A hand invisible hath been,
And left his autograph behind,
This image from th' eternal mind;
A work of skill surpassing sense,
A labour of Omnipotence!
Though frail as dust it meets the eye,
He form'd this gnat who built the sky.
Stop – lest it vanish at thy breath –
This speck had life, and suffered death!

James Montgomery

The Gnat

When the ark
reached Mt. Ararat,
why didn't Noah swat
the gnat?

Or if he was too drunk
to strafe it,
couldn't he hand the job
to Japhet?

Or Shem perhaps,
or even Ham?
Or send a prepaid
cablegram

to God in heaven,
"May I plug
this perfectly
disgusting bug?"

Instead of which
he let a pair
go practically
anywhere,

and the first nudged
the second gnat.
(You know their ways!) and that
was that.

Humbert Wolfe

The Forest Fly

So have I seen ere this a sillie flie
With mastiff-dog in summer-heate to play,
Sometimes to sting him in his nose or eie;
Sometimes about this grizzly jaws to stay,
And buzzing round his eares to flie,
He snaps in vaine, for still she whips away,
And oft so long she dallies in this sort,
Till one snap comes, and marreth all her sport.

"Harrington"

Flies of the genus *Stomoxys* cannot be told apart from an 'ordinary'
fly, especially when they are doing little beyond flying around one's

legs. But they pack a powerful punch, and their bite is painful and lasting. They usually fly only a short distance when one attempts to swat them, before returning again and again to exposed flesh. They can – and do – also bite through loosely woven and thin clothing. With no mandibles to make a wound, blood-sucking *Stomoxys* have modified mouthparts with sharp teeth on the inner surface which they manipulate through muscular contractions.

A mosquito cried out in pain:
"A chemist has poisoned my brain!"
The cause of his sorrow
Was para-Dichloro
Diphenyl-Trichloroethane

[or]

A mosquito was heard to complain,
That a chemist had poisoned his brain.
The cause of his sorrow
Was para-Dichloro
Dimethyldiethylpropane

Author unknown

Dichloro-Diphenyl-Trichloroethane is the full name of one of the best-known – and certainly the most controversial – pesticides, DDT. It was successfully used to control disease-bearing mosquitoes during the Second World War, and in 1948 Swiss chemist Paul Müller was awarded a Nobel Prize for his discovery of the remarkable efficiency of DDT as a contact poison. When it became commercially available as an agricultural pesticide, its use was widespread. Unfortunately, its side-effects on the environment were catastrophic and the publication (and accompanying public outcry) of Rachel Carson's 1962 book *Silent Spring*, in which she questioned indiscriminate use of DDT and other chemicals, can be said to have played a significant part in starting the environmental movement. Some effects of DDT were not immediately apparent:

225

for example, DDT was largely responsible for the significant decrease in birds of prey because the cumulative total amount ingested resulted, among other things, to very thin egg shells, which led to eggs breaking very easily and a serious decline in some bird populations. Agricultural use of DDT is now banned worldwide.

The Fly

Little Fly,
Thy summer's play
My thoughtless hand
Has brushed away.

Am not I
A fly like thee?
Or art not thou
A man like me?

For I dance
And drink, and sing,
Till some blind hand
Shall brush my wing.

If thought is life
And strength and breath
And the want
Of thought is death;

Then am I
A happy fly,
If I live,
Or if I die.

William Blake

The Greenbottle

Lucilia caesar, illustrious name,
In your coat of emerald armour gleaming;
A bright metallic jewel with flight insane,
Your tinsel kept without a stain,
By hind legs polishing and cleaning.
In summer sun he loves to bask,
When he is fully fed;
And then resumes his grisly task,
What can it be? I hear you ask,
Why! Sniffing out the dead.
Phallus impudicus makes him a fool,
With its carrion smell;
Attracted to this foul toadstool,
He carries off its slimy drool,
Spreading its spores amongst the pimpernel.

Robert Lawson

It is well known that flies carry diseases from walking on their pretty unsavoury food. *Phallus impudicus*, known as the Common Stinkhorn, is a widespread fungus renowned for a foul odour and for its resemblance to a phallus when mature. Rather than distributing airborne spores, Stinkhorns produce a sticky spore mass with an accompanying odour of decaying meat which attracts insects (including the greenbottle in this poem). Spores stick to the flies' legs and the flies unwittingly distribute the spores to other localities. Immature Stinkhorn fungus is consumed in parts of Europe.

The Blue-Fly

Five summer days, five summer nights,
The ignorant, loutist, giddy blue-fly
Hung without motion on the cling peach,
Humming occasionally: 'O my love, my fair one!'
As in the Canticles.

Magnified one thousand times, the insect
Looks farcically human; laugh if you will!
Bald head, stage-fairy wings, blear eyes,
A caved-in chest, hairy black mandibles,
Long spindly thighs.

The crime was detected on the sixth day.
What then could be said or done? By anyone?
It would have been vindictive, mean and what-not
To swat that fly for being a blue-fly.
For debauch of a peach.

Is it fair, either, to bring a microscope
To bear on the case, even in search of truth?
Nature, doubtless, has some compelling cause
To glut the carriers of her epidemics –
Nor did the peach complain.

Robert Graves

Drosophila In Paradise

Far east of the china plate
The earth breaks, leaks, and clots
And repeats . . .
Fire into water; earth into air.

In the main the islands come and go
Forming an archipelago.

Endless emigrants from living land
Stream forth by sea and air to found
Or founder . . .
A striking and attenuated few
Trickle their bits from a wealthy heritage
Into half-baked gene pools
About this insulated and eclectic range,
A patchwork world that naturally selects
In new directions its kaleidoscope
Of species in genetic revolution.
The hotstage of ultrarapid evolution
Awaits the leading player.

Enter from afar the gravid female fly
Or a pair of dipterans that fly united
Ours is not to reason why
But here they are
With everything they could have wanted;
Beaucoup de Lebensraum
A steamy potpourri of plants.
(Although these flies herbivorous
Would rather phyte than switch,
In a future evolutionary hitch
Some will—to spider eggs!)

Inbred offspring swell the beachhead
Generate their own invading force
And penetrate erratically
A monolithic ecologic vacuum.
To some, put off by numbers,
Falls the vagrant lot;
An offbeat drifter takes another isle . . .
With reproductive ties that bind
Dissolved by water in between,
The replicated colonies
Evolve in part in parallel
But mostly come to see
Sporadic interimmigrants
No longer as their kind.

So species in division multiply.
Among the shifty lava flows, the island flies
Continually colonize and differentiate,
Settling back from time to time to coexist.
Cycle after cycle amplifies
This rich endemic fauna to create
A matchless, if outlandish, marbled layer cake
Mushroomed out of all expected size and shape.
Though countless pieces have gone down
The lubricated gullet of extinction,
There are (by latest estimate)
In the Hawaiian Islands
Some seven hundred
Drosophilid
Species of
Distinc-
Tion.

John M Burns

The fruit fly genus *Drosophila* is used extensively in biological and molecular studies. Although the theory of tectonic plate movement was proposed in 1912, it was not generally accepted until the 1950s. The volcanic explosion which destroyed the Indonesian island of Krakatau in 1883 is well known and documented: the island is often referred to as Krakatoa, and even as a child the title of a well known film of the time, *Krakatoa, East of Java* was inexplicable to me, since I knew perfectly well that it was *west* of Java. I was lucky enough to visit Krakatau almost 25 years ago. The island itself is now dormant, unlike nearby Anak Krakatau (son of Krakatau) which came into existence in 1927 and has been carefully studied by scientists who note the order of natural succession by which flora and fauna colonise new land. At the time I set foot on Anak Krakatau it was being slightly troublesome, and the local fisherman who had taken me there was not keen to stop long.

A fly, Sir, may sting a stately horse, and make him wince; but one is but an insect, and the other a horse still.

Dr Samuel Johnson

GRASSHOPPERS AND CRICKETS

Grasshoppers, bush crickets and crickets, all of which belong to the Order Orthoptera, are arbitrarily lumped together here, although each has significant differences. "True" grasshoppers are often referred to as short-horned grasshoppers because their antennae are generally shorter than their body. Many species that make audible noises generally do so by either "snapping" the wings in flight or by stridulating – rubbing the hind legs against the abdomen or forewings. Some grasshoppers have both solitary and gregarious phases; in the latter phase, when they are known as locusts, they may swarm in phenomenal numbers and cause substantial damage to crops as they migrate. Long-horned grasshoppers, which have more segments in their very long, filamentous, antennae than grasshoppers are known as bush crickets (katydids in North America). True crickets are mainly nocturnal and are more closely related to bush crickets than to grasshoppers, despite a body structure similar to the latter. Male crickets stridulate by rubbing their raised left forewing against the right forewing, and do so at different rates depending not only on species but also the ambient temperature.

The Locust

I have speared the wild bug of the prairie,
I have hunted the tiger moth down,
You should just see me stalk the great elephant hawk,
And other fierce beasts of renown

But I've only once seen a live locust,
In a bunch of bananas he came,
He could only just creep and he seemed half asleep,
So I killed, pinned, and mounted the same

On a single authentic occasion
He has been of some use to mankind,
Since a person named John dined and breakfasted on
Native honey and locusts combined

Very often in tropical climates
He is rather too common they say
Never singly as spies, but in armies he flies,
Like the bestial Hun of today

He has only one point in his favour
As against the foul beast aforesaid,
Though destructive and low, like the Kaiser & Co.,
At a pinch you can eat him when dead

Harry Eltringham

Whole books have been written on eating insects, and the locust is one of many insects that probably have significant nutritional value. My friend, colleague and mentor Dick Vane-Wright, head of the Entomology Department at the Natural History Museum prior to his retirement, once appeared on the Terry Wogan show to prove that insects are not only edible and nutritious, but that some are tasty. Unfortunately, Terry Wogan could not be persuaded. I recall passing through Laos and Burma on public transport a few years ago. At every stop, children would appear at the bus windows offering numerous different insect species speared on shards of bamboo for sale like giant kebabs. Like Wogan, it was easy not to be tempted!

There was an old person in black,
A grasshopper jumped on his back;
When it chirped in his ear,
He was smitten with fear,
That helpless old person in black

Edward Lear

The Cricket

As in spacious days of old
When our gallant knights were bold,
Fighting battles for their chattels
Or the Lady Guinevere;
So the cricket takes objection
To a rival in affection,
And in mortal combat shows himself
A doughty cavalier

Though it's something of a libel
He's referred to in the bible;
You may eat a little "beetle"
If your appetite should pall.
But the word's a mistranslation,
Since the further explanation
Says the animal "hath legs above
Its feet to leap withal"

Though his voice is not contralto
For indeed it's worse than alto,
Yet a cricket in a thicket
Is a cheery little mate;
Still his music never varies
Half so much as a canary's,
And it's rather like a pencil
Going wrong way up a slate

There's a moral that is famous
Known to every ignoramus,
That if you bluff with noise enough
However small you be,
With the help of borrowed motors

You'll impress the county voters.
Though the method may'nt be "cricket",
It may lead to M.C.C.

Harry Eltringham

Male crickets stridulate (chirp) to attract females. The song of each species is different. While this is of obvious survival value to the crickets, a discerning entomologist can easily count the species present in a summer meadow by ear. Number of calls per minute may also be an indicator of the male's size. To some people, their constant "chirping" is intensely irritating; others find it rather soothing. In Japan and China, crickets have been kept in small bamboo cages as indoor pets for many centuries. Various predators hunt crickets by homing in on the sound, which is why they fall quiet when they sense something approaching.

On The Grasshopper And Cricket

The poetry of earth is never dead:
When all the birds are faint with the hot sun,
And hide in cooling trees, a voice will run
From hedge to hedge about the new-mown mead:
That is the grasshopper's – he takes the lead
In summer luxury, – he has never done
With his delights, for when tired out with fun,
He rests at ease beneath some pleasant weed.
The poetry of earth is ceasing never:
On a lone winter evening, when the frost
Has wrought a silence, from the stove there shrills
The Cricket's song, in warmth increasing ever,
And seems to one in drowsiness half lost,
The Grasshopper's among some grassy hills.

John Keats

Orthoptera
"grasshoppers and relatives"

Grasshoppers and locusts damage our crops.
Their feeding is voracious and rarely stops.
When food becomes scarce they take to the sky.
Locusts are just grasshoppers on the fly.
Most people are aware of their long migrations,
But few understand their stridulations.

Al Grigarick

Grasshoppers

Grasshoppers go in many a thrumming spring
And now to stalks of tasselled sour-grass cling,
That shakes and sways a while, but still keeps straight;
While arching oxeye doubles with his weight.
Next on the cat-tail grass with farther bound
He springs, that bends until they touch the ground.

John Clare

The Grasshopper

Happy insect, what can be
In happiness compared to thee?
Fed with nourishment divine,
The dewy morning's gentle wine!
Nature waits upon thee still,

And thy verdant cup does fill;
'Tis fill'd wherever thou dost tread,
Nature self's thy Ganymede.
Thou dost drink, and dance, and sing;
Happier than the happiest king!
All the fields, which thou dost see,
All the plants belong to thee,
All that summer hours produce,
Fertile made with early juice –
Man for thee doth sow and plough;
Farmer he, and landlord thou! –
Thou dost innocently enjoy;
Nor does thy luxury destroy;
The shepherd gladly heareth thee,
More harmonious than he.
Thee country minds with gladness hear,
Prophet of the ripened year!
Thee Phoebus loves, and does inspire;
Phoebus is himself thy sire.
To thee of all things upon earth,
Life is no longer than thy mirth.
Happy insect, happy thou,
Dost neither age nor winter know.
But when thou'st drunk and danc'd, and sung
Thy fill, thy flow'ry leaves among,
(Voluptous and wise withal,
Epicurean animal!)
Sated with thy summer feast,
Thou retir'st to endless rest.

Abraham Cowley

To The Cricket

Sprightly cricket, chirping still
Merry music, short and shrill;
In my kitchen take thy rest
As a truly welcome guest;
For, no evils shall betide
Those with whom thou dost reside.
Nor shall thy good-omened strain
E'er salute my ear in vain.
With the best I can invest,
I'll requite the compliment;
Like thy sonnets, I'll repay
Little sonnets, quick and gay.
Thou a harmless inmate deem'd,
And by housewives much esteem'd,
Wilt not pillage for thy diet,
Nor deprive us of our quiet,
Like the horrid rat voracious,
Or like lick'rish mouse sagacious;
Like the herd of vermin base,
Or the pilfering reptile race:
But content art thou to dwell
In thy chimney-corner cell;
There unseen we see thee greet,
Safe and snug, thy native heat.

Rev. T. Cole

The early poets were keen on using insects to provide moral illustrations of many things. The industry of the ant, compared with the perceived uselessness of many other creatures, was used very commonly. Jean de La Fontaine's 1668 poem, originally written in French, has been translated several times; three – each different – are reproduced over the next pages and illustrate a certain freedom in translation.

The Ant And The Cricket

The cricket, having passed her spring
In singing,
Felt the pangs of hunger's woe,
When chill winds began to blow:
Bare was every pantry shelf,
Not a crumb to cheer herself.
To her neighbour's home she fled,
Begging for a loaf of bread;-
"Sweet, my lady," she implored,
"Grant me of your bounty's hoard
What will ease my hunger-pain
Till the summer comes again.
Prompt repayment? Be at rest!
Principal and interest
I'll engage to satisfy
Ere the harvest-time goes by."-
Neighbour ant is not impressed;
Monks outdo her in their giving! –
"Pray, how came you by your living?"
Asked she of this waif distressed. –
"Night and day, where'er I went,
I sang. Perchance you will not censure?" –
"You sang? My word! The fond adventure!
Well, dance now to your heart's content."

A version of Jean de La Fontaine
by William Bacon Evans, *ca* 1939

The Grasshopper And The Ant

Grasshopper had blithely sung
All the long
Summer through: her cupboard bare,
Now that frost is in the air.
Not a morsel can she spy,
Neither earthworm, grub nor fly.
To the ant, her neighbour, crying
That of hunger she is dying,
She repairs and, with a groan,
Asks a few crumbs as a loan.
"Save my life, I do adjure you!
I'll return it, I assure you,
Interest and principal,
Sure as I'm an animal!"
But the ant, who is no spender,
Has no mind to be a lender.
"What was then your occupation
Through the summer's long duration?"
"Please ma'am, I sang night and day
Unto all who came my way."
"Sang through the summer? That's entrancing!
Now's your time to do some dancing!"

A version of Jean de La Fontaine
by Alan Condor, 1951

The Grasshopper And The Ant

A grasshopper gay
Sang the summer away,
And found herself poor
By the winter's first roar.
Of meat or of bread,
Not a morsel she had!
So a begging she went,
To her neighbour the ant,
For the loan of some wheat,
Which would serve her to eat,
Till the season came round.
'I will pay you,' she saith,
'On an animal's faith,
Double weight in the pound
Ere the harvest be bound.'
The ant is a friend
(And here she might mend)
Little given to lend.
'How spent you the summer?'
Quoth she, looking shame
At the borrowing dame.
'Night and day to each comer
I sang, if you please.'
'You sang! I'm at ease;
For 'tis plain at a glance,
Now, ma'am, you must dance.'

A version of Jean de La Fontaine
by Elizur Wright

DRAGONFLIES

The dragonfly has evolved into a highly efficient hunting machine, with remarkable aerial manoeuvrability including an ability to hover, like a cross between a kestrel and a helicopter. Metamorphosis from caterpillar to butterfly through a pupal stage is well known – but the metamorphosis of the dragonfly is every bit as extraordinary. The female dragonfly lays her eggs in or near water; the larva, known as a nymph, is a voracious predator, hunting and eating other invertebrates, tadpoles and small fish. The nymphal stage lasts for between two months and five years, depending on the species; when ready to emerge as an adult, the nymph climbs a grass or reed stem and never returns to the water. The skin splits, and the adult dragonfly emerges. Adult dragonflies typically eat small insects, including flies, bees, mosquitoes and butterflies which they catch on the wing with apparent ease, facilitated by speed of flight and superb eyesight through large compound eyes. Adults are said not to bite humans, although as any inquisitive small boy who has handled a dragonfly carelessly will testify, this is not quite true – some large dragonflies can deliver a surpringly sharp nip. Both dragonflies and damselflies belong to the insect Order Odonata, a name derived from the Greek "odanto-", meaning toothed, referring to the strong mandibles. They often used to be referred to as "The Devil's Darning Needle".

The earliest fossils of winged insects date from the mid-Carboniferous period, *ca* 320 million years ago. There are a number of remarkably well-preserved fossil dragonflies in existence; some of them were enormous by modern dragonfly standards, with a wingspan of 20cm or more. The largest dragonflies today occur in Central America and Hawaii, although *Petalura* dragonflies in Australia may be bulkier. Damselflies look rather like dragonflies, but are more slender – adults can be separated by the fact that the wings of dragonflies are generally held flat whilst at rest, or depressed below horizontal, whilst those of damselflies are held together, vertically above the body. There are also differences in wing shape and position of the eyes.

The Two Voices

A still small voice spake unto me,
"Thou art so full of misery,
Were it not better not to be?"

Then to the still small voice I said;
"Let me not cast in endless shade
What is so wonderfully made."

To which the voice did urge reply;
"To-day I saw the dragon-fly
Come from the wells where he did lie.

An inner impulse rent the veil
Of his old husk: from head to tail
Came out clear plates of sapphire mail.

He dried his wings: like gauze they grew;
Thro' croft and pastures wet with dew
A living flash of light he flew."

Alfred, Lord Tennyson

This is plate 12 from Moses Harris' 1782 book *Exposition of English Insects*. It depicts two adult dragonflies; a close up of the mandibles; and the aquatic larva (© Royal Entomological Society).

The Dragonfly

If you should seek in accents meek
The dragonfly to wheedle,
You'll come to rest the second best,
He's sharper than a needle

It is to me a mystery
Whence comes his education,
His youthful days are spent in ways
Of constant irrigation

Till nature brings his gauzy wings
His life must be in a muddle,
He spends his time in leaves and slime
At bottom of a puddle

Then up he flies with compound eyes
These last his skill is due to,
When at his lair you cast a snare,
Don't think he can't see you too

Now should you get one for a pet,
You'll soon discover what'll
Provide a treat for him to eat;
A freshly caught blue-bottle

Harry Eltringham

My Dragonflies

Of all the insects in the skies
The brightest are my dragonflies.
My dragonflies are stained-glass men
Who loop and turn and loop again.
On crystal wings they catch the light,
Like neon shards in jump-jet flight.

The sun and wind combine to make
A million diamonds on the lake;
Ripple-flash echoes on the mill —
My dragonflies are brighter still.

Ruary Mackenzie Dodds

And forth of floating gauze, no jewelled queen
So rich, the green-eyed dragon-flies would break,
And hover on the flowers – most aerial things,
With little rainbows flickering on their wings.

Jean Ingelow

Silent noon

'Tis visible silence, still as the hour-glass.
Deep in the sun-searched growths the dragon-fly
Hangs like a blue thread loosened from the sky, —
So this wing'd hour is dropped to us from above.

Dante Gabriel Rossetti

The Dragonfly

There was once a terrible monster
lived in a pond, deep under the water.

Brown as mud he was, in the mud he hid,
among murk of reed-roots, sodden twigs,
with his long hungry belly,
six legs for creeping,
eyes like headlights
awake or sleeping;
but he was not big.

A tiddler came to sneer and jeer
and flaunt his flashing tail –
Ugly old stick-in-the-mud
couldn't catch a snail!
I'm not scared –
when, like a shot,
two pincers nab him, and he's got!

For the monster's jaw hides a clawed stalk
like the arm of a robot, a dinner fork,
that's tucked away cunningly till the last minute –
shoots out – and back with a victim in it!

Days, weeks, months, two years and beyond,
fear of the monster beset the pond;
he lurked, grabbed, grappled, gobbled and grew,
ambushing always somewhere new –

Who saw him last? Does anyone know?
Don't go near the mud! But I must go!
Keep well away from the rushes! But how?
Has anyone seen my sister? Not for a week now –
she's been eaten,
for certain!

And then, one day, it was June, they all saw him.
He was coming slowly up out of the mud,
they stopped swimming. No one dared
approach, attack. They kept back.

Up a tall reed they saw him climbing
higher and higher, until
he broke the surface, climbing still.

There he stopped, in the wind and the setting sun.
We're safe at last! they cried. *He's gone!*

What became of the monster, was he ill, was he sad?
Was nobody sorry? Had he crept off to die? Was he mad?

Not one of them saw how, suddenly,
as if an invisible knife had touched his back,
he has split, split completely –
his head split like a lid!
The cage is open. Slowly he comes through,
an emperor, with great eyes burning blue.

He rests there, veils of silver a cloak for him.
Night and the little stars travel the black pond,
and now, first light of the day,
his shining cloak wide wings, a flash, a whirr,
a jewelled helicopter,
he's away!

O fully he had served his time,
shunned and unlovely in the drab slime,
for freedom at the end – for the sky –
dazzling hunter, Dragonfly!

Libby Houston

When, o'er the vale of Balbec winging
Slowly, she sees a child at play,
Among the sunny wild flowers singing,
As rosy and as wild as they;
Chasing, with eager hand and eyes,
The beautiful blue damsel flies
That fluttered round the jasmine stems,
Like winged flowers or flying gems ...

Thomas Moore

Flower-de-Luce

The burnished dragonfly is thine attendant,
And tilts against the field,
And down the listed sunbeam rides resplendent,
With steel-blue mail and shield

Henry Wadsworth Longfellow

The Dragonfly

Who gave thee for thy wings the bar
upon a jewelled scimitar,
to cleave the air as though the brand
were whistled in a master-hand
with snapping flashes from the cruel
cold condescensions of the jewel?
Who taught thee to outspeed the eye
in thy green motion, dragon-fly,

and leave the dazzled sense in vain
to follow, elfin aeroplane,
the soaring beams, the dropping jambs
of starry parallelograms?
Idle to ask! Enough to trust
that this bright figment of the dust,
these spilt and Indian inks, designed
to scribble beauty on the mind,
come on the air, on air are spent
a brief and coloured accident,
crumbs shaken from the garment's hem
(unnoticed as they tumbled them)
into existence by the forces
that nail the planets to their courses,
in these as in the dragon-fly
asserting the eternal "aye".

Humbert Wolfe

Good Night, Children

I was saying Good Night to my children,
Not old enough to have wings
They're still living under the water,
The greediest, ugliest things;

In the lake as smooth as a mirror
I can hardly believe what I see,
When saying Good Night to my children
I've fallen in love with ME!

To the feast and the ball have now flitted
Dragonflies red, green and blue,
You can't spend all night at your mirror
So what are you going to do?

Me? As I am a glittering beauty,
Though I too was ugly when small,
Of course I must rush off to show off
My beautiful self at the Ball!

William Plomer

Fable

A hungry sparrow chanced to spy
A brightly painted dragon-fly;
This gaudy fly, who was most vain,
Bespoke the sparrow with disdain;
"Just gaze upon my turquoise wings,
Are they not resplendent things?
And then my slender, graceful tail,
Admire it, you cannot fail".
But the sparrow cast a cynic's eye
Upon this boastful dragon-fly;
"I think this tail is far too long":
Then snapped it off – and so do I!

Author unknown

SPIDERS

Spiders are not insects of course, they are arachnids with eight legs (insects have six), two body segments (insects have three), and no chewing mouth parts. But they are closely associated with insect prey, and are given honorary status for the purpose of this anthology. Almost all spiders are predatory, and although some larger species prey on small birds and lizards, most feed on other small invertebrates. Males of some spider species are killed and eaten by the female after mating – the male spider is often tiny in size, in comparison with the female, and must approach the act of mating with great caution. In the hope of avoiding being eaten before they can mate, male spiders identify themselves by complex rituals.

A bite from some spiders (eg. funnel web spiders and redbacks in Australia) can be potentially fatal, but modern anti-venom is effective and few deaths have been reported from these particular spiders in recent years. The Australian redback spider, *Latrodectus hasseltii*, has occasionally been reported from the UK, presumably as a result of accidental importation with trade goods. A good friend in Canberra has a population of redbacks occurring naturally on her balcony and takes the very practical view that if she doesn't disturb them they won't be any trouble.

Spider silk, also known as gossamer, is a remarkably strong material with a tensile strength comparable to that of steel per weight of unit length. It is also extremely ductile (able to stretch up to 40% of its length without breaking) and light (it is estimated that a strand of spider silk long enough to circle the earth would weigh about 450 grams in total). Gossamer webs most commonly seen covering fields in the autumn were thought by some old writers to be the result of dew burnt in the sun; they are actually silk threads used by small spiders for what biologists call "ballooning", a method of transporting themselves to pastures new. The spider extrudes threads of silk and lets itself be carried away on the air currents, sometimes for considerable distances.

The Spider And The Fly

"Will you walk into my parlour?"
    Said the Spider to the Fly,
"'Tis the prettiest little parlour
    That ever you did spy;
The way into my parlour
    Is up a winding stair,
And I have many curious things
    To show when you are there."
"Oh no, no," said the little Fly,
    "To ask me is in vain,
For who goes up your winding stair,
    Can ne'er come down again."

"I'm sure you must be weary, dear,
    With soaring up so high;
Will you rest upon my little bed?"
    Said the Spider to the Fly.
"There are pretty curtains drawn around,
    The sheets are fine and thin;
And if you like to rest awhile,
    I'll snugly tuck you in!"
"Oh no, no," said the little Fly,
    "For I've often heard it said,
They never, never wake again,
    Who sleep upon your bed!"

Said the cunning Spider to the Fly,
    "Dear friend, what can I do
To prove the warm affection
    I've always felt for you?
I have within my pantry
    Good store of all that's nice;

I'm sure you're very welcome—
    Will you please to take a slice?"
"Oh no, no," said the little Fly,
    "Kind sir, that cannot be,
I've heard what's in your pantry,
    And I do not wish to see."

"Sweet creature," said the Spider,
    "You're witty and you're wise;
How handsome are your gauzy wings,
    How brilliant are your eyes!
I have a little looking-glass
    Upon my parlour shelf,
If you'll step in a moment, dear,
    You shall behold yourself."
"I thank you, gentle sir," she said,
    "For what you're pleased to say,
And bidding you good morning now,
    I'll call another day."

The Spider turned him round about,
    And went into his den,
For well he knew the silly Fly
    Would soon come back again;
So he wove a subtle web,
    In a little corner sly,
And set his table ready,
    To dine upon the Fly.
Then he came out to his door again
    And merrily did sing;
"Come hither, hither, pretty Fly,
    With the pearl and silver wing;
Your robes are green and purple –
    There's a crest upon your head;

Your eyes are like the diamond bright,
    But mine are dull as lead."

Alas, alas! How very soon
    This silly little Fly,
Hearing his wily, flattering words,
    Came slowly flitting by;
With buzzing wings she hung aloft,
    Then nearer and nearer drew,
Thinking only of her brilliant eyes,
    And green and purple hue;
Thinking only of her crested head –
    Poor foolish thing! At last,
Up jumped the cunning Spider,
    And fiercely held her fast.

He dragged her up his winding stair,
    Into his dismal den,
Within his little parlour –
    But she ne'er came out again!

And now, dear little children,
    Who may this story read,
To idle, silly, flattering words,
    I pray you ne'er give heed;

Unto an evil counsellor,
    Close heart, and ear, and eye,
And take a lesson from this tale,
    Of the Spider and the Fly.

Mary Howitt

Or Was That When I Was Grass

I was putting a bandage of cobweb on the sudden cut
In the pain the fly told me what the web was like
The spider's face with its rows of diamond studs
And my skin crackling as the pincers drove in
That crackling pain went all over me
I knew I would never grow well again, my shell crazed,
And the acid came from the jaws and began to turn me liquid
And I felt a terrible pressure all over with the suction
And I was drawn up through the tusks into that face.
Then I woke up as though I were in a distillery
Humming with energy, retorts of horn and transparent tubes
Buzzing with juices, but I was at rest
Sealed like wine in crystal vases, and I looked down myself
With my eyeskin which was the whole egg, and I felt
The wine condense and become smoky and studded with rows
Of the eyes through which I saw that the mother watched
Benevolently from the roof of the factory which was herself
And my father whom she had eaten was with me too
And we were many flies also contributing to the personality
Of the eight-legged workshop, and I began to remember the
man
I had fed on as a maggot or was that when I was grass
Or the snail slying from my shell crackled on the thrush's
anvil?
And whenever my eyes closed or my shell crackled in pain,
It was as though I stepped out of black winged habits.

Peter Redgrove

I have fought a grizzly bear,
Tracked a cobra to its lair,
Killed a crocodile who dared to cross my path;
But the thing I really dread
When I've just got out of bed
Is to find that there's a spider in the bath.

I've no fear of wasps or bees,
Mosquitoes only tease,
I rather like a cricket on the hearth;
But my blood runs cold to meet
In pyjamas and bare feet
With a great big hairy spider in the bath.

What a frightful-looking beast –
Half an inch across at least –
It would frighten even Superman or Garth.
There's contempt it can't disguise
In the little beady eyes
Of the spider glowering in the bath.

Now it's time for me to shave
Though my nerves will not behave,
And there's bound to be a fearful aftermath;
So before I cut my throat
I shall leave this final note:
DRIVEN TO IT – BY THE SPIDER IN THE BATH!

Michael Flanders and Donald Swann

There was an old person of Putney
Whose food was roast spiders and chutney,
Which he took with his tea,
Within sight of the sea,
That romantic old person of Putney

Edward Lear

There was an old person of Bromley,
Whose ways were not cheerful or comely;
He sat in the dust,
Eating spiders and crust,
That unpleasing old person of Bromley

Edward Lear

A Noiseless Patient Spider

A noiseless patient spider,
I mark'd where on a little promontory it stood isolated,
Mark'd how to explore the vacant vast surrounding,
It launch'd forth filament, filament, filament, out of itself,
Ever unreeling them, ever tirelessly speeding them.

And you O my soul where you stand,
Surrounded, detached, in measureless oceans of space,
Ceaselessly musing, venturing, throwing, seeking the
    spheres to connect them,
Till the bridge you will need be form'd, till the ductile
    anchor hold,
Till the gossamer thread you fling catch somewhere, O my
    soul.

Walt Whitman

Low Love Life

The female spider
Can't abider
Husband
Till he's tucked
Insider

Ivor C. Treby

To The Insect Of The Gossamer

Small, viewless aëronaut, that by the line
Of Gossamer suspended, in mid air
Float'st on a sunbeam. Living atom, where
Ends thy breeze-guided voyage? With what design
In ether dost thou launch thy form minute,
Mocking the eye? Alas! Before the veil
Of denser clouds shall hide thee, the pursuit
Of the keen swift may end thy fairy sail!
Thus on the golden thread, that Fancy weaves,
Buoyant, as Hope's illusive flattery breathes,
The young and visionary Poet leaves
Life's dull realities, while sevenfold wreaths
Of rainbow-light around his head revolve;
Ah! Soon at Sorrow's touch the radiant dreams dissolve.

Charlotte Turner Smith

A spider I know is quite bright.
He has wisdom and wit and insight.
There's no one who's shrewder;
He has a computer,
And soon he will have a web site.

Al Willis

Spyder, Spyder

Spyder, spyder, burning bright
Sitting in the loo all night.
What mere mortal hand or eye,
Can make you choke before you die?

When JT comes, he's more than ready,
Just hold the red can very steady
And spray the mix at spyder's head
Moments later, the beast is dead.

And did he smirk, to see his work?
You bet he did. Well actually it was more of a snigger

John Tennent

I don't like spiders. In fact, I loathe spiders. Despite the fact that this is an entirely irrational concern (fear would be the wrong word – one has to deal with them, but to do so is not a joyful event), I will go a long way to avoid a confrontation. Sleeping on the floor of a native hut on the western Louisiade island of Basilaki, a rat got inside my mosquito net one night – it didn't really bother me; I shooed it out and went back to sleep. But an hour later, I saw a large house spider silhouetted against the sky. I was outside the

260

mosquito net in seconds flat, and couldn't rest until I knew I'd got rid of it with half a tin of fly spray. I slept little for what remained of that night. Many years previously, my wife and I went to sleep on our first night in our Hong Kong flat, with the ceiling fan whirling quietly. I woke up in the wee small hours, aware that there was a large spider sitting, James Bond style, on my bare chest. Waking my wife without moving or shouting wasn't easy, but eventually I got her to understand that there was an enormous spider on my chest. Ever practical, she got up and put the light on, managing to keep a straight face whilst she looked down at me laying there in rigid terror. She didn't look as concerned as I thought she should, and eventually admitted that the breeze from the fan was making the edge of the sheet flap intermittently on my chest.

I have spent many months carrying out fieldwork in Papua New Guinea in the last few years. When sleeping on uninhabited islands, or anywhere some distance from a village or near the sea, going to the loo in the middle of the night is an easy process, although one must be wary of salt water crocodiles if too close to the beach. But in a village environment, one is obliged to use a toilet, which usually consists of a leaf hut enclosing a deep hole, over which one stands or squats. There are invariably spiders – big ones – living in every toilet cubicle, and shining a light on them reflects a bright orange light from their compound eyes. Their presence can be a serious distraction from the business in hand, and getting out of there unscathed is always a relief.

I habitually keep a comprehensive diary on these long periods of fieldwork, and send "letters" home with an account of my travels, largely to appease family concern for my safety. The above poem was scribbled on a biscuit wrapper on one of the Trobriand islands, in 2010, following a particularly traumatic experience with a very large spider lurking in the loo. And why shouldn't I put my own poem in here ...?

The Spider

Still at the centre she her warp begins
Then round, at length, her little thread she spins,
And equal distance to their compass leaves;
Then neat and nimbly her new web she weaves,
With her fine shuttle circularly drawn
Through all the circuit of her open lawn;
Open, lest else the ungentle winds should tear
Her cypress tent, weaker than any hair;
And that the foolish fly might easier get
Within the meshes of her curious net;
Which he no sooner doth begin to shake,
But straight the male doth to the centre make,
That he may conquer more securely there
The humming creature hamper'd in his snare.

Joshua Sylvester

Twas an elderly mother spider
Grown gaunt and fierce and grey
With her little ones crouched beside her
Who wept as she sang this lay

Curses on these here swatters
What kills off all the flies
For me and my little daughters
Unless we eats we dies

Swattin and swattin and swattin
Tis little else you hear
And we'll soon be dead and forgotten
With the cost of livin so dear

Don Marquis

FLEAS

Fleas are parasitic insects, with long legs; the hind pair are extremely well adapted for jumping and a flea can jump around 200 times its own body length. They are difficult to dislodge, and to kill, because of their extremely tough bodies. An adult flea must feed on blood from warm-blooded animals, including humans, in order to be able to breed successfully and can survive for several months between meals. Not all animals have fleas. In general, animals must live under conditions and in an environment where flea larvae can feed and develop. Aquatic animals like whales and seals have no fleas, and roving animals – polar bears, for example – seldom harbour significant numbers of fleas (see Robert Service's 'Lucille'). The only primate to provide a home for fleas is *Homo sapiens*.

The best known couplet regarding fleas appears in various forms and versions, some of which follow. The original is by Jonathan Swift, author of *Gulliver's Travels*, who wrote a long poem commenting on issues affecting poets, referring to philosopher Thomas Hobbes, who noted that predator/prey relationships were common in Nature. Swift drew an analogy with the way poets of his day related to each other. Earlier, Robert Hooke (1635-1703), father of microscopy had claimed that the microscope was "able to make no greater discoveries of the flea than the naked eye", but Antonie Philips van Leeuwenhoek, the first microbiologist, who created over 400 different kinds of microscope, was able not only to describe the flea, but the mite that was parasitic on its pupa. A Turkish proverb declares: "An Englishman will burn a bed to catch a flea"!

from On Poetry: A Rhapsody

Hobbes clearly proves that every creature
Lives in a state of war, by nature:
So, naturalists observe, a flea
Hath smaller fleas that on him prey;
And these have smaller fleas to bite 'em,
And so proceed *ad infinitum*.
Thus every poet, in his kind,
Is bit by him that comes behind.

Jonathan Swift

Great fleas have little fleas upon their backs to bite 'em,
And little fleas have lesser fleas, and so *ad infinitum*.
And the greater fleas, themselves, in turn, have greater
    fleas to go on;
While these in turn have greater still, and greater still, and
    so on.

Augustus de Morgan

Big fleas have little fleas to plague, perplex and bite 'em,
Little fleas have lesser fleas, and so *ad infinitum*.

R R Fielder

The Flea

There is no living thing
Whether on foot, fin or wing,
Can boast a genealogy
More ancient than the common flea.
It is the flea that chews
Moslems, Christians, Jews,
And has chewed the ancestral skin
Since man invented sin,
And even before the fall
There were fleas inside the wall
To mortify the least
Of each Edenic beast;
And if fleas have fleas to bite em
And so ad infinitum,
Then it is possible that
Some thoughtless flea begat
The universe and its laws
By nipping the Primal Cause,
Which, when it felt the bite,
Scratched, and lo! There was light!

Well, if that's how things were begot
It would account for a lot.

Isabella Fey

The Flea

For insinuating ways
And a life of happy days
Joining *suaviter in modo* with the *fortiter in re*,
Habits modest and retiring,
Stimulating and inspiring,
I feel sure I can't do better than refer you to the flea

With a joyous roving eye
Fresh adventures he'll descry,
And will jump to his conclusions without waiting to be pressed.
Every danger has its relish,
Manner Scarlet Pimpernelish,
Goes on toiling through the darkness without thinking of a rest

David Harum used to count
That a reasonabl' amount
Of these lively little playmates was a benefit to pups,
Since cutaneous irritation
Interferes with meditation
On the fact that downs in canine lives predominate the ups

Harry Eltringham

Lady B's Fleas

Lady Barnaby takes her ease
Knitting overcoats for fleas
By this kindness, fleas are smitten
That's why she's *very rarely* bitten

Spike Milligan

Epitaph For A Flea

Who With Nine And Twenty Others
Was Most Cruelly Burnt Alive
A.D. MCMLXXVII

Feare no more the heat o' th' incubator,
Nor th' thermometer's immolator
Caused has thy swift demise.
Siphonaptera all must
Leap their last, and come to dust.

Feare no more the tests of the Great,
Thou art past all stimulus.
Care no more to jump and mate,
No blood-meal gives the impetus.
Yet comfort thee! Fleaologists must
Eventually too come to dust!

Frances Whistler

from Fleas

The flea inhabits many lands.
He's found, in varied size and form,
From snowy peaks to desert sands,
But favors places where it's warm.

He has no wings with which to fly
And when he walks he barely creeps.
Important moves are chiefly by
Prodigious catapulting leaps.

He rolls and tumbles through the air;
He's apt to land most any place.
And where he lands he doesn't care;
He sometimes lands upon his face.

He jumps again, and after that
He jumps again with all his might
Until he finds a dog or cat
Of whom he takes a juicy bite.

The flea in shrouded mystery
Has spread the dread bubonic plague
And changed the course of history
As much as Kissinger or Haig.

They say a few of them can sing;
But then, of course, they have no ears.
It seems a quite preposterous thing!
What good is music no one hears?

This singing business lacks the ring
Of truth. To me it all appears
Some overzealous ding-a-ling
Has soaked up one too many beers.

If you need fleas identified
I hope you'll use this little guide.
If I were you, however I'd
Employ a strong insecticide.

William J Brown

The Flea

Marke but this flea, and marke in this,
How little that which thou deny'st me is;
It suck'd me first, and now sucks thee,
And in this flea our two bloods mingled bee;
Thou know'st that this cannot be said
A sinne, nor shame, nor losse of maidenhead,
Yet this enjoyes before it wooe,
And pamper'd swells with one blood made of two,
And this, alas, is more than wee would doe.

Oh stay, three lives in one flea spare,
Where wee almost, yea more than married are.
This flea is you and I, and this
Our marriage bed, and marriage temple is;
Though parents grudge, and you, w'are met,
And cloysterd in these living walls of jet.
Though use make you apt to kill mee,
Let not to that, selfe murder added bee,
And sacrilege, three sinnes in killing three.

Cruell and sodaine, hast thou since
Purpled thy naile, in blood of innocence?
Wherein could this flea guilty bee,
Except in that drop which it suckt from thee?
Yet thou triumph'st, and saist that thou
Find'st not thy selfe, nor mee the weaker now;
'Tis true, then learne how false feares bee;
Just so much honour, when thou yeeld'st to mee,
Will waste, as this flea's death tooke life from thee.

John Donne

The bubonic plague, which decimated some human populations worldwide in the 1340s (a quarter of the population of Europe died as a result of the Black Death) and intermittently thereafter, is widely considered to have been spread by black-rat fleas (although recent research suggests it might have originated from Asian gerbils). The disease appears to be absent now, although some consider it to be merely dormant. Most fleas are host-specific, in the sense that each species is a parasite of a specific animal species, or group of species, and will not survive on a different animal. Many fleas will not transfer to humans; but not so in the case of these particular plague-carriers. The connection between fleas and the plague was not made until the end of the 19th century – a bite from a rat flea may inject up to 100,000 plague bacilli, which frequently overwhelms the human immune system. John Donne was one of a group of metaphysical poets – an early 17th century style which examined abstract questions relating to the physical world. It was often characterised by the use of some ordinary object (in this case a flea) to make some higher point (relating here to love, marriage etc.). One wonders whether Donne would have used the flea in such an innocent or benign way if he had known that fleas were vectors of plagues which would kill some 15% of the population of London in 1603 and 1665-1666.

The Song of the Flea

There ruled a king long, long ago,
And he had a very fine flea,
Who could have been the king's own son,
He so adored that flea.
He called for his private tailor,
And when his tailor came
Cried, "Measure my boy for breeches
And coats to go with the same!"

So the flea was dressed in velvets
And silks, which were of the best,
He had ribbons on his clothing,

A cross was hung on his chest.
He became a minister soon,
So he wore a star as well,
His family became very grand at court,
And that gave the courtiers hell.

Those persons of both sexes
Excessively were bitten
And the Queen and her waiting ladies
Were all abominably stricken,
And they didn't dare to scratch,
Or catch those fleas and whack 'em, -
But you and I can scratch
And we catch our fleas and crack 'em!

Goethe

Lucille

Of course you've heard of the *Nancy Lee*, and how she
    sailed away
On her famous quest of the Arctic flea, to the wilds of
    Hudson's Bay?
For it was a foreign Prince's whim to collect this tiny cuss,
And a golden quid was no more to him than a copper to
    coves like us.
So we sailed away and our hearts were gay as we gazed on
    the gorgeous scene;
And we laughed with glee as we caught the flea of the wolf
    and the wolverine;
Yea, our hearts were light as the parasite of the ermine rat
    we slew,

271

And the great musk ox, and the silver fox, and the moose
and the caribou.
And we laughed with zest as the insect pest of the marmot
crowned our zeal,
And the wary mink and the wily "link", and the walrus and
the seal.
And with eyes aglow on the scornful snow we danced a
rigadoon,
Round the lonesome lair of the Arctic hare by the light of
the silver moon.
But the time was nigh to homeward hie, when, imagine our
despair!
For the best of the lot we hadn't got – the flea of the polar
bear.

Oh, his face was long and his breath was strong, as the
skipper he says to me:
"I wants you to linger 'ere, my lad, by the shores of the
Harctic Sea;
I wants you to 'unt the polar bear the perishin' winter
through,
And if flea ye find of its breed and kind, there's a 'undred
quid for you."
But I shook my head: "No, Cap," I said; "it's yourself I'd
like to please,
But I tells ye flat I wouldn't do that if ye went on yer
bended knees."
Then the Captain spat in the seething brine, and he says:
"Good luck to you,
If it can't be did for a 'undred quid, supposin' we call it
two?"
So that was why they said good-bye, and they sailed and
left me there –
Alone, alone in the Arctic Zone to hunt for the polar bear.

Oh the days were slow and packed with woe, till I thought
    they would never end;
And I used to sit when the fire was lit, with my pipe for my
    only friend.
And I tried to sing some rollicky thing, but my song broke
    off in a prayer,
And I'd drowse and dream by the driftwood gleam: I'd
    dream of a polar bear;
I'd dream of a cloudlike polar bear that blotted the stars on
    high,
With ravenous jaws and flensing claws, and the flames of
    hell in his eye.
And I'd trap around on the frozen ground, as a proper
    hunter ought,
And beasts I'd find of every kind, but never the one I
    sought.
Never a track in the white ice-pack that humped and
    heaved and flawed,
Till I came to think: "Why, strike me pink! If the creature
    ain't a fraud."
And then one night in the waning light, as I hurried home
    to sup,
I hears a roar by the cabin door, and a great white hulk
    heaves up,
So my rifle flashed, and a bullet crashed; dead, dead as a
    stone fell he,
And I gave a cheer, for there in his ear – Gosh ding me! – a
    tiny flea.

At last, at last! Oh, I clutched it fast, and I gazed on it with
    pride;
And I thrust it into a biscuit tin, and I shut it safe inside;
With a lid of glass for the light to pass, and space to leap
    and play;

Oh, it kept alive; yea, seemed to thrive, as I watched it
night and day.
And I used to sit and sing to it, and I shielded it from
harm,
As many a feed it had at need on the heft of my hairy arm.
For you'll never know in that land of snow how lonesome a
man can feel;
So I made a fuss of the little cuss, and I christened it
"Lucille."

But the longest winter has its end, and the ice went out to
sea,
And I saw one day a ship in the bay, and there was the
Nancy Lee.
So a boat was lowered and I went aboard, and they opened
wide their eyes –
Yes, they gave a cheer when the truth was clear, and they
saw my precious prize.
And then it was all like a giddy dream; but to cut my story
short,
We sailed away on the fifth of May to the foreign Prince's
court;
To a balmy land and a palace grand, and the little Prince
was there,
And a fat Princess in a satin dress with a crown of gold on
her hair,
And they showed me into a shiny room, just him and her
and me,
And the Prince he was pleased and friendly-like, and he
calls for drinks for three.
And I shows them my battered biscuit-tin, and I makes my
modest spiel,
And they laughed, they did, when I opened the lid, and out
there popped Lucille.

Oh the Prince was glad, I could soon see that, and the
    Princess she was too;
And Lucille waltzed round on the tablecloth as she often
    used to do.
And the Prince pulled out a purse of gold, and he put it in
    my hand;
And he says: "It was worth all that, I'm told, to stay in that
    nasty land."
And then he turned with a sudden cry, and he clutched at
    his royal beard;
And the Princess screamed, and well she might – for Lucille
    had disappeared.

"She must be here," said his Noble Nibs, so we hunted all
    around;
Oh, we searched that place, but never a trace of the little
    beast we found.
So I shook my head, and I glumly said: "God darn the
    saucy cuss!
It's mighty queer, but she isn't here; so ... she must be on
    one of us.
You'll pardon me if I make so free, but – there's just one
    thing to do:
If you'll go for half a mo' I'll search me garments through."
Then all alone on the shiny throne I stripped from head to
    heel;
In vain, in vain; it was very plain that I hadn't got Lucille.
So I garbed again, and I told the Prince, and he scratched
    his august head;
"I suppose if she hasn't selected you, it must be me," he said.
So *he* retired; but he soon came back, and his features
    showed distress:
"Oh, it isn't you and it isn't me." ... Then we looked at the
    Princess.

So she retired; and we heard a scream, and she opened
    wide the door;
And her fingers twain were pinched to pain, but a radiant
    smile she wore:
"It's here," she cries, "our precious prize. Oh, I found it
    right away ..."
Then I ran to her with a shout of joy, but I choked with a
    wild dismay.
I clutched the back of the golden throne, and the room
    began to reel ...
What she held to me was, ah yes! A flea, but ... *it wasn't
my Lucille*.

Robert William Service

If flies are flies because they fly,
And fleas are fleas because they fell,
Then bees are bees because they be.

Author unknown

Flighty Flies

An odd little thing is the flea
You can't tell a he from a she
But he can, and she can –
    Whoopee!

L R Palmer

The Flea

The male and female flea to you
Do not appear distinct;
But fleas can tell which one is who
When maritally linked.

Horace Jakes

Actually, the male flea is generally noticeably smaller than the female.

I never know why it should be
So rude to talk about the flea.
What funny folk we are.
I think we've got the jealous hump
Because we know we'll never jump
So skillfully and far.

Author Unknown

from The Man And The Flea

His contemplation thus began:
"When I behold this glorious show,
And the wide wat'ry world below,
The scaly people of the main,
The beasts that range the wood or plain,
The wing'd inhabitants of air,
The day, the night, the various year,
And know all these by Heav'n designed
As gifts to pleasure human kind,

I cannot raise my worth too high;
Of what vast consequence am I!"

"Not of th' importance you suppose,"
(Replies a flea upon his nose;)
"Be humble, learn thyself to scan:
Know, pride was never made for man.
'Tis vanity that swells thy mind.
What Heav'n and earth for thee design'd!
For thee! made only for our need,
That more important Fleas may feed."

John Gay

What must surely be the shortest poem in existence also concerns
fleas:

Adam
'Ad 'em

Anonymous

RAGBAG (other Orders and general)

This contains some general poems which do not obviously fit elsewhere; it includes various insects – and some "honorary" insects of very small groups, or about which little appears to have been written.

These rather crudely drawn insects, including butterflies, moths, bees, a grasshopper and other insects fill a plate in Domenico Cyrilli's *Entomologiae Neopolitanae Specimen Primum* of 1787 (© Royal Entomological Society)

The Insect Race

Observe the insect race, ordain'd to keep,
The lazy Sabbath of a half-year's sleep;
Entomb'd beneath the filmy web they lie,
And wait the influence of a kinder sky;
When vernal sun-beams pierce their dark retreat,
The heaving tomb distends with vital heat:
The full-form'd brood, impatient of their cell,
Start from their trance, and burst their silken shell;
Trembling awhile they stand, and scarcely dare
To launch at once upon the untried air;
At length, assur'd, they catch the favouring gale,
And leave their sordid spoils, and high in ether sail:
Lo, the bright train their radiant wings unfold!
With silver fringed and freckled o'er with gold:
On the gay bosom of some fragrant flower,
They idly fluttering live their little hour;
Their life all pleasure, and their task all play,
All spring their age, and sunshine all their day.
What atom-forms of insect-life appear!
And who can follow Nature's pencil there?
Their wings with azure, green, and purple gloss'd,
Studded with coloured eyes, with gems emboss'd,
Inlaid with pearl, and mark'd with various stains
Of lively crimson through their dusky veins.

Anna Laetitia Barbauld

My Little World

Each time that we went walking,
My gran and Jack and me,
They saw many birds and animals
That I just couldn't see.

Bowerbirds and fairy wrens,
And kangaroos they spied,
But I could never spot them,
However hard I tried.

When I had found the branch they meant,
There was no bird at all.
The wallabies I couldn't see –
The grass was much too tall.

But then one bright and sunny day,
We were going for a walk,
And I noticed something crawling
Along a thin green stalk.

It had two little squinting eyes,
And spikes upon its back,
Like little wavy feeler-things,
So I called out to Jack.

He came across and sat with me,
And was surprised to see,
The strangest little creature there
That had been found by me.

Then underneath a curl of bark,
Peeling from a tree,
I saw a spider in the gap,
Looking back at me.

A dark and shaggy spider,
With greedy, beady eyes,
Crouching on eight hairy legs,
Waiting for some flies.

I called for Gran and Jack to see,
But by the time they came,
The little thing had scuttled off,
They'd missed it – what a shame!

I saw a beetle marching
On a plant that shone with dew –
I lay down very close to it,
To get a better view.

Its head and back were armoured,
With a bright metallic sheen,
Which mostly was an orange-red,
But now and then looked green.

Its legs were brown and shiny,
Its tummy shaggy grey,
It had antennae just like feathers –
Whoops! – it's flown away.

Along a branch across the path,
My careful eyes then found
A smooth, light-coloured caterpillar,
Its body soft and round.

It had the strangest type of crawl,
Stretched out then all bunched in.
And it looped itself along like this,
Almost like measuring.

We watched it move along the branch,
Pausing now and then
To lift its head and look about,
Then move on once again.

And then upon a smooth-barked tree,
I found the oddest mark.
Like a funny zigzag pencil line,
Scribbled on the bark.

The owner of the tag was gone –
Perhaps it's very shy?
What sort of thing could make this mark?
And how and when and why?

Gran couldn't read the writing,
And it made no sense to me.
Could it be an insect code,
Written on the tree?

As we went past a soggy patch
A small plant caught my eye,
So tiny and so delicate
Just centimetres high.

Its leaves looked just like little suns,
But each one was quite wet,
As I stared, a midge got caught!
In each leaf, a trap was set!

Gran missed this capture from up high,
The ground too hard for her.
She was so sad she had to stand.
"My knees aren't what they were!"

I found a little butterfly,
Fluttering around.
It settled on a toadstool
Growing on a mossy mound.

I didn't try to catch it
Or even stroke its wings,
For I felt that it was better
Just to look, not touch, these things.

Its wings were strangely coloured,
With orange, brown and blue,
And it had spots that looked like eyes
That seemed to stare at you.

Imagine how much we had missed,
What critters there must have been!
A million beasties hiding there,
It's just they're rarely seen.

So next time you're out walking,
Look carefully all around,
For under rocks, on leaves and stalks,
They're waiting to be found!

That day I found so many things,
So many things to see,
And Jack and Gran would have missed them all –
If it hadn't been for me!

Julia Cooke

For comment on the source of the "funny zigzag pencil line", see
the note following Judith Wright's poem 'Wriggly-gum'.

Insects

These tiny loiterers on the barley's beard,
and happy units of a numerous herd
Of playfellows, the laughing summer brings,
Mocking the sunshine in their glittering wings,
How merrily they creep, and run, and fly!
No kin they bear to labour's drudgery,
Smoothing the velvet of the pale hedge-rose;
And where they fly for dinner no one knows –
The dew-drops feed them not – they love the shine
Of noon, whose sun may bring them golden wine.
All day they're playing in their Sunday dress –
When night reposes, for they can do no less
Then, to the heath-bell's purple hood they fly,
And like princes in their slumbers lie,
Secure from night, and dropping dews, and all,
In silken beds and roomy painted hall.
So merrily they spend their summer day,
Now in the cornfields, now in the new-mown hay,
One almost fancies that such happy things,
With coloured hoods and richly burnished wings,
Are fairy folk, in splendid masquerade
Disguised, as if of mortal folk afraid,
Keeping their merry pranks a mystery still,
Lest glaring day should do their secrets ill.

John Clare

Creepy-crawlies

If you happen to have an ant in your pants,
A fly in your eye or a flea,
Don't get in a state, there's nothing to hate,
They're beautiful creatures like me.

They live in this land, and just as God planned,
They all have a task to get through,
With young ones to rear, you've nothing to fear,
They're beautiful people like you.

They're here for a reason, and change every season,
Feeding the birds on the lawn,
And birds, for their part, all feathers and heart,
Will wake you up early each morn.

But if you despise those horrible flies,
That tickle your nose when asleep,
Just see that your lips are tighter than zips,
Or into your mouth they might creep.

And next time you see, a wasp or a bee,
Don't swat him, shout 'got him' and run,
Just leave him alone, he's fine on his own,
Or maybe he'll sting you for fun.

If you're troubled with fleas, just treat them with ease,
Don't wish you were blooming well dead,
Biological control is good for your soul,
Just sleep with a spider in bed.

When the weather is fine, and ants form a line,
And start to depart with your dinner,

Just watch them go past, it's a good chance to fast,
  And maybe you'll grow a bit thinner.

If a wasp or a bee, falls into your tea,
  And you can't close the teapot much tighter,
Don't give it much thought, just be a good sport,
  And rescue the poor little blighter.

Should termites invade, the home that you've made,
  Remember the reason they do it,
And try to be kind, if one day you find,
They've thanked you by chewing right through it.

When cockroaches roam, through your family home,
  Don't panic, just do what I say,
Remember with love, the Lord up above,
And say to each other 'Let's pray' (Let's spray).

John Seville

Tettigonia australasiæ Cicada maura pellucida carnifex

This picture, also on the front of the dust jacket, is a plate from Edward Donovan's *General Illustrations of Entomology: Part 1. An epitome of the natural history of the Insects of New Holland, New Zealand, New Guinea, Otaheite, and other islands in the Indian, Southern, and Pacific Oceans, &c.* published in 1805 (© Royal Entomological Society). In the tropical rainforest you can almost set your watch by the cicadas, hundreds of which seem to begin stridulating at almost exactly the same time; easy to hear, but difficult to see, since they are usually well camouflaged and fall quiet when approached.

Locust-Lovers Attention!

My attention has been recently focussed
Upon the seventeen-year locust.
This is the year
When the seventeen-year locusts are here,
Which is the chief reason my attention has been focussed
Upon the seventeen-year locust.
Overhead, underfoot, they abound,
And they have been seventeen years in the ground,
For seventeen years they were immune to politics and class
    war and capital taunts and labour taunts,
And now they have come out like billions of insect
    debutantes,
Because they think that after such a long wait,
Why they are entitled to a rich and handsome mate,
But like many other hopeful debutante they have been
    hoaxed and hocus-pocussed,
Because all they get is another seventeen-year locust.
Girl locusts don't make any noise,
But you ought to hear the boys.
Boy locusts don't eat, but it's very probable that they take
    a drink now and again, and not out of a spring or a
    fountain,
Because they certainly do put their heads together in the
    treetops and render Sweet Adeline and She'll be Comin'
    Round the Mountain.
I for one get bewildered and go all hot and cold
Everytime I look at a locust and realize that it is seventeen
    years old;
It is as fantastic as something out of H. G. Wells or Jules
    Verne or G. A. Henty
To watch a creature that has been underground ever since
    it hatched shortly previous to 1920,

Because locusts also get bewildered and go hot and cold
    because they naturally expect to find Jess Willard
still the champ,
And Nita Naldi the vamp,
And Woodrow Wilson on his way to Paris to promote the
    perpetually not-yet-but-soon League,
And Washington under the thumb of Wayne B. Wheeler and
    the Anti-Saloon League.
Indeed I saw one locust which reminded me of a
    godmotherless Cinderella,
Because when it emerged from the ground it was whistling
    Dardanella.
Dear locusts, my sympathy for you is intense,
Because by the time you get adjusted you will be defunct,
    leaving nothing behind you but a lot of
descendants who in turn will be defunct just as they get
    adjusted seventeen years hence.

Ogden Nash

Although widely known as the "seventeen-year locust" (Orthoptera),
this refers to several remarkable species of North American cicadas
of the genus *Magicicada* (Hemiptera), which have a 17-year life
cycle. In any one location, development of the population is
synchronised so that adults emerge from their life underground
feeding on plant roots only every 17 years (some other species have
a 13-year cycle), often in vast numbers measured in millions of
individuals per acre. The reason for this is believed to be that such
a mass emergence overwhelms predators, allowing a majority of the
new population to breed, whilst at the same time emerging so
infrequently as to remove the possibility of a mammalian or avian
predator adjusting their own development to coincide. Of about
3,000 known cicada species worldwide, fewer than ten are
periodical in this way.

And though the Impudence of flies be great,
Yet this has so provoked the angry wasps,
Or, as you said, of the next nest, the Hornets,
That they fly buzzing, mad, about my Nostrils,
And like so many screaming Grasshoppers
Held by the Wings, fill every Ear with Noise.

Benjamin (Ben) Jonson

The grasshoppers referred to here are almost certainly cicadas, which are sometimes referred to colloquially (especially in America) as locusts. Male cicadas have complex membranes (tymbals) on the side of the abdomen which, together with an enlarged resonance chamber to greatly amplify the sound, they use to produce the very loud "singing" sound so universal in tropical forests and elsewhere. The noise produced by an individual cicada has been measured at almost 120 decibels, among the loudest of all insect-produced sounds. In tropical regions, in late afternoon, before dusk, it is quite usual for a large number of cicadas to begin "singing" at exactly the same time – to a degree where it is possible to set the time by them. They are, however, not easy to see, since they are well camouflaged on tree trunks and fall silent when approached.

The Cockroach

The cockroach has long hairy legs
And many folded wing
With beetling brows he will carouse
On almost anything

He loves the kitchen warm and dark
He runs like any hare
You aim a blow he goes below
In fact he isn't there

He's in and out, he comes and goes
And then he's up and down
He casts his skin, looks white and thin
And then grows fat and brown

He hates being called blackbeetle as
A term of strong reproach
But then again one can maintain
He's neither cock nor roach

I fear I cannot recommend
The cockroach as a pet
His sense is crude of gratitude
I've never loved one yet

Harry Eltringham

dedicated to don marquis

Scuttle, scuttle, little roach —
How you run when I approach:
Up above the pantry shelf.
Hastening to secrete yourself.

Most adventurous of vermin,
How I wish I could determine
How you spend your hours of ease,
Perhaps reclining on the cheese.

Cook has gone, and all is dark —
Then the kitchen is your park:
In the garbage heap that she leaves
Do you browse among the tea leaves?

How delightful to suspect
All the places you have trekked:
Does your long antenna whisk its
Gentle tip across the biscuits?

Do you linger, little soul,
Drowsing in our sugar bowl?
Or, abandonment most utter,
Shake a shimmy on the butter?

Do you chant your simple tunes
Swimming in the baby's prunes?
Then, when dawn comes, do you slink
Homeward to the kitchen sink?

Timid roach, why be so shy?
We are brothers, thou and I.
In the midnight, like yourself,
I explore the pantry shelf!

Christopher Morley

Cake Shop

lights out soon
oh, the treats, the treats

doughnuts and sugar – always a fragment
the broom can't reach

I'd like to raise a family in the skirting board
maybe tonight I'll spy that special someone

cavorting in the crumbs
the chocolate patina of a carapace ...

my antennae twitch
I feel another clutch coming on

Janis Freegard

Like most people, I am no great fan of cockroaches, and remember once making a massive mistake. My wife and I went to the small island of Sandakhan, off the east coast of Borneo, to a renowned turtle beach, to watch female turtles coming onto the beach at night to lay their eggs. The only accommodation available in those days can be best described as basic; the kitchen included a large empty wooden cupboard below the sink, and it was obvious that this was a prime cockroach home because they scuttled out of sight into the cracks of the woodwork when the door was opened, exposing them to the light. I made the mistake of treating the cupboard to a long, lingering spray of insecticide. After a pregnant pause, the cupboard came alive as thousands of cockroaches scrabbled out of the woodwork and scuttled in every direction. As anyone who has sprayed large cockroaches will know, they can take a very long time to die, and they were absolutely everywhere for the whole of our stay of several days. I have never disturbed a kitchen sink again.

On another occasion, I was staying on a small island in the Russell Island group in the Solomon Islands. In common with most small islands in the Pacific there was no electricity, and on the day I arrived I was entertained in the chief's house with freshly caught fish eaten at a wooden trestle table. As is usually the case, there were no utensils and one ate with one's fingers. My hand rested on the table in the dark, and I felt something nip the end of my finger ... when I put my head torch on I saw the table was alive with cockroaches scavenging the leftovers.

Collembola
"springtails"

Collembola are renowned for their flippant tails,
And their questionable ancestors in Devonian shales,
With their furcula poised they strain and they leap –
Such exuberant behavior warrants their keep.
We should pity these creatures without a wing –
They have no idea, what the next spring will bring.

Al Grigarick

Embioptera
"webspinners"

Webspinners have forelegs with special glands,
Scurrying backwards they spin silken strands.
The strands are used as building materials,
For making tubes with connecting arterials.
This shelter protects them from external strife.
A home is provided for communal life.

Al Grigarick

Phthiraptera
"sucking lice"

Body lice suck my blood for food –
They make me itch but to scratch is rude.
I've tried the comb, I've tried shampoo –

I've tried the ointment that turns me blue.
Alas, there has been no relief for me –
Since the ban of DDT.

Al Grigarick

To A Louse, On Seeing One On A Lady's Bonnet, At Church

Ha! Whare ye gaun, ye crowlin ferlie!
Your impudence protects you sairlie:
I canna say but ye strunt rarely,
Owre gawze and lace;
Tho' faith, I fear ye dine but sparely,
On sic a place.

Ye ugly, creepin, blastit wonner,
Detested, shunn'd, by saunt an' sinner,
How daur ye set your fit upon her,
Sae fine a Lady!
Gae somewhere else and seek your dinner,
On some poor body.

Swith, in some beggar's haffet squattle;
There ye may creep, and sprawl, and sprattle,
Wi' ther kindred, jumping cattle,
In shoals and nations;
Whare horn nor bane ne'er daur unsettle.
Your thick plantations.

Now haud you there, ye're out o'sight,
Below the fatt'rels, snug and tight,

296

Na faith ye yet! Ye'll no be right,
Till ye've got on it,
The vera tapmost, tow'ring height
O' Miss's bonnet.

My sooth! Right bauld ye set your nose out,
As plump an' gray as onie grozet:
O for some rank, mercurial rozet,
Or fell, red smeddum,
I'd gie you sic a hearty dose o't,
Wad dress your droddum!

I wad na been surpris'd to spy
You on an auld wife's flainen toy;
Or aiblins some bit duddie boy,
On's wyliecoat;
But Miss's fine Lundardi, fye!
How daur ye do't?

O Jenny, dinna toss your head,
An' set your beauties a' abread!
Ye little ken what cursed speed
The blastie's makin!
Thae winks and finger-ends, I dread,
Are notice takin!

O wad some Pow'r the giftie gie us
To see oursels as others see us!
It wad frae monie a blunder free us
An' foolish notion:
What airs in dress an' gait wad lea'e us,
And ev'n Devotion!

Robert Burns

Genesis Of "British Ichneumons,"
Vols. A to Z

Should you ask me, whence these Insects,
Whence their names, those fearsome compounds,
With the Story of their doings
In the forest and the meadows;
With their bastard Greek and Latin,
With their strangely sounding titles;
With their constant repetitions
And their synonyms confusing,
As across your view they hurry ?

    I should answer, I should tell you:
From the lands of northern Europe,
From the homes of Norse and Teuton,
From the source of German sausage;
From the land of Swede and Viking,
From the mountain, moor and fenland,
Where the Parasite, ICHNEUMON,
Feeds upon the juicy larvae.
I repeat them as they're written

               "Ellnest Eriott" and "Maude Clorley"

This is part of a longer poem, written in the metre of Longfellow's
Hiawatha. Morley was an authority on Ichneumons, a widespread
group of parasitic wasps which lay their eggs by piercing the skin of
living larvae of other insect species. The eggs hatch, and the ichneumon
larvae feed on the living tissue of their host, leaving vital organs until
the end so as to prolong the supply of fresh tissue. This horrible way
of life (a parasitic lifestyle is actually one of the most successful survival
strategies in the natural world) caused some early thinkers to question
the existence of a benevolent God, who would surely not have created
or allowed such cruelty! As Erasmus Darwin noted:

The Origin Of Society

The wing'd Ichneumon for her embryon young
Gores, with sharpt horn, the catterpiller throng,
    The cruel larva mines its silky course,
And tears the vitals of its fostering nurse.

Erasmus Darwin

The Green Fly

In a state of calm repose
On the tender budding rose
Sits the Green-fly, in a world of peace and plenty,
Every one in sweet content,
Taking liquid nourishment
With a general air of *dolce far niente*

But it's quite a different song
When the gardener comes along,
With a bucket and a tin of something slimy,
And conducts a wholesale slaughter
With a squirt and soapy water,
Using funny words like "dangem" and "gorblimey"

So you see you can't rely
On what merely meets the eye,
And a tragedy may lurk in beds of roses
Always be prepared to cope
With a stranger and soft soap;
Be more fly and not so green as he supposes

Harry Eltringham

Greenflies (aphids) gain sustenance from plant sap, and are the bane of gardeners and horticulturalists. They reproduce asexually in the spring and can increase in numbers quite dramatically over a short period.

The scale of things

A very simple bug am I;
Without legs, wings or compound eye.
Stuck to a leaf, I am so small
I might not be insect at all!
I live beneath a home-made roof;
But my partner is the proof.

He's all the insect I am not,
Antennae, legs and wings he's got;
Yet I have a mouth, which he lacks;
My pheromone trail he tracks.
He's ephemeral, I'm a long-lived cat.
As insects go, how cool is that?

I can't see Boy, he can't see me,
Fragrance is my identity.
How, you ask, is there selection
Making patterns on my rear section?
Ah, there I have no explanation,
I just give rise to speculation!

When my dapper Boy comes calling,
It's my pheromone that draws him;
But he can't see beneath my scale.
Only my scent says I'm for sale.
Boy settles on my roof and blindly
He feels underneath to find me.

To pass on genes is Boy's sole aim;
To find the scattered girls, his game.
He last fed three long moults ago,
So he must hurry, not be slow.
If he's lucky, in his brief life
He'll pass from wife to wife to wife.

Gillian Watson

Armoured scale insects are approximately 1.5-2.5 mm long and feed
on plant sap, a non-moving food source. Their main life activities
have become divided between different developmental stages and
sexes. The hatchlings disperse to locate and settle at a suitable
feeding site. The females are sedentary and live several months
beneath a non-living scale cover that they secrete. They do not
expend energy on developing legs, wings or elaborate antennae;
instead, their effort is entirely reproductive. Male armoured scales
only feed in the first and second stages; then they go through three
non-feeding stages to produce legs, wings and elaborate antennae,
so that they can search out and fertilize as many females as possible.
Adult male scales cannot eat or drink, so they only live a few days.

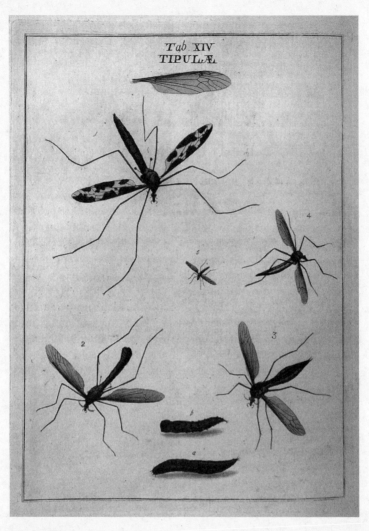

Plate 14 from Moses Harris' *Exposition of English Insects*, published in 1782, depicting Daddy Long-Legs. In its widest sense, the Tipulidae embrace some 15,000 species, of which an estimated 300 occur in the UK (© Royal Entomological Society).

The Daddy-Long-Legs

The Daddy-long-legs gets up late
And spends the night in jollity
He shows a tendency to terp-
sichorean frivolity

Though if you look upon his face
His air is one of gravity
Still, truth to tell, he's guilty of
Occasional depravity

But since his early life is spent
In studying geology
In view of these his strata days
We'll grant him some apology

To Daddy-long-legs you'll extend
Both latitude and charity
And with indulgence pardon his
Paterfamiliarity

Harry Eltringham

The Daddy-long-legs (or more correctly, the cranefly) is the adult stage of that other bane of gardeners, the leatherjacket. The cranefly deposits eggs on turf and on hatching, the larva (the name leatherjacket indicates the tough, leathery outer skin) feeds on grass roots. In cold winters they cause little damage, but mild winters allow leatherjackets to develop quickly and they may cause obvious damage to lawns in late winter or early spring. They continue feeding during the summer and pupate in the soil, with adults emerging in late summer and early autumn. Craneflies have become much more common with our recent mild winters, and are often found in quite large numbers inside houses in the autumn.

The Daddy Long-Legs And The Fly

Once Mr Daddy Long-Legs,
Dressed in brown and grey,
Walked about upon the sands
Upon a summer's day;
And there among the pebbles,
When the wind was rather cold,
He met with Mr Floppy Fly,
All dressed in blue and gold.
And as it was too soon to dine,
They drank some Periwinkle wine,
And played an hour or two, or more,
At battlecock and shuttledore.

Said Mr Daddy Long-Legs
To Mr Floppy Fly,
"Why do you never come to court?
I wish you'd tell me why.
All gold and shine, in dress so fine,
You'd quite delight the court.
Why do you never go at all?
I really think you *ought!*
And if you went, you'd see such sights!
Such rugs! And jugs! And candle-lights!
And more than all, the King and Queen,
One in red, and one in green!"

"O Mr Daddy Long-Legs,"
Said Mr Floppy Fly,
"It's true I never go to court,
And I will tell you why.
If I had six long legs like yours,
At once I'd go to court!

But Oh! I can't, because *my* legs
Are so extremely short.
And I'm afraid the King and Queen
(One in red and one in green)
Would say aloud, 'You are not fit,
You Fly, to come to court a bit!'"

"O Mr Daddy Long-Legs,"
Said Mr Floppy Fly,
"I wish you'd sing one little song!
One mumbian melody!
You used to sing so awful well
In former days gone by,
But now you never sing at all;
I wish you'd tell me why:
For if you would, the silvery sound
Would please the shrimps and cockles round,
And all the crabs would gladly come
To hear you sing, 'Ah, Hum di Hum!'"

Said Mr Daddy Long-Legs,
"I can never sing again!
And if you wish, I'll tell you why,
Although it gives me pain.
For years I could not hum a bit,
Or sing the smallest song;
And this the dreadful reason is,
My legs are grown too long!
My six long legs, all here and there,
Oppress my bosom with despair;
And if I stand, or lie, or sit,
I cannot sing one single bit!"

So Mr Daddy Long-Legs
And Mr Floppy Fly
Sat down in silence by the sea,
And gazed upon the sky.
They said, "This is a dreadful thing!
The world has gone all wrong,
Since one has legs too short by half,
The other much too long!
One never more can go to court,
Because his legs have grown too short;
The other cannot sing a song,
Because his legs have grown too long!"

Then Mr Daddy Long-Legs
And Mr Floppy Fly
Rushed downward to the foaming sea
With one sponge-taneous cry;
And there they found a little boat
Whose sails were pink and gray;
And off they sailed among the waves
Far, and far away.
They sailed across the silent main
And reached the great Gromboolian plain;
And there they play for evermore
At battlecock and shuttledore.

Edward Lear

The Midge

So long as midges are so small
And I am to be chatty,
You will at least admit that they
Are rather neat and gnatty

What would a summer eve be like
Without their marked attentions?
Be thankful they do not attain
More generous dimensions

Let us recall how great effects
Proceed from causes tiny,
And disregard false quantities
And search *ab origíne*

Harry Eltringham

As anyone who has been on a camping holiday in Scotland will know, the unwelcome attentions of midges and gnats can put a serious dampener on events. It is interesting to note how very small insects are capable of causing some of the greatest discomfort to people, despite our alleged cleverness and technology.

The Little Gnat

The little Gnat, in beauties, may compare
With all his rival brothers of the air;
Transparent feathers, purple, green and gold,
His wings, small feet, and fringed tail enfold,
Four sharpen'd spears his head with weapons arm,
And his pearled eyes, with liveliest graces charm.

Moses Browne

from Ode To Autumn

Where are the songs of Spring? Ay, where are they?
Think not of them, thou hast thy music too, -
While barred clouds bloom the soft-dying day
And touch the stubble-plains with rosy hue;
Then in a wailful choir the small gnats mourn
Among the river-sallows, borne aloft
Or sinking as the light wind lives or dies;
And full-grown lambs loud bleat from hilly bourn;
Hedge-crickets sing; and now with treble soft
The redbreast whistles from a garden-croft;
And gathering swallows twitter in the skies.

John Keats

The Gnat

When by the green-wood side, at summer eve,
Poetic visions charm my closing eye;
And fairy-scenes, that fancy loves to weave,
Shift to wild notes of sweetest Minstrelsy;
'Tis thine to range in busy quest of prey,
Thy feathery antlers quivering with delight,
Brush from my lids the hues of heav'n away,
And all is Solitude, and all is night!
—Ah, now thy barbed shaft, relentless fly,
Unsheathes its terrors in the sultry air!
No guardian sylph, in golden panoply,
Lifts the broad shield, and points the glittering spear.
Now near and nearer rush thy whirring wings,
Thy dragon-scales still wet with human gore.

Hark, thy shrill horn its fearful larum flings!
—I wake in horror, and dare sleep no more!

Samuel Rogers

In fact, it is only the male gnat (*Culex pipiens*) which has feathery
'antlers' (*i.e.* antennae) – but the male never sucks blood. It is the
female gnat, whose antennae are less complex, which requires
proteins provided by blood for development of its eggs.

To A Mosquito

Fair Insect, that, with thread-like legs spread out,
And blood-extracting bill, and filmy wing,
Dost murmur, as thou slowly sails't about,
In pitiless ears, full many a plaintive thing,
And tell how little our large veins should bleed,
Would we but yield them to thy bitter need.

Unwillingly, I own, and what is worse,
Full angrily, men hearken to thy plaint;
Thou gettest many a brush and many a curse,
For saying thou art gaunt and starved and faint:
E'en the old beggar while he asks for food
Would kill thee, hapless stranger, if he could.

William Cullen Bryant

The pubic or crab louse, *Phthirus pubis*, is a parasitic insect that has inspired lavatorial poets to indulge their creative talents in graffiti because of its association with human nether regions. Crab lice are transmitted by close physical contact, usually close encounters of a sexual kind, and toilet seats are unlikely to play any part in their spread, although it must be said that pubic lice are actually able to survive for about 24 hours without a blood meal, so it's not impossible. The following is occasionally seen (usually among less amusing offerings) in gentlemen's lavatories:

It's no good standing on the seat,
The crabs in here can jump ten feet

The retort to which, usually penned below, is:

If you think that's rather high,
Go next door, the buggers fly.

Body lice (probably more accurately referred to as clothing lice) are closely associated with poverty and the clothes of those who rarely wash or change these garments. Part of the reason for this is that lice prefer an environment with a constant temperature; thus they are most comfortable on clothes that are seldom changed. Sensitive to a marked change in temperature, they tend to move away from bodies which are "overheated" (e.g. feverish) or from bodies recently deceased. When Thomas Becket's clothing was being removed from his lifeless body in Canterbury Cathedral following his murder in 1170, the haircloth garment next to his skin "boiled over with [lice] like water in a simmering cauldron". The following poem describes the departure of a louse from a lady's corpse.

A louse crept out of my lady's shift –
Ahumm, Ahumm, Ahee –
Crying "Oi! Oi! We are turned adrift;
The lady's bosom is cold and stiffed,
And her arm-pit's cold for me."

"The lady's linen's no longer neat" –
Ahumm, Ahumm, Ahee –
"Her savour is neither warm nor sweet;
It's close for two in a winding sheet,
And lice are too good for worms to eat;
So here's no place for me."

The louse made off unhappy and wet –
Ahumm, Ahumm, Ahee –
He's looking for us, the little pet;
So haste, for her chin's to tie up yet,
And let us be gone with what we can get –
Her ring for thee, her gown for Bet,
Her pocket turned out for me."

Gordon Bottomley

Sarcoptes scabiei, which causes scabies, is another parasitic creature that burrows into human skin. It was not until experiments were conducted with pacifist volunteers in the 1940s that it became clear clothing/bedding were unimportant in the spread of scabies. The following poem is rather non-pc, which makes it even more delightful.

Recondite research on *Sarcoptes*
Has revealed that infections begin
At home with your wives and your children
Or when you are living in sin.
Except in the case of the clergy
Who accomplish remarkable feats
And catch scabies and crabs
From doorhandles and cabs
And from blankets and lavatory seats

D A Burns

There's a squeak of pure delight from a matey little mite,
As it tortuously tunnels in the skin.
Singing furrow, Folly furrow, come and join me in my burrow,
And we'll view the epidermis from within.

Author unknown

The treatment most in vogue of late
Concerns the benzyl benzoate,
Made up with water it's applied
All over every patient's hide.
It cures a very high proportion
When used with care and skill and caution.

Derris root yields rotenone
Which some say will cure alone
Without a bath or scrub or soap
(This surely is the soldier's hope)
This treatment seldom has a failure
But woe betide the genitalia

But if you must be safe and sure,
Use the good old-fashioned cure.
Cover the victim with soft soap
Then in hot water let him soak,
A scrubbing next is his appointment
And finish off with sulphur ointment!

Author unknown

The note accompanying this poem which, like that which precedes it, is from "*A potpourri of parasites in poetry and proverb*" by D A Burns published in the *British Medical Journal* in 1991, reads as follows "… many remedies for scabies have been suggested, but for centuries the standard treatment was with sulphur. In fact, sulphur ointment is still used by some dermatologists. Rotenone, an extract of derris root, was used in the 1940s to treat scabies. Although it was effective, it was rather irritant, particularly to the delicate body parts of the male. In 1937 Kissmeyer introduced benzyl benzoate as a scabicide, and it has remained in use ever since. These three therapeutic agents are celebrated in this offering from the 1940s".

A Game Of Squash

If there's one thing that's worse than a Headlouse,
Then it must, I suppose, be a Bedlouse.
But as I've understood lice
(And excepting Woodlice)
Why, the only good louse is a dead louse.

Dick King-Smith

The Louse And The Mosquito

In the King's bed, Creep the louse
Lived in her ancestral house.
They had dwelt here as of right
For three decades, and each night
She and her enormous brood
Drank the King's blood for their food.
Once the signal came from Creep
That the King was fast asleep,
Quietly, discreetly, they
Nipped and sipped and drank away.
Sons and grandsons, sisters, brothers,
Great-granddaughters, great-grandmothers,
Second cousins and their wives

Thus pursued their gentle lives
– Lives of undisturbed delight –
Growing plump and smooth and white.

One day a mosquito flew
Through the window. As he drew
Closer to the velvet bed
Canopied with gold, he said:
'Lovely! Just the place for me.
Ah, what perfume – let me see –
Rose – no, jasmine. And the quilt –
Smooth as banks of Ganges silt!
Let me test the bedsprings now.'
So he jumped up – and somehow,
In a parabolic leap,
Landed not too far from Creep.

'Sir Mosquito, flap your wings.
Leave at once. This bed's the King's.'
'Who may you be, Lady Louse?'
'I'm the guardian of this house.'
'House?' 'This quilt. It's mine,' said Creep;
'There's no place for you, Sir Leap.'
'Let me sleep here for one night
And I'll catch the morning flight.'
Thus the sad mosquito pleaded,
And at last his prayers were heeded
For the tender-hearted Creep
Could not bear to watch him weep.

'Well, come in,' she said at last,
'But tonight you'll have to fast,
For on no account may you
Bite him, as we're trained to do.

We can drink and cause no pain,
Loss of royal sleep, or stain.
You, I fear, would cause all three.
I can't risk my family.'
But the glib mosquito cried:
'Now you've let me come inside,
Lady Louse, how can you be
Cold in hospitality?
Just one bite – I ask no more –
For I've learned from learned lore
That the royal blood contains
Remedies for aches and pains –
Ginger, honey, sugar, spice,
Cardamom, and all things nice.
Save me. I'm in broken health.
Let me bite him – once – by stealth.
He won't even shift or sigh.
Cross my heart and hope to die.'

Finally the louse agreed.
'Right!' she said, 'but pay close heed.
Wait till wine, fatigue, or deep
Dream-enriched, unbroken sleep
Has enveloped him. Then go:
Lightly nip his little toe.'
'Yes, yes, yes. That's all old hat,'
Said Sir Leap; 'I know all that.
Keep your stale advice.' He smiled:
'Seriously – I'm not a child.'

It was only afternoon
– Fairly early, fairly soon –
When the king came for a snooze,
Doffed his crown and shirt and shoes,

315

Lay down on the bed, and sighed.
The mosquito almost died
From excitement, shock, and sweat.
'No!' the louse cried: 'No! Not yet!'
But too late! The self-willed bumbler
– Oh, if only he'd been humbler –
Rushing to the rash attack,
Leapt upon the royal back,
And with fierce and fiery sting
Deeply dirked the dozing king.

'Help! a scorpion! a snake!'
Screamed the King, at once awake.
'I've been bitten! Search the bed!
Find and strike the creature dead!'
When they made a close inspection
The mosquito foiled detection,
Hidden in the canopy;
But the louse clan could not flee.
All were killed without ado.
    Meanwhile, the mosquito flew,
Looking out for further prey,
Humming mildly on his way.

Vikram Seth

The Earwig

The earwig's an affectionate amusing little soul
And his favourite games are "catch me quick" and "hidey"
He loves the hospitality of any sort of hole
For he isn't what you'd call the least bit "sidey"

316

He has the most artistic filmy iridescent wings
Though you'd never think to look at him he'd got any
He loves to make while ever seeking after higher things
Researches in experimental botany

Now if you should by any chance on second thoughts decide
To cherish a few earwigs without failures
Remember that in sponges and in beds they like to hide
Don't let them out at night and don't grow dahlias

Harry Eltringham

Earwigs do not, of course, habitually take refuge inside ears, and can hardly be regarded as "amusing little souls". The name earwig may be a corruption of "ear wing", from the delicate, folded, wing of an earwig which may look vaguely like an ear to some people when expanded: the creature is also known as "forkytail" – because of the pincer-like clasps on the end of the abdomen – or "clipshear". Earwigs are very successful creatures found on every continent on earth except Antarctica. Until recently, there was a Giant Earwig, *Labidura herculeana*, found only on the South Atlantic island of Saint Helena, measuring over 8cm in length. It may now be extinct.

Hear! Hear!

Though you may feel a little fear
If there's an Earwig in your ear,
There is no cause for utter dread –
It can't get right inside your head.
But on the whole it might be best
To shift the creature, lest it nest.
An ear that's used for Earwig-rearing
Could cause you partial loss of hearing.

Dick King-Smith

The Earwig

'Tis vain to talk of hopes and fears
And hope the least reply to win,
From any maid that stops her ears
In dread of ear-wigs creeping in!

Thomas Hood

On The Dance Of The May-Fly

Some to the sun their insect-wings unfold,
Waft on the breeze, or sink in clouds of gold,
Transparent forms, too fine for mortal sight,
Their fluid bodies half dissolv'd in light.
Loose to the winds their airy garments flew,
Thin glitt'ring textures of the filmy dew;
Dipt in the richest tincture of the skies,
Where light disports in ever-mingling dies,
While ev'ry beam new transient colours flings,
Colours that change whene'er they wave their wings.

Alexander Pope

A plate from James Barbut's 1781 *Les Genres des Insectes de Linné constatés par divers échantillons d'insectes D'Angleterre, copies d'apres Nature*. The plate depicts dragonflies, damsel flies and mayflies (© Royal Entomological Society).

The May-Fly

The sun of the eve was warm and bright
    When the May-fly burst from his shell,
And he wanton'd awhile in that fair light
    O'er the river's gentle swell;
And the deepening tints of the crimson sky
Still gleam'd on the wing of the glad May-fly.

The colours of sunset pass'd away,
    The crimson and yellow green,
And the evening-star's first twinkling ray
    In the waveless stream was seen,
Till the deep repose of the stillest night
Was hushing about his giddy flight.

The noon of the night is nearly come—
    There's a crescent in the sky:
The silence still hears the myriad hum
    Of the insect revelry:
The hum has ceas'd—the quiet wave
Is now the sportive May-fly's grave.

Oh! thine was a blessed lot—to spring
    In thy lustihood to air,
And sail about, on untiring wing,
    Through a world most rich and fair;
To drop at once in thy watery bed,
Like a leaf that the willow-branch has shed.

And who shall say that his thread of years
    Is a life more blest than thine!
Has his feverish dream of doubts and fears
    Such joys as those which shine

In the constant pleasures of thy way,
Most happy child of happy May!

For thou wert born when the earth was clad
    With her robe of buds and flowers,
And didst float about with a soul as glad
    As a bird in the sunny showers:
And the hour of thy death had a sweet repose,
Like a melody, sweetest at its close.

Nor too brief the date of thy cheerful race—
    'Tis its use that measures time—
and the MIGHTY SPIRIT that fills all space
    With HIS life and HIS will sublime,
May see that the May-fly and the Man
Each flutter out the same small span.

And the fly that is born with the sinking sun,
    To die ere the midnight hour,
May have deeper joy, ere his course be run,
    Than man in his pride and power:
And the insect's minutes be spar'd the fears
And the anxious doubts of our threescore years.

The years and the minutes are as one—
    The fly drops in his twilight mirth,
And the man, when his long day's work is done,
    Crawls to the self-same earth.
GREAT FATHER of each! may *our* mortal day
Be the prelude to an endless May!

Author unknown

That "butterflies only live for a day" is an old wives' tale. Some butterflies live for many months, and most live for weeks, but the mayfly really does live as an adult for a very short time, as is illustrated by the name Ephemeroptera (from the Greek *ephemeros* = short-lived and *pteron* = wing) given to the Order containing mayflies and the generic name (*Ephemera*) of the common mayfly which occurs in the UK: *E. vulgata*. It emerges from the water, where it spends approximately a year as a nymph, around 6 o'clock on a summer evening, and dies before midnight, limiting the duration of its flight and life as an adult to just a few hours.

Mealybugs

Among the bugs that plague our plants,
There are those beloved by ants.
Mealybugs to be specific,
Are among the most prolific.
Mealy wax adorns their bodies;
Soft and plump, they're insect oddies.
No wings have they; they cannot fly,
But in their mealy beds they lie,
Sucking sap from leaf and twig;
Small they are, but damage big.
Nearly all their time is spent
Pumping sap through mouth to vent.
And the stuff they void from anus
Creates a mess that's moist and heinous.
Sticky sweet this buggy poo,
And we call it honeydew.
You or I would never eat it;
Yet the ants with joy do greet it.
Sugar sweet it lifts their mood.
Soon they feed it to their brood.
Trails of ants will soon appear

To partake this formic beer
They guard their bugs with jealous zeal;
Allow no other to share their meal.
Chase away all wasps and spiders,
To protect their bug providers.
This makes life a bit more quiet
For those bugs, whose only diet
Is the sap that flows, I fear,
In the plants that we hold dear.

Jack (John) W Beardsley

Mealy bugs (Hemiptera: Pseudococcidae), otherwise known as scale insects, feed on the sap of plants and subtropical trees; their frequency as greenhouse pests makes them no friend of the gardener. Some species are serious agricultural pests, especially in the presence of ants, which protect them from predators and parasites in return for a sweet secretion (honeydew) which the ants find attractive. The name mealybug is derived from a protective powdery wax layer secreted by the female whilst feeding.

Aphids, also known as plant lice, are another bane of the gardener's life and an agricultural pest that count ladybirds as important natural enemies.

The countless Aphides, prolific tribe,
With greedy trunks the honey'd sap imbibe;
Swarm on each leaf with eggs or embryons big,
And pendent nations tenant every twig

Erasmus Darwin

A bug and a flea went out to sea
Upon a reel of cotton,
The bug was drowned
but the flea was found
Biting a lady's bottom

Author Unknown

Bedbug

The June bug hath a gaudy wing,
The lightning bug a flame,
The bedbug hath no wings at all
But he gets there just the same.

Anonymous

The common bedbug, *Cimex lectularius*, belongs to a family of blood-sucking bugs recognised as human parasites for millenia. Both immature and adult feed by sucking blood, and do not have wings at any stage of their development. They have historically been used for a variety of ills; in powdered form they were believed to relieve fever; crushed bedbugs mixed with salt and human milk was thought to be an effective eye ointment. Yeuk!

The Termite

Some primal termite knocked on wood
And tasted it, and found it good,
And that is why your Cousin May
Fell through the parlor floor today.

Ogden Nash

I have seen few poems on termites. The one above is typical Ogden
Nash: short, funny and to the point. The poem following is a parody
of Gilbert & Sullivan's 'A Policeman's Lot Is Not A Happy One' from
The Pirates of Penzance.

A Termite's Lot Is Not A Happy One

O the termites have no problem re: employment —
Re: employment;
No need of an organization man —
'Zation man.
They have no time for frivolous enjoyment —
'V'lous enjoyment,
For each one fits into a master plan —
A — Master — plan!

When the termites finish tending to their mothers —
To their mothers,
They work, not shirk, and always shun the sun —
Shun the sun,
For the miner-mason-joiner sister-brothers —
Sister-brothers,
A termite's work is never ever done —
'Er — ever — done!

When engaged in making nests of pulp and paper —
Pulp and paper,
Their masticating jaws work all the time —
All the time;
And any that attempts to dance or caper —
Dance or caper,
Is very quickly made to toe the line —
To — toe — the — line!

The workers work with labours never-ending —
Never-ending.
A termite should be working, never seen —
Never seen!
The soldiers guard as menders are a-mending —
Are a-mending,
And nasutiforms squirt substances obscene —
'Stan — ces — ob — scene!

There are others that construct and repair runnels —
Repair runnels,
Or cultivate their fungi, or feed young —
Or feed young;
The inspectors go inspecting all the tunnels —
All the tunnels,
While the sextons consume all the dead and dung —
The — dead — and — dung!

And even when it comes to procreation —
Procreation.
The poor old Queen has hardly ever fun —
Any fun.
In the maintenance of any termite nation —
Termite nation,
Of them all, we can but envy only one —
'Vy — on — ly — one!
Guess which!

Keith McE Kevan

The Mantispid

One night I spied a mantis-fly
Midst leaves upon a tree.
The mantis-fly to me did cry
"Why spiest thou on me?"
So thus I did to her reply:
"Art thou Mantispidae?"

"I am," she said, "for I have fed
When young on spider's eggs,
But now instead, for daily bread,
Gnats catch I with my legs –
My claws embedded 'til they're dead –
With mantid spine-like pegs."

So I was right on yester night
She was a mantid-fly –
Mantispid slight, mantispid wight,
That reached toward the sky
And in my sight, her eyes quite bright,
Prayed to the Lord on High!

Keith McE Kevan

Mantispids (or mantidflies) are a group of insects in the Order
Neuroptera, the adults of which bear a superficial resemblance to
praying mantids (others are wasp mimics). They are active predators
on insects, which they catch with modified front legs, as do mantids.
Female mantispids lay their eggs on stalks of vegetation; the larvae
of many species parasitise eggs and young of insects and spiders.

The Centipede

I objurgate the centipede,
A bug we do not really need.
At sleepy-time he beats a path
Straight to the bedroom or the bath.
You always wallop where he's not,
Or, if he is, he makes a spot.

Ogden Nash

I learned an early lesson when I first met one of the foot-long venomous centipedes in the Far East in my early 20s. I was living in tented accommodation near Jahore Bahru, Malaysia. Somehow, it got inside my suitcase which was stored under the bed, and frightened the life out of me when I opened the lid and it scuttled up my arm. Since then I have been vaguely paranoid about hanging personal belongings off the ground when in the tropics, checking my boots very carefully before I put them on, and always tightly tie the neck of anything that creepy crawlies could conceivably find an attractive home.

A centipede was happy quite,
Until a toad in fun
Said, "Pray which leg comes after which?"
This raised her mind to such a pitch,
She lay distracted in a ditch
Considering how to run

Mrs Edmund Craster

Best Foot Forward

You thought the Centipede possessed
Exactly fifty pairs of feet?
Is that the figure you'd have guessed?
The answer isn't quite so neat.
For scientific men who've seen
Each centipedal cousin,
Find some have only got fifteen
And some have fifteen dozen.

Dick King-Smith

Having more than three pairs of legs, centipedes are not insects, but belong to the Class Chilopoda in the Phylum Arthropoda. They are exclusively predatory, and have a pair of poison claws, in addition to a pair of legs per body segment. The pairs of walking legs are always uneven in number, ranging from 15 to 171 or more. By comparison, millipedes, which belong to the Class Diplopoda (formerly Chilognatha) always have two pairs of legs per segment, and are largely vegetarian.

Luther's Saddest Experience

Luther, he was persecuted,
Excommunicated, hooted,
Disappointed, egged, and booted;
Yelled at by minutest boys,
Waked up by nocturnal noise,
Scratched and torn by fiendish cats,
Highwayed by voracious rats.

But the saddest of all
I am forced to relate:
Of a diet of worms
He was forced to partake-
Of a *diet of worms*
For the Protestant's sake;
Munching crawling caterpillars,
Beetles mixed with moths and millers;
Instead of butter on his bread,
A sauce of butterflies was spread.
Was this not a horrid feast
For a Christian and a priest?

Anonymous

HEMIPTERA.

Mantis Oculata. Mantis Flabellicornis.

London Published as the Act directs by E. Donovan May 1798.

This plate, depicting praying mantids, comes from Edward Donovan's *An Epitome of the Natural History of the Insects of China: comprising figures and descriptions & Co.* of 1798 (© Royal Entomological Society).

331

In Days Of Old And Insects Bold

In days of old and insects bold
(Before bats were invented),
No sonar cries disturbed the skies –
Moths flew uninstrumented.

The Eocene brought mammals mean
And bats began to sing;
Their food they found by ultrasound
And chased it on the wing.

Now deafness was unsafe because
The loud high-pitched vibration
Came in advance and gave a chance
To beat echo-location.

Some found a place on wings of lace
To make an ear in haste;
Some thought it best upon the chest
And some below the waist.

Then Roeder's keys upon the breeze
Made sphingids show their paces
He found the ear by which they hear
In palps upon their faces.
Of all unlikely places!

David Pye

In later years some further ears
Were found in other forms.
The more we know just goes to show
There are no real norms.

Two beetles go some way to show
How all this seems to check:
One has its ear upon its rear
The other on its neck.

In butterflies the eardrum lies
On *either* pair of wings.
This helps them hear with all the clear
Advantages that brings.

The mantis tries to hear bat cries
Without a stereo pair:
Makes one ear do instead of two
(But then relies on prayer)

Bullacris rates this risk too great.
Its ears are ranged in ranks,
(the normal two are still too few)
with *twelve* along its flanks!

The katydid has made a bid
To listen with its shins,
And though they chat a hungry bat
Very seldom wins.

In bee and fly new rules apply —
Not pressure but the motion.
Such nearfield sounds move hairs around
Like seaweeds in the ocean.

The dancing bee just cannot see
(the hive is dark and loud).
But nearfield sound helps those around
To hear her in the crowd.

An am'rous fruit fly paying suit
Wafts air at her antennae.
His lovesong's sweet and so discreet —
For one and not the many.

Mosquitoes who set out to woo
Can quickly find a mate.
Her wingbeat is the rate that his
Antennae resonate.

Tachinid flies use a surprise
To locate cricket song.
Their baseline ought not be so short
But works as if it's long!

This list is long, the contrasts strong
And may go on for ever.
And so we end with no clear trend—
For Nature is so clever.

David Pye

These two poems by Professor David Pye represent parodies of the poem, 'In days of old, when knights were bold ...'. They relate to the fact that the enormous variety of insects are nevertheless based on a very consistent body plan, except for their hearing organs which are remarkably diverse. Apart from grasshoppers, crickets and cicadas, many insects developed hearing only as a protective measure in order to hear predatory bats that hunt them by echolocation. This threat came long after the evolutionary origin of most insect groups and each then evolved hearing organs independently, exploiting existing mechanoreceptors in different parts of the body. The first poem was published in the journal *Nature* in 1968; the sequel was 'commissioned' to illustrate further examples discovered subsequently, and was published in a special edition of the journal *Microscopy Research and Technique*, in 2004. *Bullacris* refers to a genus of nocturnal orthopterans from Africa known as "bladder grasshoppers".

Lowly Origin

When apes began to groom their mates
In hunts for lice and fleas, they found
They liked the interchange of grunts
At each success, enjoyed caress
Of mutual combing bouts. These stunts
Became the start of talk for fun,
Apart from calls to warn of death
From eagle's swoop or pounce of lion.
It's thus I seize elusive words
To share my thoughts and feelings felt
To be of worth beyond the fog
Of blanket fur of daily noise.
Perhaps our reach for truths and light
Began with quest for vermin hid
From sight or out of range apart
From help of mate. So let us praise
The humble flea and thank the louse
Who chose our forbears as their house.

Henry Disney

Henry Disney wrote this response to my appeal for unusual insect poetry in *Antenna*, the in-house journal of the Royal Entomological

Society. As a matter of interest, apes very rarely suffer infestations of fleas, although they do suffer from the attentions of lice and other parasites. Social grooming, or allogrooming, is a major activity in reinforcing social structures.

The Sunday School Picnic

Then the girls they'll all be a yippin',
'cause a bug is in the cream;
And a daddy-long-legs skippin'
Round the butter makes 'em scream.

Joseph Crosby (Joe) Lincoln

The Butterfly's Ball, And The Grasshopper's Feast

Come take up your hats, and away let us haste
To the *Butterfly's* Ball, and the *Grasshopper's* Feast.
The Trumpeter, *Gad-fly*, has summon'd the Crew,
And the Revels are now only waiting for you.

So said little Robert, and pacing along,
His merry Companions came forth in a Throng.
And on the smooth grass, by the side of a Wood,
Beneath a broad Oak that for Ages had stood,
Saw the Children of Earth, and the Tenants of Air,
For an Evening's Amusement together repair.

And there came the *Beetle,* so blind and so black,
Who carried the *Emmet,* his Friend, on his Back.
And there was the *Gnat* and the *Dragon-fly* too,

With their Relations, Green, Orange, and Blue.
And there came the *Moth*, with his Plumage of Down,
And the *Hornet* in Jacket of Yellow and Brown;

Who with him the *Wasp*, his Companion, did bring,
But they promis'd, that Evening, to lay by their Sting.
And the sly little *Dormouse* crept out of his Hole,
And brought to the Feast, his blind Brother, the *Mole*.
And the *Snail*, with his Horns peeping out of his Shell,
Came from a great Distance, the Length of an Ell.

A Mushroom their Table, and on it was laid,
A Water-dock Leaf, which a Table-cloth made.
The Viands were various, to each of their Taste,
And the *Bee* brought her Honey to crown the Repast.
Then close on his Haunches, so solemn and wise,
The *Frog* from a Corner, look'd up to the Skies.

And the *Squirrel* well pleas'd such Diversions to see,
Mounted high over Head, and look'd down from a Tree.
Then out came the *Spider*, with Finger so fine,
To show his Dexterity on a tight Line.
From one Branch to another, his Cobwebs he slung,
Then quick as an Arrow he darted along,

But just in the Middle, – Oh! shocking to tell,
From his rope, in an Instant, poor Harlequin fell.
Yet he touch'd not the Ground, but with Talons outspread,
Hung suspended in air, at the end of a Thread.
Then the *Grasshopper* came with a Jerk and a Spring,
Very long was his Leg, though but short was his Wing;

He took but three Leaps, and was soon out of Sight,
Then chirp'd his own Praises the rest of the Night.

With Step so majestic the *Snail* did advance,
And promis'd the Gazers a Minuet to dance.
But they all laugh'd so loud that he pull'd in his Head,
And went in his own little Chamber to Bed.

Then as Evening gave Way to the Shadows of Night,
Their watchman, the *Glow-worm*, came out with a Light.
Then Home let us hasten, while yet we can see,
For no Watchman is waiting for you and for me.
So said little Robert, and pacing along,
His merry Companions returned in a Throng.

There are a number of versions of this childrens' fantasy – *The Butterfly's Ball, and the Grasshopper's Feast*. The original (above), which appeared in illustrated form, was written by William Roscoe in 1807. The following (insect sections only), from William Plomer (1973), was also lavishly illustrated:

The Butterfly Ball, And The Grasshopper's Feast

This is the day!

As night turns to dimness and draws back its curtain,
Stars, those bright sequins, now all disappear,
As dimness grows radiant, dawn makes it certain
That butterfly weather, quite perfect, is here;

Thundery cumulus masses are drifting
Very far off; overhead, very high,
Cirrus clouds spread their pink feathers, then lifting,
Dissolve and are lost in the turquoise-blue sky;

Up comes the Sun, and the very long shadows
Grow shorter; his light is like amber; the glow,
Where grey mists have melted away from the meadows,
Starts dewdrops all sparkling like jewels below;

Creatures that fly, or that creep, hop, or run,
Now wake all at once at a loud trumpet-call
To tell them this greatest of days has begun –
The day of the Feast and the Butterfly Ball!

At the sound of the trumpet the dozens invited
Now jump out of bed, squealing, "This is the day!
Oh, goody! The Ball! Aren't you madly excited?
Get up and get ready! Let's be on our way!"

Major Nathaniel Gnat

Major Nathaniel Gnat
With his fine-feathered Cavalier hat
Is off on a spree,
So with you or with me
He cannot stop now for a chat.

He sleeps in a four-poster bed
With a canopy over his head,
He lives in great state,
He dines off gold plate,
And oh, what a life he has led!

On camels' and elephants' backs
In deserts and forests and shacks,
In Tibet or Peru

He has known what to do
In ambushes, raids and attacks.

The call to adventure he hears
Has made him shoot tigers and bears,
And it quickens his pace
When a beautiful face
Or an elegant figure appears.

Though asked to the Ball, I suppose
He may visit some lady he knows,
Look deep in her eyes
And bewitch her with lies
And present her, of course, with that rose.

Happy-Go-Lucky Grasshopper

Happy-Go-Lucky Grasshopper
Snatched up a gamp and clapped on a wig,
He doesn't care how he looks,
Just doesn't care a fig!

For hours he's been hopping
Without ever stopping,
Delivering cards for the Ball,
Invitations to each and to all,
And he's taken great care
To plan and prepare
Good things for the Feast, so that every guest
May have for a treat the food he likes best –
Nuts for Squirrels and Worms for Moles,
And little titbits for Beetles and Voles.

Happy-Go-Lucky Grasshopper,
What awful risks he takes!
As Grasshoppers have no brakes
He doesn't always land
Exactly where he planned,
To be happy and hoppy and free,
Is every Grasshopper's wish –
Happy-Go-Lucky, STOP! Or you'll be
A snack for a big-mouth Fish!

SAFE! He straightens his wig
And breathes a sigh of relief;
The shock was almost too big
For the boatman on his leaf,
But Grasshopper's not afraid in the least
And with hugest hops goes off to the Feast

Magician Moth

When it's dusk or dark on earth,
Dusky, misty, ghostly,
It's then Magician Moth goes flitting mostly,
Softer than a breath.

Marked with a skull since birth
He knows no fear of death,
And when he folds his patterned velvet wings
Keeps very still, as midnight darkens,
Keeps very still, and hearkens
To the faintest, strangest, and most secret things.

They say that whispers from some very far,
Never-seen and nameless star
Give him power to foresee
Happenings unknown to you and me.

Before the Ball was even thought of, he
Knew just when it would be,
So here he is, in the clear light of day,
Famous Magician Moth outside this place of call,
The busy old White Lion,
Buying a jug of honey, something to rely on
Before he flits away
(But not till after sunset) to the Ball.

Lizzy Bee

Flowers hold for honeybees
Drops of purest nectar,
And Lizzy Bee, of all the bees,
Is the busiest collector.

Humming to herself for hours
Lizzy visits many flowers,
Honeysuckle, thyme, and clover;
Yellow pollen powders over
Lizzy's legs, as round she goes
Probing into every rose –
Lizzy knows, Lizzy knows
Where the sweetest nectar lies.
Oh today a big surprise!
Not a single flower will see
Anything of Lizzy Bee;

Today's her happy holiday
(She deserves one day at least),
She's left the hive to buzz away
With loads of honey for the Feast.

The Hornet And The Wasp

Invitations were sent to the Hornet and Wasp
On condition they laid by their stings.
"They might as well ask us," protested the Wasp,
"To fly to the Ball without wings."

"I hate you," the Hornet replied, "but for once
What you say does seem perfectly true.
I'll never go stingless so long as I live
And if I get a chance I'll sting *you*."

"This Ball," said the Wasp, "means nothing to me,
And nothing *you* say means a thing,
So long as I'm airborne, so long as I'm armed,
I shall fight for my freedom to sting."

Those who stick to their principles stick to their stings
And those who have guns will take aim,
But after they've stung, or after they've shot,
What they never will take is the blame.

The Grasshopper's Feast

Everyone had heard the Feast would be
Spread out under the broad oak tree,
At toadstool tables here are we
Happily eating, as you can see.

The Grasshopper's given us each a treat
By getting us *just* what we like to eat;
On every table there's different food,
Some to be nibbled, some to be chewed.

Moths and Butterflies suck what is sweet,
Squirrels crack nuts, they don't like meat.
Green stuff pleases Hares and Rabbits,
But some of us Insects have cannibal habits.

Caterpillars keep chumbling away
At nice green salads night and day,
But Moles and Frogs like Worms for their tea –
To eat bread-and-butter they'd *never* agree.

What a lot of trouble Grasshoppers take!
There goes one with a strawberry cake,
And Grasshopper, look, this glass is mine,
Please fill it up again with blackberry wine.

The Butterfly Ball

The Ball is beginning! From every direction
Guests are all crowding to join in the fun;
Was ever there seen such a varied collection
Of beautiful creatures? The Ball has begun!
First the Damsel-Flies' Ballet, so nimble on tiptoe,
With glittering wings, and so famous, these four,
They can kick in a can-can, or dance a calypso,
And whatever they do always gets an encore.

Homeward

Such a Ball and such a Feast
No one can forget:
Oh, if both would last, at least,
One more hour, not finish yet!

Some are sleepy, some could madly
Dance away till dawn,
Lovely wings are folding sadly,
One small Ant was seen to yawn.

Now the great big Moon is sinking
And goodbyes are said,
Darkness spreads, and some are thinking,
"Who will light us home to bed?"

Switching on his greenish light,
Glow-worm's heard to say
(He's so helpful and polite),
"Let me put you on your way.

"With my light I'll guide you all,
Homeward, like a friend,
While you're sleeping, Feast and Ball
In your dreams will never end."

William Plomer
Adapted from: *The Butterfly Ball and
the Grasshopper's Feast*, William Roscoe

The Triantiwontigongolope

There's a very funny insect that you do not often spy,
And it isn't quite a spider, and it isn't quite a fly;
It is something like a beetle, and a little like a bee,
But nothing like a woolly grub that climbs upon a tree.
Its name is quite a hard one, but you'll learn it soon, I hope.
So try:
   Tri-
      Tri-anti-wonti-
         Triantiwontigongolope.

It lives on weeds and wattle-gum, and has a funny face;
Its appetite is hearty, and its manners a disgrace.
When first you come upon it, it will give you quite a scare,
But when you look for it again, you find it isn't there.
And unless you call it softly it will stay away and mope.
So try:
   Tri-
      Tri-anti-wonti-
         Triantiwontigongolope.

It trembles if you tickle it or tread upon its toes;
It is not an early riser, but it has a snubbish nose.
If you sneer at it, or scold it, it will scuttle off in shame,
But it purrs and purrs quite proudly if you call it by its name,
And offer it some sandwiches of sealing-wax and soap.
So try:
   Tri-
      Tri-anti-wonti-
         Triantiwontigongolope.

But of course you haven't seen it; and I truthfully confess
That I haven't seen it either, and I don't know its address.
For there isn't such an insect, though there really might
   have been
If the trees and grass were purple, and the sky was bottle
   green.
It's just a little joke of mine, which you'll forgive, I hope.
Oh, try!
   Tri-
      Tri-anti-wonti-
         Triantiwontigongolope.

C. J. Dennis

The Universal Insect

I'm just a little insect, who tries to do his best,
But everyone's against me, they say I'm just a pest.

Although I try to please 'em, by keeping out of sight,
They scream and shout, and flush me out, then wonder
why I bite.
In my crack or crevice, just resting from the day,
Some great clown will knock me down, with his insect
spray.

It isn't very funny, to be a target type,
With everybody trying, to take the final swipe.

I'm really not too greedy, when feeding on your crop,
I do it when I'm needy, but don't know how to stop.

And even in your wardrobe, when chewing on your clothes,
I'll get no peace, till I decease, and vanish, I suppose.

Then when I'm in your carpet, a beetle or a flea,
With all the fluff and other stuff, you suck me up with glee.

Spiders fare no better, as this is what you do,
If in your bath, with violent wrath, you flush them down
the loo.

So can I ask you kindly, stop making such a fuss?
Stop lashing out so blindly, and have a thought for us.

John Seville

Do you know the pile-built village where the sago-dealers
    trade—
Do you know the reek of fish and wet bamboo?
Do you know the steaming stillness of the orchid-scented
    glade
Where the blazoned bird-winged butterflies flap through?
It is there that I am going, with my camphor, net and
    boxes,
To a gentle, yellow pirate that I know—
To my little wailing lemurs, to my palms and flying-foxes,
For the Red Gods call me out and I must go!

                                        Rudyard Kipling

I committed these lines of Kipling to memory many years ago. A
few lines of poetry can convey so much more than pages of prose,
and anyone who has spent time in a rainforest environment will
surely find these familiar, even if they have never heard them before.
They never fail to remind me of the island of Komodo in Indonesia
(where David Attenborough carried out one of his very early 'Zoo
Quests' in search of the Komodo Dragon, *Varanus komodoensis*),
which I visited for the first time in 1985. Kampong Komodo is the
archetypical pile-built village ... I can smell the fish and wet bamboo
of Komodo whenever I think of these lines. It was no great surprise
to find, some years later, these same lines in the introduction to W.
F. Cater's *Love among the Butterflies*, based on the diaries of
Victorian traveller and entomologist Margaret Fountaine. The words
are written out in Fountaine's own hand in the front of one of her
diaries.

Whilst researching this anthology, I came across the following
anonymous 'adaptation' (not attributed to Kipling), in the journal
Entomologist's Record and Journal of Variation for 1943. This
represents an attempt (highly unsuccessful in my view!) to transfer
the lines to a temperate setting:

Do you know the little village where the hills slope steeply
   down?
Do you know the scent of flowers and early morning dew?
Do you know the glorious stillness of the lonely wooded
   glade,
Where the golden wing-ed butterflies flit through?
It is there that I am going, with my cane, my net and
   boxes,
To a happy gentle pirate that I know,
To my beauteous little flies, to the woods the haunt of
   foxes,
The Red Gods call me out and I must go ...

                                        Anonymous

              Apologies are tendered here
                  To every poet buff,
            From whom we've lifted parodies
                And all that sort of stuff

                    "Ellnest Eriott" and "Maude Clorley"

The penultimate word (above) goes to Elliot and Morley, two
gentlemen who clearly had a lot of fun composing their rhymes; I
like to think of them sitting around their mercury vapour light in a
woodland glade on a balmy summer evening, surrounded by the
dancing shadows of moths and other insects attracted to the light.
Perhaps they had a glass of something too – and I fancy I hear the
occasional chuckle and even guffaw above the noise of the portable
generator.
    The final word (below), for which I make no apology despite the
fact it has absolutely nothing to do with insects, seems an appropriate
ending for a poetry anthology.

"It's not as easy as you think,"
The nettled poet sighed.
"It's not as good as I could wish,"
The publisher replied.
"It might," the kindly critic wrote,
"have easily been worse."
"We will not read it anyhow,"
The public said, "it's verse."

Robert Gilbert, Baron Vansittart

ACKNOWLEDGEMENTS

The poems presented here have accumulated over many years, and my pestering of colleagues has been in some cases unmerciful. The number of friends, colleagues and strangers in the UK, Australia, New Zealand and the USA who have helped over the years, primarily in bringing poems to my attention, is too many to mention individually, and it is acknowledged that this anthology would not have grown as it did without their interest. A particular pleasure has been the interaction with many people I would never have otherwise met, including contemporary entomologists and poets who so freely allowed inclusion of their words.

In acknowledging individuals, I run the risk of offending anyone I might inadvertently overlook. But I must take that chance – and hope that anyone I really have missed will forgive me. The following are gratefully thanked variously for their time, for pointing out suitable poems, or very generously allowing inclusion of their own material: William Anderson; Alasdair Aston; Geoff Baldwin; Mary Broomfield; Liz Brownlee; John Burns (USA); Dennis Burrows; Wesley Caswell; the late Michael Chalmers-Hunt; Robert Cowan; Roger Crosskey; Sandy Davidson; Henry Disney; Ruary Mackenzie Dodds; Trish Edwards (Australia); George Else; Alan Emmerson; Philip Entwhistle; Ian Ferguson; the late Brian Gardiner; Rosser Garrison (USA); the late Bob George; Peter Giles; Brian Goodey; the late Eric Gowing-Scopes; Peter Hardy; Robert Hoare (New Zealand); Mark Isaak (USA); Alan Kellerman; Frank Kenington; the late Robert Lawson and his daughter Catherine; Keith Lewis; Hugh Loxdale; David Manning; Paul Manton (USA); Brian Mitchell; Connor Muchmore (aged 8 when he sent me a poem, in 1998); Adrian Pont; Adrian Price; David Pye; Freda Raymont; Trevor Sampson; John Seville; Kenneth Smith; the late Ernest Taylor; Richard Tilley; Gillian Watson (USA); Len Winokur; Harry Zirlin (USA);

The Royal Entomological Society, St Albans (late of London) funded a short stay in London many years ago when I first browsed relatively aimlessly in the British Library. The Society also very generously allowed use of the illustrations and figures from specialist literature covering the last three centuries; the originals are in the Society's excellent library in St Albans. The Society's librarian, Val McAtear, dealt with enquiries patiently and efficiently, in the way of librarians everywhere.

Jill Lucas showed particular interest in this project, nudging me several times over the years. My good friend Martin Jacoby kindly waded his way through an early draft and made many constructive suggestions – inclusion of potted biographies, for example, was Martin's idea. At the end of the process, Richard Davies, of Parthian Books, welcomed the concept, and the scarily efficient Carly Holmes managed to retain her sense of humour in dealing with the often frustrating copyright and associated issues, arranging type-setting, and generally keeping on top of the process of preparing the anthology for publication.

I made every effort to check sources and accuracy, and hope I have done all the poems in this anthology justice; any errors or omissions in reproducing the poems are wholly my responsibility.

BIOGRAPHICAL NOTES

Acheta domestica (see L M **Budgen**)

Henry Gardiner **Adams** (1811 or 12 – 1881)
English author of several natural history books, on subjects including birds of prey, wildfowl, hummingbirds, butterflies, and nature generally.

John Yonge **Akerman** (1806 – 1873)
Akerman is best known for his numerous specialist works on numismatics (coin collecting). Born in Wiltshire, he also published works on local dialect, including *Glossary of Words used in Wiltshire* (1842) and *Wiltshire Tales, Illustrative of the Dialect* (1853).

Philip Bertram Murray **Allan** MBE (1884 – 1973)
Known to entomologists as "PBM Allan", he was a contributor to readers of the entomological literature for many years under the *nom de plume* "An Old Moth-Hunter", or simply "O.M.H.". His three books *A Moth-Hunter's Gossip, Talking of Moths,* and *Moths and Memories* were written in a humorous and informal style, but stimulated deep thought as befits a scientist educated at Charterhouse School and Clare College, Cambridge. His interests were varied: for many years he was editor of a well-known entomological journal and a publisher of a wide range of books. He founded *The Police Journal* and *The Journal of Criminal Law*, both of which he edited for many years – the latter until the year before his death. His research for a dictionary of mediaeval Latin resulted in his election to the Fellowship of the Society of Antiquities in 1921.

Archy and **Mehitabel** (see Don **Marquis**)

Arthur Bowden **Askey** CBE (1900 – 1982)
Popular English concert hall and radio/television variety entertainer from the 1930s until shortly before his death.

Pam **Ayres** MBE (1947 –)
Much-loved comedienne and broadcaster, Pam Ayres has entertained for almost 40 years since winning *Opportunity Knocks* in 1975. She is one of the UK's top-selling comediennes with her theatre shows. Her poetry collections include *You Made Me Late Again!, The Works, With These Hands* and *Surgically Enhanced* – and *The Necessary Aptitude* is her memoir of

growing up in Berkshire during the post war years. She has appeared three times for HM Queen Elizabeth, and was made an MBE in the Queen's Birthday Honours of 2004.

Anna Laetitia **Barbauld** (1743 – 1825)

A prominent English intellectual, poet, children's author, essayist and literary critic, whose poetry was significant during the development of Romanticism in England. Her poem 'Eighteen Hundred and Eleven' criticised British participation in the Napoleonic wars and received hostile reviews which effectively ended her literary career in 1812.

Cicely Mary **Barker** (1895 – 1973)

Barker was an Illustrator, and creator of the famous *Flower Fairies* in the form of children (always using real-life models) with butterfly wings. Largely educated at home due to her poor health, her artistic talent was recognised early in her life – she was elected a life member of the Croyden Art Society at the age of only 16, in 1911. From this time her paintings were featured regularly on postcards, greeting cards and, later, books.

Thomas Haynes **Bayly** (1797 – 1839)

An English song-writer, novelist and dramatist with a humorous bent and a talent for verse. His song 'I'd be a butterfly', written in the 1920s, became very popular.

John W (Jack) **Beardsley** (1927 – 2001)

Originally from California, Jack Beardsley became a specialist on parasitic wasps and scale insects. He was particularly associated with Hawaiian entomology and chaired the Department of Entomology in the College of Tropical Agriculture and Human Resources, University of Hawaii from 1981 until his retirement. He was closely associated with the Bernice P. Bishop Museum, Hawaii, and published more than 650 papers and notes on insects.

Joseph Hilaire Pierre René **Belloc** (1870 – 1953)

Belloc was a writer and historian born in France of an English mother and a French father. His father died in 1872, shortly after losing everything in a stock market crash, and Hilaire was brought up in West Sussex. He became a naturalised British subject in 1902. An honours history graduate from Balliol College, Oxford, accomplished writer, yachtsman and Liberal Member of Parliament, Belloc is best known now for his verse.

Arthur Christopher **Benson** (1862 – 1925)

British academic, essayist, author and poet, the son of a late 19th century Archbishop of Canterbury, Benson's best known legacy is having written the words to 'Land of Hope and Glory'. He left diaries containing four million words.

William **Blake** (1757 – 1827)

An English poet and artist, Blake's work was not accorded the critical acclaim it might have had during his lifetime, due largely to his highly idiosyncratic views on religion and his rejection of authority. He was said to be in the front rank of a mob that stormed Newgate Prison in 1780, releasing the inmates, and he had several other brushes with the law. He is remembered for his etchings and superb watercolours of religious works, as well as for his poetry.

Trevor **Blakemore** (Not known)

Little has been discovered about Trevor Blakemore. He published around the time of WW1 and his books include *Through a Glass, Darkly* (1913) and *The Flagship* (1915)

Gordon **Bottomley** (1874 – 1948)

An English poet influenced by the Romantic poets and the pre-Raphaelites, Bottomley is particularly remembered for his poetic drama, a form of verse written to be spoken, similar to the work of Shakespeare.

Vincent **Bourne** (1695 – 1747)

Vincent "Vinny" Bourne was an English classical scholar. Little seems to be known of his life beyond the fact that after being educated at Westminster School and Cambridge, he spent time as an usher at the former establishment. He published three editions of his Latin poems, notable for their mastery of Latin linguistics. His translation of English poems into Latin were acclaimed by scholars.

Henry **Brooke** (*ca* 1703 – 1783)

Irish poet, novelist and dramatist, Henry Brooke studied law at Trinity College, Dublin, but chose literature as a career. Although he began writing poetry, he turned dramatist and playwright – his play *Gustavus Vasa* was the first play to be banned by the Licensing Act of 1737, a dubious honour that made his life difficult thereafter. He was also active politically, arguing publicly against the persecution of Roman Catholics in the UK.

William J **Brown**, M.D. (Not known)
I can find no information on William J Brown.

Moses **Browne** (1704 – 1787)
A pen-cutter who became a vicar and eventually the Chaplain to Morden College, Browne wrote poetry and some religious works, but may be best remembered outside religious circles for *Piscatory Eclogues* (pastoral poetry) (1729) and later editions (from 1750) of *The Compleat Angler*, first published by Walton and Cotton in 1653.

Liz **Brownlee** (1958 –)
Liz Brownlee is a British wildlife poet, published in over 60 anthologies. She has 23 poems on display around Bristol Zoo, and is one of the National Poetry Day Ambassadors 2014. Her book about endangered animals, with poetry and facts, is called *Animal Magic*, and is available from Iron Press.

William Cullen **Bryant** (1794 – 1878)
William Bryant was born near Cummington, Massachusetts; his mother was able to trace her ancestry directly to the Mayflower, which brought the Pilgrim Fathers from the UK in 1621; his father to colonists arriving some years later. He developed an interest in poetry early in his life, trained as a lawyer and was admitted to the bar in 1815. A collection of his poetry published in the 1820s included *The Ages*, an account of the history of civilisation culminating in the establishment of the United States of America written as a result of an invitation to address Harvard University. An expanded version of his poetry volume was published in America and the UK in 1832 and resulted in his recognition as one of America's leading poets of the day.

Miss L M **Budgen** (Not known)
Acheta domestica is the scientific name of the House Cricket, a widespread species known in the USA as the Grey Cricket. It is also the pseudonym of Miss L M Budgen, who published three slim volumes of insect verse (1849 - 1850) called *Episodes of Insect Life*, containing many humorous poems relating to insects.

John **Bunyan** (1628 – 1688)
John Bunyan began his working life as a tinker – mending pots – and was known by his peers as "the ungodliest fellow for swearing" they had ever heard. His life changed when he had a spiritual experience. An English preacher, best known for *Pilgrim's Progress* (full title: *The Pilgrim's Progress*

358

from this World to that which is to come, delivered under the Similitude of a Dream, wherein is Discovered, the Manner of his Setting out, his Dangerous Journey, and Safe Arrival at the Desired Countrey [sic]), a significant work of religious English literature published in 1678 and translated into more than 200 languages. The Restoration of the monarchy by Charles II, beginning in 1660, required regular attendance for everyone at their Anglican parish church, and made preaching outside the rituals of the church a punishable offence. A popular and notorious preacher, *Pilgrim's Progress* was started whilst Bunyan was serving a prison sentence for his religious activities.

John M **Burns** (1932 –)

Curator of Lepidoptera in the Smithsonian Institution's National Museum of Natural History since 1975, John Burns's book entitled *BioGraffiti* grew from poems he wrote to introduce speakers at a Natural History Seminar he ran when a professor at Harvard University. His research deals with evolution and taxonomy of skipper butterflies in the New World, and emphasises geographic and ecological distribution, life history, morphology, and DNA barcodes (as well as colour and pattern).

Robert (Rabbie) **Burns** (1759 – 1796)

Widely regarded as the national poet of Scotland, and often referred to simply as "The Bard", Robbie Burns is the best known poet to have written in the Scots dialect. Many of his poems and ballads are internationally famous, and he himself is annually celebrated in Scots' communities around the world on the 25th of January at Burns Supper.

George Gordon **Byron** (1788 – 1824)

One of the greatest and best known English poets, Lord Byron was a leading figure in what later became known as Romanticism: the Romantic poets, including Blake, Wordsworth, Keats and Shelley, favoured the pastoral in preference to the urban. A colourful figure of his day, famously described by Lady Caroline Lamb as "mad, bad and dangerous to know", Byron travelled widely in Europe, took part in Italy's struggle against Austria and fought against the Ottoman Empire in the Greek War of Independence. He died from fever in Greece in 1824. Although Byron was christened George Gordon Byron, his father took the surname "Gordon" to facilitate his entitlement to his wife's claim to a Scottish estate, and Byron was enrolled at school as George Byron Gordon. He inherited the Barony of Byron (becoming simply "Lord Byron") at the age of 10, but when his mother-in-law died he changed his name to Noel by Royal Warrant in order to be able to inherit half of her estate; from then he signed himself "Noel Byron", apparently because this gave him the same initials as his hero Napoleon Bonaparte.

Lewis **Carroll** (1832 – 1898)

Charles Lutwidge Dodgson, much better known by his pseudonym Lewis Carroll ("Lewis" is an anglicised form of "Ludovicus", which is in turn Latin for Lutwidge; "Carroll" a surname similar to the Latin "Carolus", derivation of the name Charles), was an English author, mathematician, photographer and Anglican deacon. His best known works are those of literary nonsense including *Alice's Adventures in Wonderland*, *Through the Looking Glass*, 'Jabberwocky' and 'The Hunting of the Snark'. Although there are only a few lines of his in the anthology, his poems 'The Walrus and the Carpenter' (from *Through the Looking Glass*), and 'The Hunting of the Snark' are parodied by others, and names from 'Jabberwocky' have been given to several Pacific butterflies. Although highly conservative, he was interested in philosophy and a founder member of the Society for Psychical Research. The first work under the pseudonym that was to make him famous was a romantic poem, 'Solitude', published in the same year (1856) that Henry Liddell arrived at Christ Church College, Oxford, where Lewis Carroll was at that time employed. Although denied by Carroll later in his life, it is widely assumed that Liddell's daughter Alice was the "model" for the adventures in wonderland and through the looking glass.

Charles Edward **Carryl** (1841 – 1920)

Charles Carryl was born in New York and became a very successful American businessman and stockbroker, becoming a member of the New York Stock Exchange in 1874, a seat he held until 1908. Due to his contribution to children's "nonsense" literature, Carryl was hailed in the United States as the American Lewis Carroll at the end of the 19th century.

John George **Children** (1777 – 1852)

British chemist, minerologist and entomologist, John Children was educated at Tonbridge School, Eton College and Queen's College, Cambridge. He was elected a Fellow of the Royal Society in 1807, serving for a period as the society's secretary, and was founding President of what became the Royal Entomological Society, in 1833. The rare mineral childrenite was named after him, as were an Australian snake, a stick insect, an American beetle, and *Childrena childreni*, a large Himalayan nymphalid butterfly.

John **Clare** (1793 – 1864)

English poet John Clare, also known as the "Northampton Peasant Poet" was the son of a labourer and, with little formal education, his original work contained a lack of punctuation which was generally corrected by publishers. His work also incorporates Northamptonshire dialect; he became known for his powerful celebration of the English countryside and his lamentation of its disruption during the time of the industrial and agricultural revolutions. His work celebrates the countryside and illustrates keen observation and wide knowledge of the natural world.

Maude **Clorley** (see Claude **Morley**)

Rev. T. **Cole** (early 19th century)

Several poems written by the "Rev. T. Cole" have been considered, although only one – 'To the Cricket' – is presented in this anthology. He is mentioned in *The Poetical Register, and Repository of Fugitive poetry for 1805*, published in London two years later, and in the second edition of *The Naturalist's Poetical Companion* selected by Rev. Edward Wilson, published in 1852. It cannot be said with confidence that these refer to the same Cole; one refers to "the late Rev. Thomas Cole LL.B.", but no further information directly linked to Cole or poetry has been seen. An early edition of *The Spectator* magazine (established in 1828) referred to "On Tuesday last, the Lord Bishop of Peterborough instituted the Rev. H. W. Cottle to the Vicarage of Watford, in the county of Northampton, vacant by the resignation of the Rev. T. Cole. Patron, the King."

Julia **Cooke** (1981 –)

A Lecturer in Ecology at the Open University, UK since 2015, Dr Julia Cooke is a plant ecologist. She was awarded her PhD in 2012 from Macquarie University, Sydney, for her research on the functions of plant silicon. Her children's book, *My Little World*, began as a school English assignment. In her writing and teaching, Julia works to inspire a sense of wonder in the natural world.

Grace Wilson **Coplen** (Not known)

Little has been discovered about this poet, although searches found a Grace A Wilson Coplin, born in 1877. I do not even know whether she was a poet.

Stephen **Cordwell** (Not known)

Little has been discovered about this poet. I presume he is a current writer, but aside from an entry in *Very Rude Limericks* (which fits) I have not found anything more specific.

Barry **Cornwall** (see Bryan Waller **Procter**)

Nathaniel **Cotton** (1705 – 1788)

A little-known English physician and poet who is believed to have studied medicine at Leiden University. He specialised in the care of mental health patients and set up and maintained the Collegium Insanorum at St Albans in Hertfordshire. His most famous patient was William Cowper. Cotton contributed to various periodicals. His *Visions in Verse*, a collection of moral verses for children, was first published in 1751.

Robert (Bob) D. **Cowan** (1919 –)

An American physicist and Fellow of the American Physical Society, Optical Society of America, and the Los Alamos National Laboratory. Cowan is the recipient of numerous awards for his work in atomic spectroscopy, and is author of a book: *The Theory of Atomic Structure and Spectra*. His computer programmes for the calculation of atomic spectra are widely used throughout the world. The light-hearted fly limerick included here was the winner of a poetry competition run by the American Physical Society in 1997.

Abraham **Cowley** (1618 – 1667)

An English poet born in London, Cowley became a leading 17th century poet. He composed an epic romance at the age of 10, followed by other mature works whilst still a young teenager. Numerous printings of his works were published between 1668 and 1721.

William **Cowper** (1731 – 1800)

William Cowper had a fundamental effect on 18th Century nature poetry through his writing of everyday life in the English countryside. He also wrote the words to many hymns, and was responsible for several well-known sayings (e.g. "variety's the very spice of life").

Mrs Edmund **Craster** (? – 1874)

Aside from the fact that she died in 1874, and the poem 'The Centipede' is attributed to her, very little information has been found.

Tom **Crew** (20th century)

Author of *Health First in Verse, Prose and Epigram* (1931) from which the lines of 'Song of the Fly' were taken. No further information available.

John **Cunningham** (1729 – 1773)

A Dublin born playwright, poet and actor, who spent much of his life in Newcastle, Northumberland, where he also died. He began to write at the age of 12 and his first play, *Love in a Mist*, written at the age of 17, was performed in Dublin. His book of poems was published in 1766, and the fable presented in this anthology appeared in several 19th century collections, often attributed to just "Cunningham" or, in at least one case, merely "C".

Dante (*ca* 1265 – 1321)

Durante degli Alighieri, commonly known as Dante Alighieri or plain Dante, was an Italian poet of the Middle Ages. He is best known for his *Divine Comedy*, a work divided into three books: *Inferno*, *Paradiso* and *Purgatorio*.

Erasmus **Darwin** (1732 – 1802)

Grandfather of the rather more famous Charles, Erasmus Darwin was a leading intellectual of his day, who speculated on how species might change in time through natural selection. He based his theories on his own detailed observations of domestic animals, and published much of his work in the form of poetry.

Jean **de La Fontaine** (1621 – 1695)

A famous 17th century French poet, commemorated most recently by a set of postage stamps in 1995 and a film of his life in 2007. Jean de La Fontaine was a prolific writer, best known for his *Fables* and *Contes* (fairy tales).

Walter John **de la Mare** (1873 – 1956)

An English poet and novelist noted for his imagination, remembered most for his works for children and his famous poem 'The Listeners', first published in a newspaper in 1911. Descended from French Huguenots, he was born in what is now Greenwich, London, and published his first book (*Songs of Childhood*) under the name Walter Ramal – representing a part of his name backwards. Later work included ghost and horror stories.

Augustus **de Morgan** (1806 – 1871)

A Victorian mathematician, with mathematical laws and a moon crater named after him. Blind in one eye almost from birth, de Morgan's numerical abilities became obvious as a teenager and he entered Trinity College, Cambridge. A witty writer on a variety of subjects, his few lines in this anthology provides a twist to Swift's biting fleas.

Clarence Michael **Dennis** (1876 – 1938)

Australian journalist and writer Clarence Michael James Stanislaus Dennis was better known as C. J. Dennis. He is best known for *The Songs of a Sentimental Bloke*, which sold 65,000 copies in the first year following its publication in 1916.

Emily **Dickinson** (1830 – 1886)

An American poet born in Amherst, Massachusetts, Emily Elizabeth Dickinson was something of an eccentric recluse who conducted much of her life through correspondence. She was a prolific poet, although very few of her poems were actually published during her lifetime – indeed, the extent of her work did not become known until her poems were discovered by her younger sister following her death: her *Complete Poems* were not published until 70 years later. She was a keen botanist and an active gardener with a penchant for exotic scented flowers: the family garden was locally notable during her lifetime. Much of her written work illustrates a melancholy preoccupation with death.

Henry **Disney** (1938 –)

Henry Disney was born in Dorset in 1938. Following National Service in the Royal Artillery, he read Natural Sciences at Cambridge University before becoming Assistant Warden of the Flatford Mill Field Centre in Suffolk. He then took up entomological research posts overseas, at the Dermal Leishmaniasis Research Unit (Belize) and Helminthisasis Research Unit (Cameroon), before returning to the UK to become Director of the Field Centre and National Nature Reserve at Malham Tarn in North Yorkshire. From 1984-1998 he was the Field Studies Council Research Fellow in the Department of Zoology of Cambridge University, primarily researching the natural history and taxonomy of scuttle flies (Phoridae) of the world. He is the author or co-author of 550+ scientific papers, and enjoys a wide variety of other interests: he was co-founder and co-editor of the acclaimed *Naturalists' Handbooks* series and he has served or is serving on a number of governmental committees and advisory panels; as a school governor, and churchwarden. He is a Director of Dervish Mine Clearance Limited (concerned with clearing antipersonnel landmines). He currently continues his research activities at Cambridge University's Department of Zoology.

Ruary Mackenzie **Dodds** (1946 –)

A Scots writer and broadcaster, Dodds' interest in dragonflies began in 1985 when he was a businessman in London, and a dragonfly landed on his shirt. In 1989 he set up Europe's first dragonfly reserve, Ashton Water Dragonfly Sanctuary, and in 1995 he founded the National Dragonfly Museum at Ashton Mill near Oundle, Northamptonshire. The Museum closed due to external factors after seven successful years, but he and his team were subsequently instrumental in setting up the Dragonfly Centre at Wicken Fen in Cambridgeshire. He was elected a Fellow of the Linnean Society in 2013, and is a strong supporter of the British Dragonfly Society.

John **Donne** (*ca* 1572 – 1631)

A Jacobean poet, preacher and Member of Parliament noted for his romantic and religious poems, Latin translations, epigrams and eloquent sermons. Donne was ordained into the Church of England in 1615 and became Dean of St Paul's Cathedral in 1621. Well educated and well travelled, his poetry reflected intimate knowledge of English society and its problems; his works include many quotable passages, some used by later authors for book titles (e.g. Hemingway's *For Whom the Bell Tolls* and Merton's *No Man is an Island*).

Mrs Amanda Louisa Ruter **Dufour** (1822 – 1899)

American lyricist and poet.

Ernest Arthur **Elliot** (1850 – 1936)

Ernest Elliot was born in Calcutta, where his father (reputed to have declined a baronetcy and not dared to tell his wife) was the Chief Magistrate. Following a period working in London, he undertook Forestry training and became an Unteroffizier in the "Merry Black Foresters" in Saxony (1871-3). He returned to India but failed to get accepted for the Indian Forestry Service due to his poor health. Undeterred, he travelled on a cargo sailing ship around Cape Horn to Australia where he took up cattle ranching and opal mining, finally returning to the UK in 1884. He was a collector of all manner of things, including natural history artefacts. He had a particular interest in beetles and, later, Stephanidae (parasitoid wasps). His work on the latter resulted in a worldwide monograph. Ernest Elliot and his good friend Claude Morley published a poetry book, *The Beatific Babblings of Bugland's Bard* (1934), printed in only 100 copies, under the names Ellnest Eriott and Maude Clorley.

Harry **Eltringham** (1873 – 1941)

Following scientific studies at Trinity College, Cambridge, Harry Eltringham looked after the family shipbuilding business following the death of his father. He was an entomologist at the Hope Department of Entomology at Oxford for many years, with a special interest in butterfly mimicry and the systematics of some African and South American butterflies, and became a renowned histologist. President of the Royal Entomological Society (1931-32), Fellow of the Royal Society, and author of a number of scientific tomes, he achieved world-wide fame for his pioneering work on the structure of insect sensory organs. One of his more unusual accomplishments was to photograph a colleague through the compound eye of a glowworm. He left a thin volume of unpublished poems, with some line drawings, entitled *Studies in Emptyknowledgy by A Bughunter*, to the Royal Entomological Society, and some of his nonsense rhymes rival the best of Ogden Nash and Edward Lear.

Ralph Waldo **Emerson** (1803 – 1882)

Leader of the mid-19th century Transcendentalist movement, Boston philosopher Ralph Waldo Emerson was also an essayist and poet. Closely connected with the church, especially in his early years, he became disaffected and left the church in 1832, when he embarked on a tour of Europe. In Paris, he visited the Jardin des Plantes, where observation of Jussieu's system of classification promoted an interest in science. He visited England and met the Romantic poets Wordsworth and Coleridge, becoming subsequently influenced by Thomas Carlyle, a Scottish writer and historian who had also experienced a loss of faith.

Ellnest **Eriott** (see Ernest Arthur **Elliot**)

Isabella **Fey** (Not known)

I can find no information about this poet.

R R **Fielder** (Not known)

The two lines in this anthology attributed to Fielder were published in the *British Medical Journal*, volume 303 (1991) in an item entitled *A potpourri of parasites in poetry and proverb* by D A Burns.

Michael Henry **Flanders** OBE (1922 – 1975) (see also Donald **Swann**)

An English actor, broadcaster, writer and performer of comic songs, notably with Donald Swann, with whom he had a professional partnership from 1948 to 1967. Flanders was born in London to an actor father and a mother who was a professional violinist. The Flanders & Swann duo were very well known for songs which include 'The Hippopotamus', 'First and Second Law' (the laws of thermodynamics put to music), 'A Transport of Delight' (in honour of the London double-decker bus), and many others. He also wrote 'Ill Wind', to the finale of Mozart's Horn Concerto No. 4. He made numerous appearances on stage, radio and television, appeared in two films, and provided the narration for EMI's classic production of Prokofiev's *Peter and the Wolf*.

"Mr **Frankly**" (early 19th century)

Little is known of "Mr Frankly". He was the author of a charming book printed by Whittingham & Arliss, London, in 1816, entitled *The History of Frugal, the Wild Bee*. The introduction begins 'My Young Friends', and contains a meandering account of the natural history of bees in general, aimed at the level of children and young people. The book includes a large number of poetic passages and poems; such poems are clearly derived from other sources, but are unattributed.

Janis **Freegard** (1963 –)

Poet, writer and botanist Janis Freegard was born in South Shields, Northumberland, but has lived for most of her life in New Zealand. She has a Bachelor's degree in Botany from the University of Auckland, and an Honours degree in Plant Ecology from Victoria University of Wellington. The poem presented here is from her collection of poems *Kingdom Animalia: The Escapades of Linnaeus* (Auckland University Press, 2011).

Pavel **Friedmann** (1921 – 1944)

Pavel Friedmann was born in Prague on the 7th of January 1921 and deported to Thereisenstadt concentration camp at Terezín, in what is now the Czech Republic, on the 26th of April 1942. He was transported to Auschwitz on the 29th of September 1944, where he died. The text of 'The Butterfly' was discovered at Thereisenstadt after the ghetto was liberated.

Robert **Frost** (1874 – 1963)

An oft-quoted American poet, Robert Lee Francis Frost examined philosophical and social themes through rural life in New England. He was awarded four Pulitzer Prizes for Poetry during his lifetime. His first published poem, not included in this anthology, was 'The Butterfly: an Elegy' which he sold in 1894 to New York literary journal *The Independent* for $15.

John **Gay** (1685 – 1732)
English poet and dramatist best remembered for his allegorical lyrical drama *The Beggar's Opera*, which caricatured Sir Robert Walpole, the First Prime Minister of Great Britain.

Kathryn L. **Garrod** (Not known)
I can find no information on this poet.

Johann Wolfgang von **Goethe** (1749 – 1832)
A German writer and politician, whose prolific output embraced the fields of poetry, drama, literature, theology, humanism and science. His *magnum opus*, the two-part drama *Faust* is internationally acknowledged as a peak of world literature. His poems were set to music by composers from Mozart to Mahler, and his first scientific work, *Metamorphosis of Plants*, was published on his return from a tour of Italy in 1788. He gathered together what was at the time the largest collection of minerals in Europe – some 18,000 specimens, and wrote several books on morphology. By his own admission, Goethe disliked "tobacco smoke, bugs and garlic, and the cross".

Samuel Griswold **Goodrich** (1793 – 1860)
American author, bookseller and publisher born in Connecticut to a Congregational Minister and better known under the pseudonym Peter Parley. Largely self-educated, he published an illustrated annual, *The Token*, which contained some of the early work of Hawthorne, Longfellow and others, and later produced a substantial number of extremely successful books for the young which encompassed a variety of subjects including biography, geography, history and science – all under the name of Peter Parley. An active politician, he was elected a member of the Massachusetts House of Representatives in 1836, and of the State Senate the following year. He subsequently accepted the post of American Consul in Paris, and was presented with a commemorative medal for his work there.

Harry **Graham** (1874 – 1936)
Jocelyn Henry Clive Graham, known as "Harry", was educated at public schools in England and became a Captain in the Coldstream Guards, from which he took a pseudonym, "Col D. Streamer". He became well known for

his collections of wicked rhymes: *Ruthless Rhymes for Heartless Homes* and *More Ruthless Rhymes*.

Robert **Graves** (1895 – 1985)

A prolific English poet, translator and novelist, Robert Ranke Graves earned his living from writing and was a prominent translator of ancient Greek and classical Latin texts. He began to write poetry at school – where he was also a boxing champion – and later attended St John's College, Oxford, but was commissioned into the Royal Welch Fusiliers at the outbreak of the First World War in 1914. His first volume of poems, *Over the Brazier*, was published in 1916. Seriously wounded at the Somme, he became close friends with the poet Siegfried Sassoon and, later, with Wilfred Owen. Graves lived for a time in Cairo, Majorca and Pennsylvania, before returning to England. In the latter part of his life he corresponded regularly with Spike Milligan, and was one of 16 Great War poets commemorated in Westminster Abbey's Poet's Corner.

Oliver **Grey** (see Henry **Rowland-Brown**)

Al **Grigarick** (? –)

A Professor of Entomology at the University of California, Davis, Al Grigarick composed a series of poems designed to entertain and educate students in his introductory entomology class in the 1950s. These, and others, were published by the University's R. M. Bohart Museum of Entomology, with rather nice illustrations by Marina Planutiene.

Thomas **Hardy** (1840 – 1928)

Hardy considered himself primarily a poet who also composed novels, although even during his lifetime he was best known for his novels, which included *Tess of the d'Urbervilles* and *Far From the Madding Crowd*. However, his poetry has become equally well thought of and is regarded as having had a significant influence on modern English verse.

Adrian Hardy **Haworth** (1761 – 1833)

Born in Chelsea, London, Haworth was a very well known entomologist and botanist of his day. Steered towards a career in law, in which he had little interest, he devoted all his energies to natural history when he inherited his parents' estate. A founder of the Entomological Society – now the Royal Entomological Society – he compiled an important and authoritative work on British Lepidoptera, *Lepidoptera Britannica*, between 1803 and 1828. He counted Sir Joseph Banks and William Jones among his friends.

"Harrington" (probably Sir John Harington [1561 – 1612])

The poem presented here by "Harrington" came from the 2nd edition of *The Naturalist's Poetical Companion* (1852) with poems selected by Rev. Edward Wilson. The poet was probably Sir John Harington KCB (also spelled Harrington), author, poet, master of art, and courtier at the Royal Court of Elizabeth the First (his godmother). His best known work today is a poetical allegory *A New Discourse of a Stale Subject, called the Metamorphosis of Ajax* (1596), a title derived in part for his invention of the flush toilet, called the Ajax ("jakes" was a contemporary slang term for toilet: hence A "Jakes" = Ajax).

Felicia Dorothea **Hemans** (1793 – 1835)

Born Felicia Dorothea Browne in England, her first poems were dedicated to the Prince of Wales and published in 1808 when she was only 14 years old. This resulted in a brief correspondence with Percy Shelley. A marriage to Captain Hemans, an Irish army officer, lasted only 6 years; she lived in Dublin from 1831 and became a well-known literary figure.

Robert J B **Hoare** (1967 –)

Born in England, Robert Hoare emigrated to New Zealand in 1998 (after a PhD in Australia) to become lepidopterist at the New Zealand Arthropod Collection in Auckland, where he is now Head Curator. His entomological poems were originally written for the monthly meetings of the Auckland Branch of the Entomological Society of New Zealand and a number of them were later collected in the volume *Six-legged Things and Scaly Wings*, published by Magnolia Press in 2008. He has worked on the taxonomy of various groups of moths, chiefly micro-moths.

Mary Ann **Hoberman** (1930 –)

Born on the 12th of August 1930, in Stamford, Connecticut, Mary Ann Hoberman was interested in writing from an early age, editing her high school yearbook and writing for school newspapers. She was awarded a BA Degree in History from Smith College in 1951, and an MA in English Literature from Yale in 1986. She has taught literature at educational levels from elementary to college, but her primary occupation has been writing for children – she has written more than 40 books for children, and recently (2009), a historical novel, *Strawberry Hill*. In 2008, she was named US Children's Poet Laureate by the Poetry Foundation.

Joyce **Hodgson** (Not known)

I can find no information on this poet.

Thomas **Hood** (1799 – 1845)

A London-born British poet and humorist, Thomas Hood was known to his family for his fondness for practical jokes. One of his first poems, 'The Song of the Shirt', was published anonymously in an early issue of *Punch* in 1843 and became a popular and well known work. He wrote humorously on a range of subjects, and was a friend of several well known literary figures of his time, including William Makepeace Thackeray. He was never a healthy man. A monument in his memory was erected in Kensal Green cemetery some years after his death, by public subscription.

Gerard Manley **Hopkins** (1844 – 1889)

English poet Gerard Manley Hopkins came from a deeply religious background. A Roman Catholic convert and Jesuit priest, he wrote poetry from an early age, and was strongly influenced by Robert Bridges (who was to become Poet Laureate) and Christina Rossetti, but was only credited as a leading Victorian poet after his death. Most of his poetry was published posthumously. He experienced difficulty in coming to terms with his homosexuality, and believed that poetry conflicted with his religion.

Horace (65 – 8 BC)

A contemporary of Virgil, Quintus Horatius Flaccus Horace, known more commonly as Horace, was a leading Roman lyric poet during the time of the emperor Augustus. The much used phrase "carpe diem" ("seize the day") is derived from one of his poems.

Libby **Houston** (1941 –)

A British poet, born in North London, she was educated at Lady Margaret Hall, Oxford. During the 1960s she became a popular performer of her work. *A Stained Glass Raree Show* (1967), her first collection of poetry, was followed by *Plain Clothes* (1971), *At the Mercy* (1981), and *Necessity* (1988). Many of her poems succeed in combining an intention to entertain with an understated moral or philosophical seriousness. The title poem of her widely acclaimed collection, *At the Mercy*, formed an extended meditation on the death in 1974 of her first husband, the artist Mal Dean. While she is frequently concerned with aspects of fable and legend, anecdotal treatments drawn from everyday experience are equally characteristic of her work. *All Change* (1993) is a substantial collection containing mainly children's verse. Since the early 1970s, she has contributed poetry for BBC broadcasts for schools.

Mary **Howitt** (1799 – 1888)

The first line of the poem '"Will you walk into my parlour?" said the Spider to the Fly"' is very well known indeed – the remainder possibly not. Mary Howitt and her husband wrote some 180 books between them, but she will inevitably be remembered for this poem above anything else.

Jean **Ingelow** (1820 – 1897)

Ingelow was an English poet and novelist born in Boston, Lincolnshire. As a young girl, following contributions to various magazines under the pseudonym "Orris", her first – anonymously published – book, *A Rhyming Chronicle of Incidents and Feelings*, appeared in 1850, and she became friends with Tennyson, who thought it charming. She became popular following her *Poems* in 1863 (many were subsequently put to music) and went on to write a series of novels and children's stories.

Mark **Isaak** (1959 –)

Mark Isaak is a retired software engineer with wide-ranging interests, entomology prominent among them. He grew up in rural central California; after college exchanging that environment for life and work as a computer programmer in the heart of Silicon Valley. In mid-life he pursued entomology as a hobby, to the point of acquiring a Masters degree. His interests currently include (but are not limited to) biology, tai chi, puzzles, and folklore.

Horace **Jakes** (Not known)

I can find no information on this poet.

Samuel **Johnson** (1709 – 1784)

Dr Samuel Johnson, English writer and lexicographer, was born in Lichfield, Staffordshire. Despite a rather ungainly appearance and eccentric manners, he was an outstanding scholar. He attended Pembroke College, Oxford where for the two years of his residence he was hounded and ridiculed for his appearance – although the College gate was subsequently adorned with his effigy, even though he left without a degree. Throughout his life he struggled with poverty and a series of maladies and eccentricities verging on madness. At the age of 28, Johnson went to London where he eventually published (the first edition anonymously) the stately poem 'London', which was acclaimed by many people including Alexander Pope, the most eminent writer of his generation. His reputation thus made, Johnson was engaged by several eminent booksellers to compile a *Dictionary of the English Language*, the "first dictionary which could be read with pleasure", for which he became famous. His best work, some critics would argue, was the several volumes of *The Lives of the Poets*, narratives published near the end of his life.

Benjamin (Ben) **Jonson** (1572 – 1637)

A contemporary of Shakespeare, Ben Jonson was an English Renaissance dramatist, poet and actor, best known for his satirical plays (including *Volpone* and *The Alchemist*) and lyric poems. No stranger to controversy, he was imprisoned three times in his life: for co-authorship of a play considered "lewd and mutinous"; again, briefly, for killing someone in a duel; and then, again briefly, when the authorities took exception to topical allusions in one of his plays. He was questioned as a result of his presence at a supper party together with most of the Gunpowder Plot conspirators. His first significant success, *Every Man in his Humour*, cast William Shakespeare as one of the actors. An annual pension awarded in 1616 caused some to regard Ben Jonson as England's first Poet Laureate.

John **Keats** (1795 – 1821)

Together with Byron and Shelley, Keats was one of the main figures of the second generation of Romantic poets. Born in London, he became a medical student at Guy's Hospital (King's College, London) and was set to become a doctor, receiving his apothecary's licence in 1816. However, he resolved to become a poet, carrying out medical duties and literature studies at the same time. He was a successful poet in his short lifetime and is remembered for a series of Odes ('Ode to a Nightingale'; 'Ode on a Grecian Urn', etc.). Wentworth House, on the edge of Hampstead Heath, where Keats lived and wrote, now houses the Keats Museum. He died in Rome of tuberculosis.

D. Keith McE. **Kevan** (1920 – 1991)

Born in Helsinki of British parents, Keith Kevan's early years were spent in and around Edinburgh. His accountant father was a leading shell and beetle specialist, and his mother was an enthusiastic botanist – a combination that encouraged an interest in natural history. A natural academic, he earned second and third year medals in zoology and botany, and left Edinburgh University with a first class honours degree in zoology. Following stints overseas in places as diverse as Trinidad, Kenya, Ethiopia and Somalia, he returned to the UK where he became the first Head of a newly-formed Zoology Department at Nottingham University. In 1957 he accepted a Professorship and Chairmanship of the Department of Entomology of McGill

University in Quebec, and worked in Canada for most of the rest of his life. He was closely associated with the Lyman Entomological and Research Laboratory at McGill. An accomplished linguist and prolific author on a variety of entomological subjects, with 400 scientific publications, he was also known for his theatrical talent and a quick sense of humour; the latter is apparent in his verse. He is well known for his voluminous research into anything and everything, historical and cultural, in any language, concerning Orthoptera, published in more than 1,000 pages in the *Memoirs* of the Lyman Museum.

Dick **King-Smith** OBE (1922 – 2011)

Ronald Gordon 'Dick' King-Smith was a prolific author of children's books, and is best remembered for his book *The Sheep-Pig* (*Babe the Gallant Pig* in the USA) which was later adapted as the film *Babe*. He grew up in the West Country of England, served in the Grenadier Guards regiment in Italy during WW2 and was a farmer for 20 years before becoming a teacher and author. He was awarded an Honorary Master of Education degree by the University of the West of England in 1999 and appointed an OBE in the 2010 New Year Honours list. He wrote over 100 books.

Joseph Rudyard **Kipling** (1865 – 1936)

Born in Bombay, Rudyard Kipling must be one of the best known English writers and poets, remembered today for his tales and poems in support of soldiers in India, and for children's stories. Following a blissfully happy early childhood among the exotic sights and smells of India, he was sent to boarding school in England – by all accounts a dramatically less pleasurable experience for him. At the age of 16 he returned to India (Lahore) and worked on the *Civil and Military Gazette*, writing stories in his spare time. Subsequently returning to England, he wrote *Barrack-Room Ballads* (which contained the poems 'Road to Mandalay' and 'Gunga Din') as well as many short stories. He wrote *The Jungle Book* whilst living in New England with his American wife. Eventually retiring to Sussex, Kipling was regarded as the People's Laureate and the poet of Empire. So many of his stories and poems remain familiar today, including *The Just So Stories*, *Kim*, *Puck of Pook's Hill*, and the poem 'If', the last said to have been based on Dr Leander Starr Jameson, author of the infamous botched Jameson Raid in the Transvaal in 1895-6. Kipling became an international celebrity, although his conservative views were to become considered rather old-fashioned. He declined many Honours, including a Knighthood, the Order of Merit and the Poet Laureateship, but accepted the Nobel Prize for Literature in 1907.

D H **Lawrence** (1885 – 1930)

English novelist, poet, playwright, literary critic and painter David Herbert Lawrence's collected works reflect bleakly the dehumanising effects of industrialisation. His inauspicious working class beginnings – his father was a miner; his mother a teacher and then worker in a lace factory – would never have suggested that the house in which he was born, in the mining village of Eastwood, Nottinghamshire, would become the D. H. Lawrence Birthplace Museum. He was interested in books and wrote poetry from an early age, moving to London in 1908 and becoming a teacher before deciding to be a full time writer in 1911. A stream of books followed, including *Sons and Lovers* (1913), travel books, *The Rainbow* (1915), and *Women in Love* (1920). He and his German wife's contempt for war and militarism resulted in accusations of spying during the Great War and towards the end of the war, in 1917, Lawrence was obliged to leave Cornwall with three days notice under the terms of the Defence of the Realm Act. Following the war, he spent most of the remainder of his life travelling around the world, including France, Italy, Australia, Sri Lanka, the USA and Mexico. His continued travel writing, poems (*ca* 800, mainly short) and novels culminated in the notorious *Lady Chatterley's Lover* (1928), his last major novel, for which Penguin Books were prosecuted in 1960 under the Obscene Publications Act, 1959. He suffered from poor health throughout his life and returned to Europe, where he died from complications associated with tuberculosis in Vence, France. His ashes are interred in New Mexico.

Robert **Lawson** (1943 – 2013)

Scotsman Robert Lawson was born and brought up in Glasgow. Following short service as a marine engineer in the Royal Navy, he spent most of his working life as a gardener, spending as much time as possible outdoors. Always interested in wildlife, including insects, he was an enthusiastic cyclist and mountaineer; he was also something of a linguist, teaching himself Latin, Greek and French. He was in the process of learning Russian up until his death on the Isle of Bute in 2013.

Edward **Lear** (1812 – 1888)

An English writer of literary nonsense, often using made-up words, and much loved by people of all ages, Lear's best known works – in addition to his numerous limericks – include 'The Owl and the Pussycat', 'The Jumblies', and many others. Born in Holloway, London, he suffered epileptic seizures from an early age, in addition to other ailments including bronchitis, asthma and partial blindness, and lived towards the end of his life in San Remo (where he is buried) on the Mediterranean coast. He was also an accomplished painter, employed by the Zoological Society as an ornithological artist; his work was favourably compared with that of Audubon. Lear has been played in radio dramas by Andrew Sachs and Derek Jacobi.

Denise **Levertov** (1923 – 1997)

An American poet born in Ilford, Essex, Levertov declared her intention to become a writer at the age of five, and sent some of her poems to T. S. Eliot at the age of 12. Apparently he replied with a two page letter of encouragement, and she published her first poem in 1940. During World War II she served as a nurse in the London Blitz, and moved to the USA with her American husband in 1947. She published several books and in the 1960s and 70s became politically active in her life and in her work as poetry editor for *The Nation*. The Vietnam War, of which she was highly critical, was a focus for her poetry. She taught at several US universities and on retirement travelled widely in the UK and the USA giving poetry readings. She published 24 books of poetry, in addition to translations and critical works. She received many awards for her work, including a Guggenheim Fellowship.

Joseph Crosby (Joe) **Lincoln** (1870 – 1944)

Joe Lincoln was born on Cape Cod – in Brewster, Massachusetts – and became an author of novels, poems and short stories, many of which were set in a fictionalized Cape Cod. His writing frequently appeared in popular magazines, and two of his stories were made into films.

Hugh **Llewelyn** (see Hugh **Loxdale**)

Henry Wadsworth **Longfellow** (1807 – 1882)

Probably the most widely known and best-loved American poet of his time, Longfellow achieved prominence with poems such as 'Paul Revere's Ride'; 'Evangeline, A Tale of Acadie'; 'A Psalm of Life', and 'The Song of Hiawatha'. Born in Portland, Massachusetts (now Maine), he cared little for the legal career his father favoured and was saved from it by endowment of a professorship in Modern Languages at Bowdoin College, Brunswick. He travelled widely in Europe, developing an understanding of European traditions and a wide readership for romantic poetry, and was invited to Harvard as Smith Professor of Modern Languages. A prolific poet, dozens of volumes of poetry were published during his lifetime. He is honoured in Poets' Corner in Westminster Abbey, London.

Hugh **Loxdale** MBE (1950 –)

Hugh David Loxdale, was born in Horley, Surrey, and is of English, Welsh and Irish descent. Educated at Apsley Grammar School, Hemel, he studied Zoology at Reading University and gained a D.Phil. from Oxford University in insect biochemistry and physiology. He is an entomologist by profession and was Professor of Ecology at the Friedrich-Schiller University, Jena, Germany from 2009-2011. He currently works as an entomological consultant, living with his wife Nicola in Taunton, Somerset. Hugh has been interested in the natural world, especially insects, since a very early age and started writing poetry in his late teens. He has written nine books of poetry, the first of which – *The Eternal Quest* – was published under the name Hugh Llewelyn. His poetry is both eclectic and universal; it largely concerns natural history themes, but also includes human love in all its positive and negative manifestations. His poems, written in a variety of styles, have been printed in various magazines and on the BBC website and he has given recitals of his work, both in England and overseas.

Donald Robert Perry **Marquis** (1878 – 1937)

Donald Robert Perry (Don) Marquis was a New York newspaper columnist, humorist, poet, playwright, short story and screen writer. He was a determined opponent of prohibition (writing under the name "The Old Soak"), and wrote numerous newspaper sketches as the boss of 'Archy and Mehitabel', a cockroach "wise beyond his years" and an alley cat. The latter were a clever method of filling his newspaper column at times when he was short of copy, and the short, broken lines of text were explained by the fact that typing was a challenging pastime for a cockroach. As well as being highly amusing, his contributions are thoughtful and insightful.

Andrew **Marvell** (1621 – 1678)

Marvell was an English metaphysical poet and politician born and brought up in Yorkshire. A contemporary of John Donne and George Herbert, he was a colleague and friend of John Milton. Marvell's first poems, published when he was at Cambridge, recorded an outbreak of the Plague, the birth of a son to Charles I, and praised Oliver Cromwell. He was elected Member of Parliament for Kingston-upon-Hull in 1659 and again the following year to the Convention Parliament, and in 1661 to the Cavalier Parliament. Much of his poetry and many prose satires were critical of the monarchy, tyrannical government and Catholicism, and were published anonymously; his best known poem today is arguably 'To His Coy Mistress'.

David **McCord** (1897 – 1997)

An American poet born in New York City who grew up in Princeton, New Jersey and rural Oregon, McCord was well known as a children's writer, authoring or editing more than 50 books, including *Far and Few* (1952) and *One at a Time:* his *Collected Poems for the Young* (1974), which won a National Council of Teachers of English Award for Excellence in Poetry for Children. He earned a BA and an MA at Harvard University and was later awarded honorary doctorates from 22 universities, and served for many years as Executive Director of the Harvard College Fund.

Joseph **Merrin** (1820 – 1904)

Merrin was a British entomologist who published *The Lepidopterist's Calendar: giving the time of appearance of the British Lepidoptera, as far as they are known in the imago, larva, and pupal states; with a classified arrangement of the larvae-food* (1860) and *Butterflying with the Poets. A Picture of the Poetical Aspect of Butterfly Life* (1864).

Spike **Milligan** KBE (1918 – 2002)

Actor, broadcaster, comedian, musician, poet, soldier, writer, and celebrated eccentric Terence Alan Patrick Sean ("Spike") Milligan was born and brought up in India, lived most of his working life in England, and claimed his right to Irish citizenship (his father was Irish; his mother English) after the British government of the day declared him stateless following changes to the British Nationality Act 1981. He was co-creator (with Peter Sellers, Harry Secombe and Michael Bentine), main writer and a principal cast member of *The Goon Show* (the first series was aptly titled *Crazy People*), a ground-breaking BBC radio comedy which ran from 1951 to 1960, and has been re-run many times. He wrote many books, including *Puckoon* and his 7 volume biographical account of his time in the Royal Artillery during World War II (*Adolf Hitler: My Part in his Downfall* (1971), *"Rommel?" Gunner Who?: a Confrontation in the Desert* (1974), *Monty: His Part in my Victory* (1976) and *Mussolini: His Part in my Downfall* (1978)). A self-taught jazz musician, he was wounded in action in the battle for Monte Cassino and following a spell in hospital, eventually became a full time entertainer for the troops. *The Goons* came after the war and he made several sallies into television as writer-performer, although the pressures and demands of writing resulted in several mental breakdowns and a manic depression that lasted for many years. His poems were in the best tradition of literary nonsense, rivalling those of Edward Lear and Lewis Carroll – his poem 'On the Ning Nang Nong' was voted the UK's favourite comic poem in 1998.

Alan Alexander (A. A.) **Milne** (1882 – 1956)

Known universally to generations of children and adults as "A. A. Milne".
He was a noted writer and playwright, but remembered today for his
phenomenally successful *Winnie the Pooh*, and other children's stories. Born
in Hampstead, he was educated at a public school (H. G. Wells was one of
his teachers, briefly), Westminster School, and Trinity College, Cambridge
on a mathematics scholarship. At Cambridge, he edited and wrote for a
student magazine in collaboration with his brother Kenneth and came to the
attention of the editors of *Punch* Magazine, of which he later became an
Assistant Editor. In the First World War he served as an officer in the Royal
Warwickshire Regiment and Royal Corps of Signals; towards the end of the
war he wrote propaganda articles for Military Intelligence. In the Second
World War he served as a Captain in the Home Guard. He wrote several
plays and three novels and produced his children's poetry book *When We
Were Very Young* after the birth of his son, Christopher Robin. The various
stuffed toys that formed the basis of Milne's animal characters were real,
and the "Five Hundred Acre Wood", in which Pooh had many adventures,
was based on Ashdown Forest in East Sussex. Sadly – but perhaps
understandably – he became rather bitter that the success of his Pooh books
overshadowed his other work.

James **Montgomery** (1771 – 1854)

A Scots poet, hymn writer, editor and philanthropist, widely associated with
campaigns to abolish slavery and the exploitation of children used to sweep
chimneys. Born in Ayrshire to a pastor and missionary, Montgomery was
sent to study in Leeds when his parents left for the West Indies, where both
died. Apprenticed to a baker, then a storekeeper, he moved to Sheffield
where he eventually took over management of the *Sheffield Register*,
changing its name to *Sheffield Iris*. He was twice imprisoned on charges of
sedition – for printing poems celebrating the fall of the Bastille, and for
criticising a magistrate for his forcible dispersal of a political meeting in the
town – and later published a pamphlet of poems (*Prison Amusements*)
written during his incarceration. He went on to publish many poems, often
with a humanitarian bent, which were well received, but may be most
remembered today for writing hymns, notably the Christmas carol 'Angels
from the Realms of Glory'.

Thomas **Moore** (1779 – 1852)

An Irish entertainer, poet, singer and songwriter whose best known lyrics
include 'The Minstrel Boy' and 'The Last Rose of Summer'. Born in Dublin,

Moore was interested in music and the performing arts from an early age, acting in plays with his friends. Educated at Trinity College, Dublin, he moved to London in 1799 to study law, but instead found success as a poet, singer and translator. A successful society figure in London, he travelled to Bermuda in 1803 to take up the appointment of Registrar to the Admiralty, and went on to travel extensively in the United States and Canada. He returned to the UK in 1804, where he continued writing but got into debt due to a combination of his expensive tastes and embezzlement by a deputy in Bermuda, for which he became liable. He travelled in Europe and continued to write and publish a series of songs, stories, novels, biographies and poetry. Thomas Moore is considered Ireland's national bard, as Robert Burns is in Scotland. With John Murray, he was responsible for burning the memoirs of his good friend Lord Byron after his death.

Christopher **Morley** (1890 – 1957)

Born in Bryn Mawr, Pennsylvania, Christopher Morley was an American novelist, essayist and poet. He was educated at Haverford College and awarded a Rhodes Scholarship to New College, Oxford after which he moved to New York where he lived for most of the rest of his life. He suffered a series of strokes in 1951; after his death two New York newspapers published his message to his friends: "Read, every day, something no one else is reading. Think, every day, something no one else is thinking. Do, every day, something no one else would be silly enough to do. It is bad for the mind to continually be part of unanimity."

Claude **Morley** (1874 – 1951)

An English antiquary and entomologist, with a particular interest in Hymenoptera (bees, wasps, ants etc) and Diptera (flies), Morley lived and worked in Suffolk, and is best known to entomologists for his five volumes on the Ichneumons (parasitic wasps) of Great Britain, published between 1903 and 1914. His collection is deposited in the Ipswich Museum. Elected a Fellow of the Entomological Society of London (now the Royal Entomological Society) in 1896, he and his good friend Ernest Arthur Elliot privately published a collection of 37 poems – *The Beatific Babblings of Bugland's Bard* – mostly parodies of well-known poetic works, under the lightly disguised names Ellnest Eriott and Maude Clorley. The anthology was described by Morley in a 'review' as "what can (and cannot) happen to naturalists ... in the great open spaces and most particularly those of Suffolk ... 'a little nonsense now and then is relished by the wisest men. Here you have it'".

John **Morris** (Not known)
I can find no information on this poet.

Vladimir Vladimirovich **Nabokov** (1899 – 1977)
Russian born novelist and entomologist who is best known for his writing, in particular his controversial but acclaimed novel *Lolita*, first published in English (his second language) in 1955 – a rather disturbing book about the obsession of a middle-aged literature professor (Humbert Humbert) with a 12 year old girl. Perhaps it is not so well known, except to entomologists, that he was also a very keen – and capable, and respected – entomologist with a particular interest in small blue lycaenid butterflies. He grew up in a trilingual (Russian, English, French) household, but became a permanent exile following the October Revolution in 1917. The family lived briefly in England, for 15 years in Germany (his father was assassinated in Berlin in 1922), and then briefly in France before leaving for America in 1940. Nabokov began volunteer work as an entomologist at the American Museum of Natural History in New York, and joined the staff of Wellesley College as a resident lecturer in comparative literature; he became a naturalised US citizen in 1945, when he was, *de facto*, curator of Lepidoptera (butterflies and moths) at the Museum of Comparative Zoology, Harvard University. He wrote the bulk of *Lolita*, his most successful novel, and his autobiographical memoir *Speak, Memory* (he wanted to call it *Speak, Mnemosyne*, which probably refers to the scientific name of a butterfly, *Parnassius mnemosyne*) whilst travelling on butterfly collecting expeditions around the western USA. Nabokov's career as an entomologist was as distinguished as that of his writing, and he commented that if it had not been for the Russian revolution, he may well have written no novels at all; he was a serious and accomplished taxonomist – his hypothesis that certain polyommatine blue butterflies entered the New World over a Beringhian land bridge is supported by recent molecular research.

Frederic Ogden **Nash** (1902 – 1971)
An American poet born in New York, Ogden Nash was descended from the brother of Brigadier General Francis Nash (1742-1777) who gave his name to Nashville, Tennessee. The name Ogden Nash is synonymous with humorous poetry, including unconventional and crafted rhymes and lines of deliberately unequal length and metre. He lived in Baltimore, Maryland, for most of his life; he had various jobs, including as an editor for Doubleday publishing house, where he first began to write verse – although he once said in a news interview that he had thought in terms of rhyme since the

age of six. He published more than 500 comic verses in several collections, and made frequent guest appearances on comedy and radio shows in the USA and the UK. He wrote humorous poems for each movement of Saint-Saëns' orchestral suite *Carnival of the Animals*, the original recording of which was made by Colombia with Noël Coward reciting the poems. Some of his most popular writings were verses featuring animals, including insects.

Edward **Newman** (1801 – 1876)
Newman was an English entomologist and botanist born into a Quaker family. Both his parents were keen naturalists and Edward became active in entomological circles, being a founder member of the Entomological Club (extant today) and the Entomological Society of London (now the Royal Entomological Society) as well as editor of several well regarded specialist journals of the day. He published a series of books on diverse natural history subjects including British ferns, birds' nests, British moths and butterflies, and also an ornithological dictionary. He had a keen sense of humour, and in 1843 wrote a short, rather tongue-in-cheek, paper arguing that pterosaurs were marsupial bats rather than reptiles, for the first issue of *The Zoologist*, of which he was the editor. He also published the first edition of *The Insect Hunters; or Entomology in Verse* (1857) (see opening page of this anthology).

William **Oldys** (1696 – 1761)
An English antiquarian and bibliographer, Oldys was the illegitimate son of Dr William Oldys, Chancellor of Lincoln. He lost a good deal of his paternal inheritance in what became known as the South Sea Bubble, when a company formed to take advantage of a monopoly in proposed trade with South America, and other dubious schemes, peaked in 1720 and collapsed shortly thereafter. In 1738 he was appointed Secretary to the Earl of Malton, whose library he catalogued with Samuel Johnson. Oldys is most noted for editing *The Harleian Miscellany: or, A Collection of Scarce, Curious, and Entertaining Pamphlets and Tracts, as Well in Manuscript as in Print, Found in the Late Earl of Oxford's Library, Interspersed with Historical, Political, and Critical Notes*.

L R (Elsie [Lyn] Ruth) **Palmer** (1934 – 1969)
Australian poet Lyn Palmer was born in Melbourne in 1934. A sufferer from chronic asthma from childhood, she held a number of unsatisfying secretarial positions and throughout much of her short life experienced bouts of manic depression. Possessed of a sarcastically perceptive wit, she preferred to be referred to as "L. R. Palmer". Moving briefly to London in her early 20s,

she returned to Australia in 1960, and became one of the most successful and powerful agents in Australia, representing some of the most high profile entertainers of the era. Her poetry largely reflects her own pessimism and depression, but is interspersed with cheerful and often nonsensical humour.

Peter **Parley** (see Samuel Griswold **Goodrich**)

Peter **Pindar** (see John **Wolcot**)

William Charles Franklyn **Plomer** CBE (1903 – 1973)
William Plomer (pronounced Ploomer) was a South African novelist, poet, librettist and literary editor, who became well known in South Africa for *Turbott Wolfe*, his first novel. A friend of his publisher, Virginia Woolf, he moved to the UK, where he became a literary editor for Faber and Faber and a reader and literary advisor to Jonathan Cape. He edited several of Ian Fleming's Bond novels (Fleming dedicated *Goldfinger* to Plomer) in the 1950s and 60s and, with illustrator Alan Aldridge, published *The Butterfly Ball and the Grasshopper's Feast* (1973) based on William Roscoe's work of the same name (1807).

Alexander **Pope** (1688 – 1744)
An English poet known for his satirical verse and translations of Homer. Pope was born in London, and a Catholic, and was thus hampered in his education and alienated from parts of society by legislation that upheld the status of the Church of England and banned Catholics from attending University, teaching, or holding public office. Pope's early publications were well received, and he counted the likes of Joseph Addison, John Arbuthnot, John Gay, Thomas Parnell and Jonathan Swift among his friends. He began the mammoth task of translating Homer's *Iliad* around 1713: the final part was not published until 1720. Its undoubted success led him to translate Homer's *Odyssey* (1726) and present a new edition of Shakespeare's work in which he demoted some 1,500 lines to footnotes, believing them to have been of such poor quality that Shakespeare could not have written them. His poetry writing was prolific; his most famous poem is probably 'The Rape of the Lock' (1712).

Bryan Waller **Procter** (1787 – 1874)
Born in Leeds, Procter was an English solicitor and poet who wrote under the pseudonym Barry Cornwall. His contemporaries at Harrow school included Lord Byron and Robert Peel. He went on to study law and was

called to the bar in 1831. He was appointed Metropolitan Commissioner of Lunacy – and subsequently elected a Commissioner for Lunacy. Most of his poetry was written within about 20 years, from 1815 onwards. He had many literary friends and books were dedicated to him by Thackeray (*Vanity Fair*) and Wilkie Collins (*The Woman in White*).

Professor J David **Pye** (1932 –)

David Pye is Emeritus Professor of Zoology in the University of London. As something of a physicist manqué, he is now, *inter alia*, a Fellow of the Institute of Physics which published his book on polarised light in 2001. He is fascinated by the ways in which animals may exploit physics, especially in the ultrasonic 'radar' of bats and the acoustic countermeasures of their prey.

Sir Arthur Thomas **Quiller-Couch** (1863 – 1944)

A British literary critic, writer and academic who published under the pen name "Q" and is remembered for his monumental work on the *Oxford Book of English Verse 1250-1900* as well as for his literary criticism. He came from a family of accomplished academics and became a lecturer at Trinity College, Oxford. He was knighted in 1910, Commodore of Royal Fowey Yacht Club from 1911 until his death, and appointed to the King Edward VII Professorship of English Literature at Cambridge University in 1912. In 1928 he was made a Bard of Gorseth Kernow. He wrote many stories and critical works, and his poetic work is contained in *Poems and Ballads* (1896). He was also a main character in a BBC television feature, *The Last Romantics*, in 1992.

Allan **Ramsay** (1686 – 1758)

Ramsay became established as an Edinburgh wigmaker, writing occasional verse, but changed his attention to selling books and eventually publishing. He opened the first 'circulating' library in Scotland and published a large number of poems and Scottish songs. His correspondents included John Gay and Alexander Pope. He arranged construction of a new theatre in Edinburgh – an unsuccessful venture which closed a year later. Ramsay died in the same year as the publication of the tenth edition of Linnaeus' book *Systema Naturae*, which forms the basis of modern taxonomy.

Peter **Redgrove** (1932 – 2003)

Redgrove, an English poet, was born in Kingston-upon-Thames and educated at Queens' College, Cambridge, where he briefly edited *Delta* magazine. His friends there included Ted Hughes and Philip Hobsbaum. He taught at the University of Buffalo (1961-2) and was Gregory Fellow at Leeds University (1962-5). A prolific and critically acclaimed poet, he was awarded the Queen's Gold Medal for poetry in 1996.

Emma **Roberts** (ca 1794 – 1840)

"Miss Emma Roberts" was an English poet and travel writer who, initially with her sister and brother-in-law, spent much of her life in India, which influenced her writing. In India she published some poetry, stories and essays; she returned briefly to England following the death of her sister, before travelling back to India in 1839, where she died suddenly.

Samuel **Rogers** (1763 – 1855)

An English poet celebrated during his lifetime, although now much less well known than other Romantic poets – particularly his friends Byron, Coleridge and Wordsworth. Born and brought up within a well-to-do family in what is now the outer London suburbs, Rogers entered his father's banking business despite a wish to join the Presbyterian ministry. He became interested in English literature and began to write poetry himself, modelling his poems on those of Thomas Gray, and published *The Pleasures of Memory* in 1792. Extremely influential, he was elected a Fellow of the Royal Society in 1796, and in 1803 moved to 22 St James' Palace, where he entertained the cream of London Society for half a century with a notoriously ascerbic wit. On the death of Wordsworth in 1850, Rogers was invited to succeed him as Poet Laureate, but declined due to his age.

P. A. **Ropes** (Not known)

I can find no information on this poet.

William **Roscoe** (1753 – 1831)

English historian, writer and political pamphleteer, Roscoe was born in Liverpool and was well known for his outspoken opposition to the African slave trade, as well as for his children's fantasy poem *The Butterfly's Ball* which has charmed children and adults since its publication in 1807. An ardent reader, he became a solicitor, but maintained an interest in the classics and in the language and literature of Italy. He became Member of Parliament for Liverpool in 1806, standing down the following year, and following financial difficulties involving a bank with which he was associated, retired from commercial interests. He wrote many poems and conducted extensive historical research, including *Life of Lorenzo de' Medici* and *The Life and Pontificate of Leo the Tenth*. The first collected edition of his *Poetical Works* was published in 1857 but, oddly, omitted the 'Butterfly's Ball'.

Christina Georgina **Rossetti** (1830 – 1894)
An Italian poet well known for her poem 'Goblin Market', Christina (or Cristina) Rossetti was the daughter of Gabriel Pasquale Giuseppe Rossetti (1783-1854). She was also the sister of author Maria Francesca Rossetti (1827-1876), artist Dante Gabriel Rossetti (1828-1882), and critic William Michael Rossetti (1829-1919).

Henry **Rowland-Brown** (1865 – 1921)
Henry Rowland-Brown was educated at Rugby and Oxford. He was interested in Lepidoptera from his childhood days, and became a Fellow of the Entomological Society (before the Royal prefix) as well as a personal friend of Charles Oberthür, a prominent French entomologist. He contributed many papers to Oberthür's privately published series of entomological 'journals', *Études d'Entomologie* and *Études de Lépidoptèrologie comparée*. Although he was mostly a journalist by persuasion, he was an accomplished poet, and produced two published volumes of verse: *Rhymes and Rhapsodies* and *Preludes and Symphonies*. The poem presented in this anthology was written under the pseudonym Oliver Grey.

Tony **Sargeant** (20th century)
An Australian "bush poet". No further information has been found.

Robert William **Service** (1874 – 1958)
Robert Service – the Canadian Kipling – is remembered more for his poems relating to the hardships of life in the Canadian Yukon Territory, (e.g. The Shooting of Dan McGew), where he was known as the "Bard of the Yukon", than for anything else. He was English, born into a wealthy family, and spent his childhood in Glasgow before sailing to Canada to become a cowboy. He travelled extensively throughout his life and lived in Brittany, France, after leaving the Yukon.

Vikram **Seth** (1952 –)
An Indian novelist, biographer and poet. Educated at Dehradun, India; Tonbridge and Oxford, England; California, USA; and Nanjing, China. He has published eight volumes of poetry.

John **Seville** (1927 –)

John Seville's interest in the Arthropoda results from many years as a Pest control and Hygiene consultant. He is a Fellow of the Royal Entomological Society.

Monica **Shannon** (1890 – 1965)

A Canadian born children's author, Monica Sharp's family moved to the American West shortly after she was born. She lived there for the rest of her life. Her first book, *California Fairy Tales*, was published in 1926 and she is best known for her novel *Dobry*, published in 1934, for which she was awarded the Newbery Medal the following year.

William **Sharp** (1855 – 1905)

A Scottish poet and literary biographer who in his later years also wrote under the pseudonym Fiona MacLeod. Born in Paisley, Sharp was educated in Glasgow and worked briefly in a Glasgow law office before obtaining a position at a London bank. Among his friends and acquaintances were Dante Gabriel Rossetti and Charles Swinburne; he also had a conflicting relationship with W. B. Yeats who initially approved of MacLeod but not of Sharp – although he later realised they were the same person. MacLeod's correspondence was dictated by Sharp to his sister, whose handwriting maintained the feminine facade. Sharp died, and is buried, in Sicily.

Lydia Huntley **Sigourney** (1791 – 1865)

A popular American poet and philanthropist during her lifetime, most of her work was published under her married epitaph – Mrs Sigourney, although she was also commonly known as the Sweet Singer of Hartford. Born in Norwich, Connecticut, she opened schools "for young ladies" in Norwich and Hartford and published her first work, *Moral Pieces in Prose and Verse*, in 1815. Following her marriage a few years later, she chose at first to write anonymously. She became a significant role model for women, inspiring many young women to become poets. Her commitment to education, writing and charity resulted in many literary clubs and societies being named in her honour, as was the city of Sigourney, Iowa, the seat of Keokuk County. She contributed more than 2,000 journal articles, and almost 70 books.

Annie Trumbull **Slosson** (1838 – 1926)

Slosson was an American author and entomologist born in Connecticut. Many of her works were short stories published in *The Atlantic Monthly* and *Harper's Bazaar*, perhaps most notably 'Aunt Randy. An entomological sketch', published in the latter in 1887. The poem 'Uncle Jotham's Boarder' was published in the *New York Times* in 1895. Though she had no formal training, Annie Slosson devoted much of her time to entomology; in 1892 she was one of the founding members of the New York Entomological Society, which met at her house in New York and later at the American Museum of Natural History (AMNH). A number of insects were named in her honour, and her collection was donated to the AMNH.

Charlotte Turner **Smith** (1749 – 1806)

Smith was an English Romantic poet, writer and novelist. Her first book of poetry, *Elegaic Sonnets*, was written in debtor's prison where she joined her violent, unfaithful and extravagant husband; the success of the sonnets helped to procure his release. Her poetry subsequently earned the support of Wordsworth and Coleridge, and her ten, largely autobiographical, novels included *The Old Manor House* – often considered her best. Her father-in-law, Richard Smith, who owned slave plantations in Barbados, willed his considerable fortune to Charlotte's children but this inheritance, which contained significant legal difficulties, became tied up in chancery for almost four decades. It has been suggested that this may have been the basis of Charles Dickens' fictional account of Jarndyce and Jarndyce in *Bleak House*. A supporter of the ideals of the French Revolution, Charlotte Smith wrote a play, two volumes of a history of England and *A Natural History of Birds*, the last published posthumously.

Robert **Southey** (1774 – 1843)

Southey was one of the 'Lake Poets' and Poet Laureate for the 30 years from 1813 to his death. A prolific writer, his biographies include the lives of Bunyan, Cowper, Cromwell, Nelson and Wesley. His best known work is probably *The Story of the Three Bears* – the well-known Goldilocks tale.

Edmund **Spenser** (1552 or 1553 – 1599)

Born in London and educated at London and Cambridge, Spenser became secretary to the Bishop of Rochester and later went to Ireland in the service of the Lord Deputy, 14th Baron de Wilton. His most famous work, published in several books, was the epic poem *The Faerie Queene* (1590) although he was well known also for a prose pamphlet *A View of the Present State of Ireland*, circulated by hand and unpublished in his lifetime, probably because of its inflammatory views. He is buried in Poets' Corner in Westminster Abbey.

James **Stephens** (*ca* 1882 – 1950)

Irish novelist, poet and later broadcaster, known as 'Tiny Tim' because of his small stature, and remembered for his retellings of Irish myths and fairy tales. His most famous work was a modern fable *The Crock of Gold* (1912), which won the Polignac Prize for fiction.

Donald **Swann** (1923 – 1994) (see also Michael **Flanders**)

Donald Ibrahim Swann was a British musician, composer and entertainer, best known for his partnership with Michael Flanders in writing and performing comic songs (Swann wrote the music, Flanders the lyrics). He was born in Wales, to a father who was a Russian of English descent and a mother from Transcaspia – both were refugees from the Russian Revolution. In addition to his collaboration with Flanders that arose from their meeting in 1948 and continued until 1967, Swann had a prolific musical output, including operas and operettas and a setting of Tolkien's poems from *Lord of the Rings*. He also formed the *Swann Singers*.

Jonathan **Swift** (1667 – 1745)

Born in Dublin, Swift was a satirist, novelist and poet remembered for many works – most notably his book (1726) *Travels into Several remote Nations of the World, in Four Parts, by Lemuel Gulliver, first a surgeon, and then a captain of several ships*, known by its shortened title *Gulliver's Travels*, first published anonymously. His family was well connected in the world of literature. He was politically active and at one time he hoped to obtain an important church appointment in England, an ambition opposed by Queen Anne, who was angered by his satire (1704) *The Tale of a Tub*, which she considered blasphemous, and by his poem 'The Windsor Prophecy', in which Swift offered advice on which of the Queen's bedchamber ladies she could trust. Towards the end of his life, Swift became mentally ill. Swift's well known poem *The Flea* is sometimes, confusingly, attributed to "Dean Swift", referring to Jonathan's appointment as Dean of Saint Patrick's Cathedral, Dublin, where he was also buried.

Algernon Charles **Swinburne** (1837 – 1909)

A British poet known for his rebellion against the conservative values of his time, and in particular for the explicit sexual themes of *Poems and Ballads* (1866), his most important collection of poetry which shocked many of his readers – and delighted others. He is recognised as one of the most accomplished Victorian lyric poets. Born into a wealthy Northumbrian family, he was educated at Eton and Oxford, where he met the Rossetti brothers and other members of the pre-Raphaelite circle. He wrote widely diverse poems, including many on natural history subjects, which predominated in his later years.

Joshua **Sylvester** (1563 – 1618)
Sylvester was an English poet, the son of a Kentish cloth manufacturer. At the age of 43 he was given a small pension by Henry, Prince of Wales, as a court poet. In his day, Sylvester was renowned for translating the scriptural epic *Guillaume du Bartas* into English. Popularity of his work died a death with the Restoration of the monarchy which began in 1660.

Alfred **Tennyson** (1809 – 1892)
Alfred Tennyson is often referred to as "Alfred Lord Tennyson" – but more properly Alfred, Lord Tennyson. He was the first Baron Tennyson and one of the most popular English poets. He became Poet Laureate following the death of Wordsworth in 1850, and is responsible for many phrases that have become very well known and oft-quoted (eg. "nature, red in tooth and claw"; "better to have loved and lost", etc). His poems include 'The Lady of Shalott' (1832) and 'The Charge of the Light Brigade' (1854).

Ivor C. **Treby** (1933 – 2012)
A prolific poet who prior to his death had some 400 poems in print in anthologies and magazines around the world, including six published collections, and five books on the Victorian poet "Michael Field", which actually referred to Katherine Bradley and her niece and partner, Edith Cooper.

James William **Tutt** (1858 – 1911)
A prominent and remarkably industrious English entomologist who published widely on entomological subjects, including a ten volume work on British and European butterflies and moths. A teacher by training, he was Headmaster of a number of schools, and an active participant in the life of entomological societies as well as a voluminous contributor to specialist literature of the time.

Robert **Vansittart** GCB, GCMG, PC, MVO (1881 – 1957)
Robert Gilbert Vansittart, the 1st Baron Vansittart, was a senior British diplomat up to and throughout World War II. He is remembered for his opposition to Appeasement and his hard line stance towards Germany. He was also a published poet, novelist, and playwright.

Virgil (70 – 19 BC)

Publius Vergilius Maro, most commonly known as Virgil, was a classical Roman poet. His major works – the *Eclogues* (Bucolics), the *Georgics* and the *Aneid* – have had a wide influence on Western literature.

Gillian W. Watson (1954 –)

One of very few entomologists worldwide specialising in the identification and taxonomy of scale insects; Gillian Watson also works on whiteflies and thrips, particularly in agriculture and plant quarantine. Born in Kenya and educated in the UK, she currently works in California.

Isaac **Watts** (1674 – 1748)

Born in Hampshire, England, Watts was a renowned theologian and prolific writer of hymns, with some 750 to his credit, many of which are very well known today. He had a propensity for rhymes at an early age and was notable in contravening tradition by introducing Christian poetry into hymns. One of his best known poems was an exhortation against "idleness and mischief" in children, later parodied by Lewis Carroll in *Alice's Adventures in Wonderland*. He left a substantial legacy of written work. His papers are now at Yale University, Massachusetts.

Susanna **Watts** (1768 – 1842)

British author, translator and campaigner, Susanna Watts was born in Leicester and became a vocal activist and opponent of slavery. She worked on a local periodical, *The Hummingbird*, which brought together abolitionist views, and visited households and shops with a view to persuading people to boycott sugar produced in the Caribbean. Her belief that abstinence from sugar would have a positive and direct effect on West Indian slavery may count as a very early 'fair trade' campaign, and her poem 'The insects in council: addressed to entomologists', intended as a criticism of those who collected insects for a 'hobby', may be considered very early support for animal rights. Her scrapbook of interests survives in the Records Office for Leicestershire, Leicester and Rutland.

Frances **Whistler** (Not known)

I can find no information on this poet.

Walter (Walt) **Whitman** (1819 – 1892)

American poet, essayist and journalist Walt Whitman was born on Long Island, New York State and worked as a teacher and a government clerk as well as a volunteer nurse in army hospitals during the American Civil War. He founded his own newspaper, the *Long Islander*, which he ran for less than a year, selling it in 1839. His work was considered rather controversial in his time; he was no supporter of slavery and at one time called for its abolition, although he later viewed the abolitionist movement as a threat to democracy. His first collection of poetry, *Leaves of Grass*, was first published in 1855 and was heavily criticised for what were perceived to be offensive sexual themes. The collection was subject to constant editing until shortly before Whitman's death in 1892.

Ella Wheeler **Wilcox** (1850 – 1919)

American author and popular poet, whose best known lines are probably those which begin the poem 'Solitude': "Laugh and the world laughs with you / Weep, and you weep alone". She wrote poetry from an early age and was well known in her home state of Wisconsin by the time she graduated from high school. A firm believer in the occult, she also cared deeply about animal suffering – her poem 'Voice of the voiceless' begins: "I am the voice of the voiceless; / Through me the dumb shall speak, / Till the deaf world's ear be made to hear / The wrongs of the wordless weak". Her rather unorthodox poem 'The butterflies' fad', reproduced in this anthology, turns the tables rather neatly on the question of small boys collecting butterflies.

Al **Willis** (Not known)

I can find no information on this poet.

John **Wolcot** (1738 – 1819)

Wolcot was an English poet and satirist, who often wrote under the pseudonym Peter Pindar. He wrote a succession of satires on a number of subjects; his favourite victims being the "farmer king", King George III, and Samuel Johnson.

Humbert **Wolfe** CB, CBE (1886 – 1940)

The Italian-born English poet, author and translator Humbert Wolfe is probably best remembered for his cynical and amusing epigram: "You cannot hope / to bribe or twist, / thank God! the / British journalist. / But, seeing what / the man will do / unbribed, there's / no occasion to." Some of his poetic verses were set to music by Gustav Holst. He died on his 55th birthday.

William **Wordsworth** (1770 – 1850)

An English poet who, with Samuel Taylor Coleridge, is credited with launching the 'Romantic Age' in English literature with their joint publication *Lyrical Ballads* in 1798, in which his poem 'Tintern Abbey' was first published, together with Coleridge's 'Rime of the Ancient Mariner'. Oddly, neither of their names appeared in the first edition. Wordsworth is remembered for a substantial body of poetry, including his semi-autobiographical poem 'The Prelude' (titled posthumously – known as 'to Coleridge' in his lifetime), and his very well know poem 'I Wandered Lonely as a Cloud', perhaps better known simply as 'Daffodils'. In his later years he lived with his sister Dorothy in the English Lake District where his house, Dove Cottage, is a tourist attraction. He was Poet Laureate from 1843 until his death in 1850.

Judith **Wright** (1915 – 2000)

An Australian poet with a focus on the environment and indigenous affairs, Judith Wright was born in Armidale, New South Wales. She studied English, history, philosophy and psychology at the University of Sydney and went on to write and publish a large number of poems in more than 50 collections. Her first book of poetry, *The Moving Image*, was published in 1946 whilst she was a researcher at the University of Queensland. She was active in conservation and a founding member and President (1964-1976) of the Wildlife Preservation Society of Queensland. She was acutely aware of the damage humans cause to the environment and campaigned tirelessly for conservation of the Great Barrier Reef and Fraser Island. She received the Queen's Gold Medal for Poetry in 1992.

Andrew **Young** (Not known)

I can find no information on this poet.

INDEX OF FIRST LINES

395

COPYRIGHT ACKNOWLEDGMENTS

"Changing Perceptions" and "Lowly Origin" are reproduced by kind permission of Henry Disney

"My Dragonflies" is reproduced by kind permission of Ruary Mackenzie Dodds

"The Woolly Bear", "The Bumble Bee", "The Wasp", "The Glow-Worm", "The Locust", "The Cricket", "The Dragonfly", "The Flea", "The Cockroach", "The Green Fly", "The Daddy-Long-Legs", "The Midge", "The Earwig" are all taken from Harry Eltringham's unpublished *Studies in Emptyknowledgy by A Bughunter* and are reproduced by kind permission of the Royal Entomological Society

'Cake Shop' by Janis Freegard taken from *Kingdom Animalia: the Escapades of Linnaeus* (Auckland University Press, 2011) and reproduced by kind permission of Janis Freegard and Auckland University Press

'Waspish' and 'Fireflies In The Garden' taken from *The Poetry of Robert Frost* by Robert Frost, published by Jonathan Cape. Reproduced by permission of The Random House Group Ltd

'Flying Crooked' and 'The Blue-Fly' by Robert Graves taken from *Complete Poems in One Volume*. Reprinted by permission of Carcanet Press Ltd

"Lepidoptera – moths", "Orthoptera – grasshoppers and relatives", "Collembola – springtails", "Embioptera – webspinners", "Phthiraptera – sucking lice", all by Al Grigarick are reproduced from *Insect Enlightenment with Orderly Verse* by kind permission of the Bohart Museum of Entomology, University of California, Davis

"The Dream Of Betty", "The Galling Problem", "Close Encounter Of The *Calicotis* Kind", "Ode to *Tatosoma*", "Gum-Leaf Skeletonizer Blues", all taken from *Six-legged Things and Scaly Wings*, 2008. Reproduced by kind permission of Robert Hoare

'The Dream of the Cabbage Caterpillars' by Libby Houston © 1973, 1993. Taken from *All Change* (Oxford University Press 1993)

'The Dragonfly' by Libby Houston © 1973, 1999. Taken from *Cover of Darkness, selected poems 1961-1998* (Slow Dancer Press 1999). Reprinted by kind permission of Libby Houston

403